Negotiating Inseparability in China

Negotiating Inseparability in China

The Xinjiang Class and the Dynamics of Uyghur Identity

Timothy Grose

Hong Kong University Press
The University of Hong Kong
Pokfulam Road
Hong Kong
https://hkupress.hku.hk

© 2019 Hong Kong University Press

ISBN 978-988-8528-09-7 (*Hardback*)

All rights reserved. No portion of this publication may be reproduced or transmitted in any form or by any means, electronic or mechanical, including photocopying, recording, or any information storage or retrieval system, without prior permission in writing from the publisher.

British Library Cataloguing-in-Publication Data
A catalogue record for this book is available from the British Library.

10 9 8 7 6 5 4 3 2 1

Printed and bound by Paramount Printing Co. Ltd., Hong Kong, China

To the intelligent and selfless young Uyghurs
who bravely shared their stories with me

Contents

List of Figures and Tables	ix
Acknowledgments	x

Introduction — 1
    Ethnicity and the State — 6
    Ethnicity and the State in China — 8
    Fitting the Uyghurs into the Weiwu'er Minzu — 10
    Methodology — 14
    Limitations — 16
    Structure of the Book — 17

Chapter 1: Incubating Loyalty (or Resistance) in Chinese Boarding Schools — 18
    A Tried-and-Tested Method for Educating Young Uyghurs — 18
    Carving Out an Uncontested Space in the Xinjiang Class — 28
    Sanctioned Space for Weiwu'er zu Culture — 45
    Concluding Remarks — 49

Chapter 2: Asserting Uyghur Identity from China's "Central Plains" — 50
    Han-Uyghur Interactions beyond the Xinjiang Class — 51
    Uyghur Language as Ethnic Marker — 55
    Dating: "Our Future Spouse Must Be Uyghur" — 59
    Forging Transnational Islamic Bonds — 61
    Qu'ran: Reciting Piety — 62
    "She's the One That Veils" — 65
    Time for Prayer — 66
    Transnational Yet Mono-minzu Islam — 69
    Concluding Remarks — 70

Chapter 3: Ignoring CCP Calls to Return to Xinjiang — 72
    Herding Xinjiang Class Graduates back to Xinjiang — 73
    Return to Xinjiang? — 76

Escaping Inseparability?	86
Concluding Remarks	88

Chapter 4: The Disappointing Road Home — 90
- Reasons to Return — 90
- Dragging Their Feet back to Xinjiang — 91
- Reestablishing Feelings of Belonging in Xinjiang — 100
- Building a New Life in Xinjiang — 103
- Balancing Acts: Women and the Struggles of Reintegration — 104
- Finding Place in Xinjiang — 108
- Concluding Remarks — 109

Conclusion — 111

References — 117
Index — 143

Figures and Tables

Figures

Figure 0.1: The International Grand Bazaar, Ürümchi, Xinjiang: "Minzu Unity, One Family" — 2
Figure 1.1: Xinjiang Class enrollment and schools, 2000–2018 — 24
Figure 1.2: Locations of Xinjiang Classes, 2000 and 2005 — 31
Figure 2.1: Xinjiang Class graduates mingle with their Uyghur classmates at UIBE's Uyghur Student Association's Roza celebration — 53
Figure 2.2: Uyghur Xinjiang Class graduates prepare to perform *sama* at the 2010 Roza celebration — 54
Figure 2.3: Hierarchy of languages used in bilingual WeChat moments — 58
Figure 2.4: The "Uyghur" Team squeezes tightly in a huddle before a match — 71

Tables

Table 1.1: Xinjiang Class enrollment plans by minzu, 2008 and 2012 — 23
Table 2.1: Language preference for WeChat moments among Xinjiang Class, Minkaohan, and Minkaomin Uyghurs — 57

Acknowledgments

This book is the culmination of several years of studying, researching, and writing in the United States and the People's Republic of China. For the decade I have devoted to this research, I have been privileged, honored, and humbled, to work, interact, and simply be myself in the company of a large group of wonderful human beings and in excellent institutions. Although my name appears as this work's author, the book was not completed in solitude. Indeed, I would have never achieved this accomplishment without the support of the people mentioned below.

As an undergraduate student at John Carroll University, I worked with scholars committed to East Asian Studies. Dr. Susan Long opened my eyes to anthropology and provided me with the necessary tools for conducting sound ethnographic field work. Dr. Paul Nietupski urged me to "see" China from the perspective of ethnic minorities and helped me to get a foot in the door of Uyghur studies. I am also grateful to Dr. Roger Purdy, Dr. Diana Chou, and Jie Zhang for guiding my undergraduate work.

At the University of Virginia, Dr. John Shepherd nudged me in the direction of researching education in Xinjiang and helped me meet the demands of graduate school.

As a PhD student in the Department of Central Eurasian Studies at Indiana University, I was under the guidance of scholars whom I can only hope to someday half measure up to. I am especially indebted to my former dissertation committee, who saw promise in the project and in me. The late Dr. Heidi Ross stood as a pillar of stability throughout the completion of my graduate work. When each "crisis" presented itself, she calmly and patiently placed me back on course. Dr. Ron Sela taught me—with his sarcastic humor—the importance of skepticism—skepticism toward the sources, toward the dominant narratives in the field, and toward my own work. The late Dr. Elliot Sperling impressed me with his command of languages and historical sources. He instilled in me the importance and necessity of self-confidence (and I promise to never lazily pronounce 文成公主 again). Finally, Dr. Gardner Bovingdon served as an extremely generous adviser and mentor. His encouragement to "swallow the bitter medicine" of social theory is advice that has been so extremely rewarding. I cannot imagine going through the joys and trials of academia without Gardner's kindness, insightful guidance, and erudition.

Research for this project was made possible through several generous grants. Various stages of field research were funded by the International Education Exchange Fulbright Program, a National Security Education Program Boren Fellowship, Foreign Language and Area Studies Fellowships, the China and Inner Asian Council, and an Indiana University–Andrew W. Mellon fellowship.

Having lived in China for many years, I am grateful to my "China" family, who provided me with all the comforts of home. Howard Hao and Tan Qian graciously offered me a bed and late night Chinese practice during my extended stays in Beijing. Of course, I also want to thank my large group of Uyghur friends, especially those in Lukchun, who took me in as one of their own. I wish that the situation in Xinjiang allowed for me to list your names.

I'm also indebted to the many scholars in China who assisted my research. At the Minzu University of China, Dr. Yang Shengmin has been a gracious host and a caring mentor, and Dr. Zhang Haiyang who also supported my endeavors. Conversations with Dr. Abdulresit Qarluq provided me with a treasure chest of knowledge about Uyghur culture. Finally, this project would have been impossible without invitations from Dr. Zhu Zhiyong at Beijing Normal University and Dr. Luo Xin and Dr. Zan Tao at Peking University.

My colleagues at Rose-Hulman Institute of Technology lent much-needed support as I finished writing the book. A Rose-Hulman summer professional development grant in 2015, facilitated an extended stay in Xinjiang for follow-up interviews. Dr. Terrence Casey, Dr. Paul Christensen, and Dr. Andreas Michel encouraged me to stay focused on the book project when it became easy (and convenient) to be distracted. I also appreciate the useful feedback from Drs. Rebecca Dyer, Daniel Hartner, and Jody Jensen.

Many of my insights and analysis were sharpened by comments and suggestions made to earlier drafts of this manuscript. I would like to especially thank Dr. Chen Yangbin, Colin Legerton, Dr. James Leibold, Dr. Stevan Harrell, Dr. Joanne Smith Finley, Paula Szocik and two anonymous reviewers.

The book also benefited from the excellent production team at Hong Kong University Press. Dr. Susie Han—who saw potential in my pitch—worked tirelessly and patiently with me throughout the publication process. Clara Ho oversaw the copyediting and final production of the manuscript. Winnie Chau devised an excellent marketing plan, and Jennifer Lim helped secure endorsements and review articles.

Above all, I want to thank my family. To my siblings—James, Margaret, Betsy, Katherine, Alicia, Michael, and Diana—your love and support have been unwavering. I have missed births, birthdays, weddings, family reunions, but you have always understood. I especially want to thank (and hug) my parents Fay and Phyllis. Although I have spent so much time away from home, you only asked once when "man-man" was coming home. Finally, I smile when I think about sharing my research trips, the joys of daily life, and our "journey" (and, of course, each draft of each chapter) with Abi. Here's to our next adventure—parenting our twins, Josephine Mariyem and Madeline Aynur!

With all sincerity—and that happy lump in my throat I feel as I type this sentence—thank you!

August 2018

Introduction

> We must make fighting separatism our top priority in a bid to safeguard Xinjiang's social stability and closely guard against and severely crack down on the 'three evil forces'.
>
> —Nur Bekri, Former Chairman of the Xinjiang Uyghur Autonomous Region
> *People's Daily*, March 6, 2011

Although still boasting the name of an impressive landmark, the International Grand Bazaar in Ürümchi, Xinjiang,[1] appeared dilapidated in July 2017. Just a decade before, the open-air market bustled with excitement. Speakers blasted the latest synthesizer-heavy Central Asian melodies at deafening volumes; food hawkers, veiled by thick clouds of black smoke emanating from charcoal grills, filled the air with the aromas of roasted mutton generously spiced with cumin; and death-defying tightrope performances attracted throngs of people in the evenings.

Clearly, much had changed. The few visitors seeking entry to the gated marketplace solemnly queued for security checks. As tourists and shoppers approached the metal detector, they robotically opened their purses and bags while security attendants inspected the contents, paying careful attention to Uyghur visitors. Inside the market, vendors were confined to the trellised National (*Minzu*)[2] Unity Pedestrian Street (Uy. *milletler ittipaqliqidiki ülgilik kocha*;[3] Ch. *minzu tuanjie buxing jie*) and

---

1. Comprising one-sixth of China's total territory, the Xinjiang Uyghur Autonomous Region (XUAR) is the largest provincial-level political unit in the country. Neighboring Mongolia to the south, Russia, Kazakhstan, Kyrgyzstan, and Tajikistan to the east, and Afghanistan, Pakistan, and India to the northeast, Xinjiang shares more international borders than any other Chinese province. Domestically, the XUAR borders the Tibet Autonomous Region (TAR), Qinghai, and Gansu.
2. *Minzu* is the Chinese term used to describe the People's Republic of China's (PRC) fifty-six ethnic (and ethno-national) groups. The Chinese Communist Party (CCP) identified minzu groups using a loose interpretation of Joseph Stalin's four criteria for nationality: i.e., common language, territory, economy, and culture (Fei 1980). Recent research has exposed the many imperfections of the CCP's ethnic identification campaign (Ch. *minzu shibie*) (Mullaney 2011). In light of the term's inadequacies, I will not attempt to translate it into English. For more on the ambiguity of many ethnic designations in China, see Gladney 1991; Harrell 2001.
3. With the exception of commonly known Uyghur place-names such as Kashgar and Khotan, I use the Uyghur Latin alphabet (*Uyghur Latin Yéziqi*, or ULY) for the romanization of all other Uyghur terms. I have chosen the ULY for the sake of consistency and understand that Uyghurs often borrow from many "standardized" systems in their daily communication.

Figure 0.1: The International Grand Bazaar, Ürümchi, Xinjiang: "Minzu Unity, One Family"

appeared to be concerned more with sheltering themselves from the oppressive heat than selling their handicrafts and dried fruits. A large piece of engraved slate depicting "Uncle" Qurban Tulum, a poor Uyghur farmer from Khotan who supposedly rode his donkey from Xinjiang to Beijing,[4] embracing hands with Mao Zedong leaned against the rear exterior wall of the Döngköwrük Mosque. The caption below the simple engraving reads in Uyghur, Chinese, and English, "Uncl [sic] Qurban Visits Beijing." The square's focal point—and one of its few remaining "tourist attractions"—is a large statue of a pomegranate scored through the core exposing its arils. Large red Chinese characters erected in front of the faux fruit read, "Minzu Unity: One Family" (Ch. *minzu tuanjie yi jia qin*).

The pomegranate has become the defining image of minzu cohesion since General Secretary of the Communist Party of China Xi Jinping's May 2014 address to the Central Work Forum on Xinjiang. In his speech, Xi encouraged China's minzu groups to nestle tightly as if they were pomegranate seeds (*China Education Newspaper* 2014). The calyx-crowned fruit is now prominently featured in full-color posters hung throughout Xinjiang, in television commercials broadcast in every major oasis city, and in newspaper advertisements reaching every corner of the region. Despite the Chinese Communist Party's (CCP) efforts to promote this

---

4. According to the popular story, Qurban Tulum rode his donkey from Xinjiang to Beijing to meet Mao Zedong. In reality, Qurban traveled to Beijing as part of a special delegation organized by the CCP to celebrate land reform.

slogan, the pomegranate metaphor for minzu unity is only convincing if the fruit remains enclosed in its leathery outer skin. When opened, a pomegranate's red arils can be easily plucked from its membranes. Once the seeds are exposed, they will loosen and fall to the ground with a delicate tap and gentle squeeze.

The seeds of minzu unity in Xinjiang began to dislodge in bunches on July 5, 2009. While the CCP might have wished for that Sunday to resemble any other hot but placid summer day in Ürümchi, the morning instead brought public protest followed by deadly violence that afternoon. Uyghur university and high school students took to the streets demanding government action after the deaths of two fellow Uyghurs came at the hands of their Han coworkers from a toy factory in Shaoguan, Guangdong Province. In a public display of anger over the CCP's (mis)handling of the Shaoguan incident, hundreds of Uyghurs carrying Chinese flags staged mass demonstrations in the autonomous region's capital.[5] Tempers quickly swelled, and the protest spiraled into interethnic violence, with Uyghur protesters attacking Han bystanders and vandalizing Han-owned properties. On July 7 Han citizens wielding improvised weapons poured into the city's predominantly Uyghur districts seeking revenge. According to some estimates, the riots and ensuing violence claimed 197 lives and resulted in close to 2,000 injuries before order was restored (*Reuters* 2009; Ramzy 2010); the Munich-based World Uyghur Congress reported over 600 deaths (BBC 2009).[6] In a stroke of poetic irony, Liberation Road (Ch. *Jiefang lu*) and Unity Road (Ch. *Tuanjie lu*) were the epicenters of violence. The names of these heavily trafficked arterial roads provided unsubtle reminders of the "New Era" ushered in by the CCP. The riots demonstrated that many Uyghurs have yet to buy into this interpretation of history.

Nevertheless, China's state-controlled media quickly spun the story to deflect blame from CCP policy. Official reports alleged that the high-profile dissident and then president of the World Uyghur Congress Rabiye Qadir carefully orchestrated the attacks from abroad (Xinhua 2009). This is a story often recycled but rarely confirmed by independent media: malicious groups from outside have infiltrated Xinjiang and radicalized a very small segment of Uyghur society to commit heinous acts of violence (or, in the eyes of the CCP, "terrorism").

More troubling for the CCP, violence did not end that July afternoon on the streets of Ürümchi. The region has witnessed an uptick in sporadic attacks since 2010, and insurrection has spilled into other regions. However, a string of unrelated yet large-scale coordinated attacks began in 2013. On June 6, 2013, a group of Uyghur men armed with knives in Lukchun, a sleepy town near Turpan, laid siege to a police station, leaving thirty-five people dead (Powers 2013). Five people died and forty others were injured on October 28, 2013, when a Uyghur driving an SUV plowed into a crowd of people at Beijing's iconic Tiananmen Square (Demick 2014). On March 1, 2014, Uyghur assailants carried out a knife attack at a busy train

---

5. Darren Byler shared with me these important details of the Uyghur protests.
6. For academic treatments of the 2009 Ürümchi riots, see Millward 2009; Smith Finley 2011; Tobin 2011.

station in Kunming, Yunnan, which claimed twenty-nine lives and injured scores more (Powers 2014a). A September 18, 2015 ambush at a coal mine in Aksu resulted in over fifty deaths. Meanwhile, skirmishes between Uyghurs and security personnel have become common occurrences (Lee 2014; Radio Free Asia n.d.). Discontent simmers and paroxysms of violence have unsettled the region, straining an already fragile relationship between Uyghurs and the party-state.

Protracted conflict in the region brings into focus fundamental issues pertinent to the future stability of the Xinjiang Uyghur Autonomous Region (XUAR). Despite Beijing's claim that Xinjiang has been an "inalienable" part of China since "ancient times" and the Uyghurs are "inseparable" members of the country's multiethnic mosaic of peoples,[7] many Uyghurs insist their language, religion, and culture are under systematic assault, while others complain about being left out of China's booming (but Han-dominated) economy (Cliff 2016). Indeed, many Uyghurs claim to be suffering under the current order and desire meaningful reform. In a playful expression of their indignation, several of my Uyghur friends purposely substituted a near homophone for the official term "liberation," *azadliq* in the Uyghur vernacular and a reference to the founding of the People's Republic of China. Instead, they used the term *azabliq*, which means "suffering."

Has the CCP made a gross miscalculation in its "civilizing project" (Harrell 1995), which is ostensibly aimed at amalgamating (Ch. *ronghe*) China's ethnically diverse population (Mackerras 1994)? Is the CCP failing to "interpellate" or hail (Althusser 1971) the Uyghurs through state apparatuses as complaisant members of the "Chinese Nation" (referred to hereafter as the "Zhonghua minzu")?[8] How do young Uyghurs conceive, demarcate, and express their collective identities, understood here as the dynamic formation of common interpersonal relationships that define in-group and out-group membership based on shared language and culture (Melucci 1995, 45–49)? Is it possible for Uyghurs to be "separate but loyal" to the Zhonghua minzu (Tang and He 2010), or are Uyghur and Chinese identities mutually exclusive?

This study engages with these questions by critically examining and theorizing the experiences of Uyghur graduates of the "Xinjiang Class" national boarding school program (Ch. *neidi Xinjiang gaozhong ban*; Uy. *ichkiri ölkilerdiki Shinjang*

---

7. A popular Chinese dictum goes, "Han are inseparable from minority minzu, minority minzu are inseparable from the Han, and each minority minzu is inseparable from one another" (Ch. *Hanzu libukai shaoshuminzu, shaoshuminzu libukai Hanzu, gemin shaoshuminzu zhijian huxiang libukai*. See, for example, Communist Youth League Central Committee 2009, 30.
8. As a political concept, Zhonghua minzu has a rich history. James Leibold (2006, 212–13n1) traced the first usage of the term to the late Qing dynasty (1644–1911) reformer Liang Qichao, who in 1903 used the term in an attempt to formulate a multiethnic Chinese nationalism, as opposed to more narrow and Han-centric conceptualizations of Chinese nationalism advocated by anti-Manchu Han intellectuals. See also Leibold 2007. In its contemporary usage, the term captures the complex relationships between the Han majority, the fifty-five minority minzu (Ch. *shaoshu minzu*), and the Chinese party-state. The Chinese party-state acknowledges the diversity of its population yet insists on its unity, a concept China's most influential anthropologist, Fei Xiaotong (2010), termed the "pluralistic unity" (Ch. *duoyuan yiti*) of the Zhonghua minzu.

toluq ottura sinipliri).[9] The Xinjiang Class was established in the year 2000 to educate mainly ethnic Uyghur students at schools located in central and eastern China. Of course, as students in "inner China" (*neidi*),[10] the young Uyghurs did not participate in the violence that has plagued Xinjiang; in fact, they condemned it. Yet they challenged the absoluteness of CCP rule and their assigned status as minority minzu in subtle ways: they defined, embraced, and asserted markers of Uyghur and Muslim identities unsanctioned by the state. To be sure, performing Uyghur identity does not require an outright rejection of Chineseness through violent protests or calls for independence. Rather, Xinjiang Class graduates decide as individuals how to navigate their multilayered identities.

What unfolds is a dynamic and sometimes contradictory process. Xinjiang Class graduates employed their boarding school educations to resist and break free from the party-state's narrowly defined minzu category—the Weiwu'er zu (维吾尔族)[11]—and the racialized, yet inclusive Zhonghua minzu. They were instead drawn to collectivities wherein membership is more flexible. Indeed, many Xinjiang Class graduates simultaneously desired to be Uyghur, Muslim, educated, modern, and even Chinese. As such, a central argument of this study is that Xinjiang Class graduates participated in Chinese mainstream society and appropriated ethnic markers of the dominant Han people to stretch the boundaries of their ethno-national identities. More specifically, Xinjiang Class graduates used their privileged experiences in Han-dominated neidi cities to strengthen transregional bonds with other Uyghurs, connect with non-Chinese Muslims, and chart paths to other countries. These opportunities—which can be more difficult to create in Xinjiang owing to an increasingly invasive surveillance apparatus and oppressive policies (Klimeš 2018; Rajagopalan 2017; Zenz and Leibold 2017)—activated and solidified transregional and transnational identities, which oftentimes were linked to the *umma*, or the global community of Muslims.

---

9. The *neidi Xinjiang gaozhong ban* also has been translated variously into English as "Inland Xinjiang Senior Secondary School Classes (Chen 2008; Chen and Postiglione 2009) and abbreviated as "Xinjiang Classes" (Chen 2008; Chen and Postiglione 2009). I have chosen to play with the absence of plural suffixes in modern Chinese and have taken the liberty of translating this program as the "Xinjiang Class" despite the Uyghur language use of *sinipliri*, or "classes." I have chosen to leave "class" in its singular form to show that, although there are multiple schools hosting Uyghur senior high students across China, these schools are part of one overarching program that is managed with a considerable degree of uniformity.
10. I use the term *neidi* throughout this book because my informants distinguished the Han-majority provinces as such. Their use of this term vis-à-vis Xinjiang (as well as the Tibet Autonomous Region) implies that inner China is defined by cultural, linguistic, and religious practices that differ greatly from those predominating in Uyghur-majority communities in Xinjiang.
11. Throughout this book, I use *Weiwu'er*—the Chinese rendering of *Uyghur*—to refer to the state-defined identity offered to Uyghurs.

Ethnicity and the State

Scholars have gone to great lengths to produce a taxonomy for malleable and ambiguous social units such as "nation," "ethnic group," and "ethnic minority" (Atkin 1992; Bromley and Koslov 1989; Cheboksarov 1970; Connor 2004; Gellner 1983; Harrell 2001; Hobsbawm 1990; Shanin 1989, 409–13; Smith 1998). Space prevents recapitulating every influential argument on these topics here, but it is worth noting the several important works informing the current study. Ethnic groups are but one of many "reference groups" available to individuals (Ardener 1972). Members of an ethnic group constellate, delimit social boundaries, and crystallize feelings of shared belonging through the identification, maintenance, and performance of ethnic markers (Harrell 2001), or "styles" (Royce 1982)—which may include language, religion, culture, and common kinship—deemed different from those of another group. Therefore, attachment to one's ethnic group intensifies because of social interaction (Barth 1969; Butler 1990), and the decision to identify with a particular ethnic community over other social groupings is situational and strategic (Atkin 1992; Gladney 1994; Royce 1982; Shahrani 1984).

Instead of understanding ethnic groups as ancient, natural, and enduring, social scientists have recognized the state's increasingly active role in codifying ethnic categories and reifying ethnic loyalties so they appear to be concrete social realities (Brubaker 1996; Smith 1998, 145–58). Although we should be careful not to treat ethnic groups as coherent and homogeneous social units (Brubaker 2002, 166), we cannot ignore the real consequences of ethnic mobilization for political gains. Sometimes this process works in favor of state interests; sometimes it does not.

If mishandled by the state, ethnic diversity can breed political discord. The potential for an otherwise benign ethnic identity to become "malignant" and "fester" into ethno-nationalism, (i.e., the convergence of ethnic identity and sovereignty—or at least the aspiration for this political configuration) (Connor 1973)—threatens a multiethnic state's territorial integrity. Clifford Geertz (1973, 260–61) reminds us:

> To an increasing degree national unity is maintained not by calls to blood and land but by a vague, intermittent, and routine allegiance to a civil state. . . . Economic or class or intellectual disaffection threatens revolution, but disaffection based on race, language, or culture threatens partition, irredentism, or merger, a redrawing of the very limits of the state, a new definition of its domain.

To be sure, ethnic identity and national consciousness do not follow a neatly charted teleology—a topic Prasenjit Duara (1995) discusses in greater detail—and others have convincingly shown the difficulties predicting which ethnic groups are likely to engage in separatist movements (Horowitz 1981; Smith 1979). Indeed, ethnic identity remains an important social phenomenon precisely because it fluctuates, is in constant negotiation, and its boundaries shift unpredictably. Nevertheless, I want to draw attention to the tendency for outbreaks of protest and violence framed in terms of "ethnic conflict" (Leibold 2016b) to be direct responses to a state's ethnic praxes (Horowitz 1981, 167–68).

If communitarian violence (often referred to in its shorthand as "ethnic") is precipitated by domestic policies, a fundamental question presents itself: Can modern states—or perhaps more accurately, their institutions—effectively squeeze multiple and sometimes oppositional ethnic identities into a coherent national vision? Marxist treatises stipulate that the state subjugates its citizenry through the use of violence carried out by a tightly bound institution (e.g., the government, the army, courts, prisons), or the repressive state apparatus (RSA) (Althusser 1971, 140–48). According to Althusser, this blueprint overlooked the ideological state apparatus (ISA)—that is, the myriad social domains (e.g., the media, literature, arts, and public schools) strung together by the ideology of the dominant class (Althusser 1971, 144–45). The ideology of the ruling class is infused into the ISA and confers to the individual his identity vis-à-vis the state. Operating on a subconscious level, the ideology of the ISA compels an individual to respond to the hypothetical police officer who is shouting "Hey, you there!" (Althusser 1971, 174).

Nation-building projects have turned to state schooling to "interpellate" disparate populaces. For example, colonial schools in British India sought to bring "peripheral" Indians into the cultural fold of the British metropole. In his "Minute on Education," Thomas Macaulay (1835) urged to educate "a class of persons Indian in blood and colour, but English in tastes, in opinions, in morals and in intellect." Even in ostensibly "homogeneous" late nineteenth- and early twentieth-century France, readily accessible and free public education was perhaps Paris's most useful institution in its attempt to acculturate and "civilize" the people of the French countryside (Weber 1976, 303–38). The former Soviet Union provides a crowning example illustrating the potential for a vast centrally controlled education system to inculcate a national consciousness in culturally disparate peoples. Vladimir Lenin (1870–1924) initially championed the use of indigenous languages (i.e., non-Russian) for many social settings, and early Soviet education—reflecting Lenin's position—was, in fact, multilingual (Smith 1997). However, by the late 1930s, the Soviets, under the direction of Joseph Stalin (1878–1953), shifted their policy to effect the gradual Russification of education throughout the union (Fierman 2009; Kirkwood 1991; Laitin 1996).

The governments of the United States, Canada, and Australia employed similar policies toward indigenous peoples, and to similar ends. Throughout the nineteenth and twentieth centuries, the US federal government used schooling as a means to assimilate multitribal Native American children. As early as 1819, Congress passed legislation to appropriate funds for the education of Native American children. Decades later, in passing the 1887 Dawes General Allotment Act, sometimes referred to as the "Indian Emancipation Act," Congress sought to accelerate the assimilation of native peoples by dividing tribal lands and reservations into private plots, a strategy lawmakers believed would dissolve tribal affinities.

Off-reservation boarding schools for native children were established shortly after Congress passed the Dawes Act. The first off-reservation schools were spearheaded by Richard H. Pratt (1840–1924), a Civil War veteran who commanded regiments of former slaves (Child 2000, 5–6; Lomawaima 1994, 2). Pratt predicted the removal of native children from their families combined with a Christian education far from their homes would destroy tribal loyalties. Pratt's strategy to "immerse [the Native American] in civilization and keep him there until well soaked" (Utley 1964, xxi, cited in Lomawaima 1994, 4) was well received by state and federal legislators, and off-reservation Native American boarding schools began to spring up across many parts of the United States.

Though the US government did not establish or run the boarding schools according to a common plan, one can descry consistent goals among these institutions. Similar regulations and the common purpose of assimilating Native American children tied together the otherwise unconnected schools (Szasz 2005). Or as one informed observer has summarized, "The [Native American boarding school] was designed to separate children from all that was familiar to them—their families, tribes, languages, traditions, their very identities" (Child 2000, 6) while providing a space to instill discipline and teach students "practical" skills such as proper grooming habits, etiquette, and employable trades.[12]

Ethnicity and the State in China

Likewise, the CCP has devoted great energy and care to molding minzu identities since 1949, but its policies have been inconsistent. Although amalgamation (Ch. *ronghe*), or the melting together of Han and non-Han minzu, has undergirded the CCP's ethnic praxes (Mackerras 1994; Zang 2015, 20–27), policies on minzu minority rights have vacillated between assimilatory and conciliatory phases. Other national campaigns underwent similar cycles of "tightening" (Ch. *shou*) and "loosening" (Ch. *fang*) (Baum 1997). For example, in the early 1950s CCP officials expected minority minzu to demonstrate only minimal loyalty to the party and its programs (Dreyer 1976, 25; Zang 2015, 23–24). In fact, officials believed minority minzu would be drawn naturally to the economically and culturally "superior" Han (Hyer 2016, 78) and therefore exercised patience toward the persistence of minority minzu customs (Dreyer 1968, 97–98; Mackerras 1994, 146; McMillen 1979, 113–14). However, large-scale radical socialist campaigns such as the Great Leap Forward (1958–1962) and the Great Proletarian Cultural Revolution (1966–1976) violently suppressed expressions of minority minzu culture (Zang 2015, 23–24) to the point that some individuals denied their own minority status (Wu 1990).

---

12. The US Congress passed a bill in 2010 that recognized "years of official depredations, ill-conceived policies, and the breaking of covenants by the federal government regarding Indian tribes." The bill also urged then-president Barack Obama to issue a formal apology (US Congress 2010).

The Reform Era's (1978–) first two decades witnessed a return to more loosened policies toward ethnic and religious expression. For example, minority minzu have been afforded a package of preferential policies (Ch. *youhui zhengce*) in family planning, education, and employment to help them gain their footing in an otherwise Han-dominated society (Ma 2009; Sautman 1998, 1999). Mosques have been restored and rebuilt (Gillette 2000; Gladney 1991, 162 and 175; Hillman 2004; McCarthy 2009, 147–48); Tibetan monasteries have once again become active centers for Buddhist learning, albeit under the party's watch (Goldstein and Kapstein 1998; Slobodník 2004); and the annual state-led hajj has been reinstated (Ma 2008, 10–12). Many minority minzu communities have even benefited economically from China's opening by constructing "ethnic villages" to attract domestic and foreign tourists (Oakes 1993; Schein 1997).

However, since taking office in 2012, Xi Jinping has tightened his grip on religious and cultural expression, especially among Muslims. Throughout Hui (Tungan or Chinese Muslim) communities, officials are "sinicizing" Islamic practices by removing crescents from mosques, halting the new construction of "Arab-style" mosques, and banning amplified calls to prayer recited in Arabic (Gan 2018). As will be discussed throughout this book, the CCP is also placing suffocating limits on the ways in which Uyghurs can express their ethno-religious identities.

Despite its inconsistent practices, the CCP attempts to preserve the integrity of its ethnic identification campaign and its system for managing its non-Han peoples by tracing and fixing contours for each minzu.[13] Therefore, minzu identity is supposed to operate in a fundamentally different way from ethnic identity or race; minzu identity is (ideally) unchanging, inherently political, and directly buttressed by state (i.e., CCP) support (Ma 2010). At various times, the CCP has created, shaped, and constrained minzu identities according to Marxist-Leninist theory while provoking countervailing (non-Chinese) ethno-national consciousness among others.

Research on minority minzu identity has reflected the uneven results of the CCP's ethnic engineering projects. Long-term ethnographic research has brought attention to the creative ways by which minority minzu internalize, redefine, and assert their identities. These studies demonstrate that official minzu designations help to foster—and in some cases create where it never existed—strong group identification, even at the expense of a corporate Chinese identity.[14] Other studies have overemphasized the role of the state and its institutions in this process, especially

---

13. Ma Rong (2011, 2012), an influential Peking University sociologist, has advocated for a "de-politicization" of ethnic issues in China. He recommends replacing the term *minzu*—when referring to the fifty-six ethno-national groups—with "ethnic group" (Ch. *zuqun*). His proposed model would also strip many minority minzu of the preferential policies that they are currently afforded. Although Ma's ideas are gaining traction within some academic and political circles, they have not replaced the current system. See also Leibold 2013.
14. Here I draw on the rich literature on ethnicity in China. For a short list, see Blum 2001; Borchigud 1995; Bovingdon 2010; Gillette 2000; Gladney 1996; Gladney 2004; Kaup 2000; Hansen; 1999; Harrell 2001; Hillman 2004; Hillman and Henfry 2006; Leibold and Chen 2014; Litzinger 2000; McCarthy 2009; Rudelson 1997; Schein 2000; Smith Finley 2013.

in the context of state schooling (Gladney 1990, 15; 1999; Kormondy 2002; Yu 2010; Zhu 2007a). As a result, this scholarship tends to overlook the importance of agency, or the ability to manipulate social structures to improve one's fortune (Sewell 1992, 20). Following this basic line of inquiry, this study will explore the tremendous scope within existing minzu and ethno-national categories for individual Uyghurs to embrace multiple identities. In doing so, it will also highlight instances when these individuals responded to competing nonstate ideologies—a process Michel Pêcheux (1982, 99–102) describes as "unevenness subordination." Although Xinjiang Class students are "interpellated" by their boarding school education, profiles of these young adults will show how minority minzu bend, pull, stretch, and sometimes break beyond the limits of their state-ascribed identities.

Fitting the Uyghurs into the Weiwu'er Minzu

The CCP did not begin its state-building projects in the Tarim and Junggar Basins—present-day XUAR—from scratch. In fact, Xinjiang's territorial incorporation within a China-based state has remained largely uninterrupted since Manchu Qing forces (1644–1911) crushed Yaqub Beg's (1820–1877) Kashgar-based Islamic emirate and reconfigured the region as a province in 1884 (Clarke 2007; Kim 2004; Jacobs 2016). From the late nineteenth century onward, there have been only two brief yet notable interruptions to "Chinese" sovereignty in Xinjiang. The First East Turkestan Republic—officially named the Turkish Islamic Republic of Eastern Turkestan (TIRET) because of its strong ties to Pan-Islam (Forbes 1986)—was announced in November 1933, following widespread rebellion in Qumul (Ch. *Hami*), Turpan, and southern Xinjiang; but it was defeated by Hui forces loyal to the Guomindang (GMD) in 1934. Subsequently, from 1934 to 1941, Sheng Shicai, with Soviet backing, administered Xinjiang as a puppet state (Millward and Nabijan Tursun 2004, 78–81). In October 1944 rebellion against Chinese rule broke out in the northwest city of Ghulja (Ch. Yining), and a coalition army declared the establishment of the second East Turkestan Republic (ETR) (Millward 2007, 215–17). A government composed of GMD and ETR leaders formed in July 1946, but internal disputes severely undermined its legitimacy (Millward 2007, 220–24). The CCP's defeat of the GMD in 1949, and the mysterious crash of an airplane transporting ETR leaders to a meeting in Beijing, dashed all hopes of an East Turkestan independent of Chinese rule.

By this time, however, indigenous intellectuals were already promoting a collective Uyghur identity. Centuries before the CCP's recognition of a Weiwu'er minzu, Soviet meetings on the "nationality problem" (Edgar 2004; Hirsch, 2005; Slezkine 1994), and even before the Qing's conquest of Xinjiang, the sedentary Turkic-speaking dwellers of the Tarim Basin's oases (which would come to be known as Altisheher in the local vernacular)[15] began cementing collective identities based on linguistic, religious, and regional loyalties. By the seventeenth century, the region had completed its conversion to Islam. Altisheher's Muslims then possessed linguistic and religious boundaries to separate them from the region's non-Muslim and non-Turkic-speaking Jews, Chinese, Mongols, and Manchu. Islam provided an essential vehicle for ethnic mobilization as it equipped its faithful with common stories, shared experiences, texts, and—through pilgrimages to important Islamic holy sites—it charted a religious landscape (Thum 2014).[16] Over time, the elements of this protonational identity coalesced into a "discrete group consciousness" (Newby 2007, 16). Individual communities, then, filled this space with "cultural stuff"—a habitus (Bourdieu 1977) in the form of an economic organization of society, common life-cycle rituals, social norms, and religious rituals (Bellér-Hann 2008).

Encroaching empires from both the East and West helped bring to fruition the region's germinating collective identities. Russian and Chinese (Qing and Republican) imperial practices "forced Uyghurs to adopt more strict perceptions of their cultural identity" (Roberts 2009, 365). Although indigenous elites debated over promoting Kashgarians in the south or Taranchis in the north as the touchstone for this national identity, they eventually rallied around the revival of the Uyghur ethnonym, a term that had fallen out of use for over five hundred years (Brophy 2016; Klimeŝ 2015). Cultural promotion societies—organizations responsible for, among other matters, popularizing education—began to "teach" this identity in their schools "making it an everyday category in the minds of literate Xinjiang people" (Schluessel 2009, 399). To be clear, Soviet, and later Chinese, bureaucrats did not invent a transregional ethnic identity and impose it on the Uyghurs (Gladney 1990). Rather, they "officialized" (Bourdieu 1999, 223–24) already existing identifications at a national level (Brophy 2005; Klimeŝ 2015; Roberts 2009).

Therefore, it should not be surprising that the Uyghurs have yet to be fully integrated into the Chinese mainstream (Clarke 2007), despite living within the borders of the PRC for over sixty years. In fact, CCP policy appears to have strengthened Uyghur ethno-national identity. By drawing administrative boundaries around the Tarim and Junggar Basins and naming it the Xinjiang Uyghur Autonomous Region, the CCP has further solidified a fluid Uyghur identity (Bovingdon 2004). In other words, XUAR's borders have bound the Uyghurs firmly to a political "homeland" (cf. Brubaker 1995), and Uyghur identity remains chthonic, or firmly rooted in the land (Dautcher 2009, 205). Facing growing numbers of Han people in the region, the promotion of Chinese language, and strict regulations on religious practices, Uyghurs choose cultural and, more recently, religious symbols to demarcate their

---

15. Meaning "six cities," *Altisheher* is an indigenous term for East Turkestan—modern-day Xinjiang—and refers to the major oases located east and south of the Tian Shan Mountains (Yarkand [Yeken], Kashgar, Khotan, Kuche, Aksu, and Uch-Turfan). See Thum 2014.
16. These ideas have been inspired by Anderson's (1991) and Gellner's (1983) canonical works on nationalism.

ethno-national identity (Bovingdon 2002; Cesàro 2000; Smith Finley 2013; Smith Finley and Zang 2015).

The CCP has pushed back forcefully with its own set of policies aimed at transforming Uyghur identity (i.e., defined by sedentary Central Asian and Islamic cultures) to a hollowed-out Weiwu'er zu identity, one of fifty-six minzu comprising the Zhonghua minzu. Over 85 percent of Kashgar's Uyghur neighborhoods built in the style of Central Asian *mehelle* (single family homes organized around a mosque) have been demolished, and residents have been relocated to high-rise apartment compounds (Powers 2014b). To curb "extremist" Islamic dress, especially imported styles of veiling, authorities in Xinjiang launched "Project Beauty" (Ch. *liangli gongcheng*) in September 2011. The "engineering project" (Ch. *gongcheng*) requires women to shed face veils (Uy. *niqab*), *hijab*, and long robes (Uy. *jilbab*) while it promotes "modern fashion" represented by free-flowing hair and colorful *etles* fabric (Leibold and Grose 2016, 12–16). In April 2017 officials imposed a ban on "extreme" Islamic names, which forbids parents to give their children names that are "overly religious" and requires parents to change the names of children under the age of sixteen (Radio Free Asia 2017). Names once included in state-published handbooks on Uyghur naming practices—such as Hajim, Imam, and Mahmut (Sidiq 2013)—have been replaced; in public demonstrations of their compliance, some individuals have even posted these changes in *Xinjiang Daily* (2017, 4), the most widely circulated newspaper in the region.[17]

State-sponsored schooling, though, has stood apart as the key arena through which the CCP attempts to reify Weiwu'er zu identity (as well as other minority minzu) and realign it more closely to mainstream (Han) culture. Party leaders have long recognized the importance of using schools to recruit minority minzu in its state-building projects. To this end, the CCP has designated twenty-two institutions of higher learning for non-Han students, the most prestigious being the Minzu University of China (Ch. *Zhongyang minzu daxue*) in Beijing. In addition to these institutions, minority minzu classes (Ch. *minzu ban*) wherein students complete a year of preparatory classes before they begin their regular coursework, have been established in many Chinese universities (Sautman 1998, 83–86).

CCP officials have prioritized the expansion of state schooling, especially since Uyghur education levels are lower than Han (SCCO 2002, 563–67).[18] Their efforts are paying off. Between 1982 and 2006 the percentage of Uyghurs over the age of six who received a primary school education increased from 37 percent to 53.1 percent;

---

17. One such post reads, "My son's former name was Qedirdin Mahmut (ID number: XXX). I changed his name to Qedirdin Memetyüsüp. We live at X County, Y Village."
18. The Chinese government rarely publicizes data revealing education levels or income broken down by minzu. However, in 2002, the State Council Census Office released statistics gathered in the year 2000 that measured the highest education level of individuals older than age six from fourteen minzu. According to these numbers, Han with a primary, middle, high school, and university education stood at 37.6 percent, 37.3 percent, 8.8 percent, and 3.8 percent, respectively. Uyghurs with a primary, junior high, high school, and university education stood at 53.1 percent 24.6 percent, 4.3 percent, and 2.7 percent, respectively.

those who received a junior high school (Ch. *chuzhong*)[19] education doubled from 12 percent to 24.6 percent; and those who received a senior high school education (Ch. *gaozhong*)[20] has hovered around 5 percent (Gladney 1999, 73; SCCO 2002, 563–67, cited in Ma 2008, 368). The percentage of college-educated Uyghur adults has also risen, albeit modestly, from 0.1 percent in 1982 to 2.7 percent in 2000 (Gladney 1999, 73; SCCO 2002, 563–67, cited in Ma 2008), and statistics released in 2006 indicate that this number has reached 3.1 percent (CASTED 2006, 71). According to numbers calculated from the 2010 census, the most recent, highest level of education attainment among Uyghurs at the primary, junior high, senior high and postsecondary (university or vocational) levels stood respectively at 41.6 percent, 42.0 percent, 6.6 percent, and 6.3 percent (Liu 2014, 73).

Despite improving education levels nationwide, the CCP remains desperate in its quest to garner the loyalties of Uyghur youth and has turned to boarding schools to deliver the results it desires. We can trace the origins of Uyghur boarding schools to the Tibet Autonomous Region (TAR) and neighboring Tibetan areas—also hotbeds of political disloyalty (Hillman and Tuttle 2016; Sautman 2005; Yeh 2013)—in 1985, when officials developed the Tibet Class boarding school program (Ch. *Neidi Xizang gaozhong ban*) (Postiglione 2009; Postiglione and Jiao 2009; Zhu 2007a). The CCP predicted that well-equipped schools in neidi, which were to be staffed by highly trained teachers and administrators, would "produce a considerable cohort of trustworthy and knowledgeable minority cadres and specialists, and meanwhile orchestrate the generosity and benevolence of the central authorities and Han majority" (Wang and Zhou 2003, 98). Nearly thirty years after its conception, the Tibet Class remains a vital part of Tibet's education system. Yearly enrollment in the Tibetan Class has reached over 1,600 individuals at the junior high level and 3,000 individuals at the senior high school level (Tibet News Online 2015), numbers which account for nearly 20 percent of school-aged children from the TAR (Postiglione 2009, 895). According to one overzealous Han scholar, the prestige associated with these boarding schools is so great that "whereas in the past, [Tibetans] considered lamas as first-class citizens (Ch. *yi deng gongmin*), now they believe those coming to neidi to study [in the Tibetan Classes] are first-class citizens" (Piao 1990, 46).

The decision to establish a similar program for Xinjiang's minority minzu students was announced in 1999, after four years of violence rattled the region. In July 1995 Uyghurs in Khotan took to the streets demanding information about two popular imams—Islamic clergy—whom Chinese authorities had arrested. A Uyghur-led demonstration, unrelated to the incident in Khotan, was organized in Ghulja (Ch. *Yining*) on August 14 (Millward 2007, 328–29). In an incident unreported in Chinese media, a Uyghur cadre and three of his family members were violently murdered in Kuchar (Ch. *Kuche*) in 1996 (Smith Finley 2013, 10 and 202).

---

19. In the PRC junior high school typically includes grades seven through nine of its twelve-year system.
20. In the PRC senior high school typically includes grades ten through twelve of its twelve-year system.

In 1997 the Ghulja Incident and the ensuing violence that erupted in Ürümchi on February 25 shook social stability in Xinjiang once again.[21] The insurrection added urgency for the CCP to enforce the policy recommendations laid out in the 1996 Central Committee drafted "Document No. 7," which identified "radical" Islam as an example of rising Uyghur nationalism (Bovingdon 2010, 67–69; Millward 2007, 342). To gain an upper hand, the CCP decided to take the fight against Uyghur separatism, radical Islam, and—after 9/11—"terrorism" outside the autonomous region's borders and into classrooms in neidi. From the perspective of the CCP, the Xinjiang Class was and is a matter of national security.

Methodology

This study seeks to "envision schools as instruments of national policy and sites for constructing social alternatives" (Ross 2000, 126). To this end, I draw on over thirty months of field research conducted in Beijing and several oases of the XUAR between February 2006 and July 2017. During this eleven-year period, I embarked on nine separate research trips to China. From February 2006 until June 2006, I was enrolled as an advanced visiting student (Ch. *gaoji jinxiu sheng*) at the Minzu University of China (MUC). While enrolled at MUC, I audited classes on the history and cultures of Xinjiang, and I was the only non-Han student participating in MUC's beginning and intermediate Uyghur language courses. I remained in China until May 2008. However, by the fall 2007 semester, I had transferred my university affiliation to the University of International Business and Economics (UIBE). In 2010 I returned to Beijing for six months as a visiting scholar at Beijing Normal University (BNU). I made seven consecutive research trips to China each summer from 2011 to 2017.

As have many other scholars, I encountered several obstacles along the way. While affiliated with MUC, I was told by the director of the university's Institute of International Education (Ch. *Guoji jiaoyu xueyuan*) that my research was too (politically) "sensitive" (Ch. *mingan*) for the school to support. I was lectured for thirty minutes about the "troubles" (Ch. *mafan*) conducting research in Xinjiang could bring to the university and myself. The school official urged me to examine the minority minzu of Yunnan province because they are "harmonious" (Ch. *hexie*). I had little choice but to change my school affiliation if I desired to carry out my research.

After completing my doctoral coursework at Indiana University's Department of Central Eurasian Studies, I returned to China in 2010 for six months of research. During this period, I attempted to gain access to one of Beijing's Xinjiang Classes.

---

21. The Ghulja Incident likely occurred in response to CCP-imposed restrictions on the practice of *meshrep*, or the secret gatherings for Uyghur men whose members abide by Islamic codes of conduct, and on other religious activities deemed "illegal" (Ch. *feifa zongjiao huodong*) (Millward 2007, 329–34; cf. Pawan, Dawut, and Kurban 2017).

My request was aided by one of BNU's senior faculty members, the individual who invited me to his school and who conducted research on national-level Tibetan boarding schools. Coincidentally, this particular faculty member was a former classmate of the principal at a local Xinjiang Class. My faculty sponsor at BNU arranged a date with the principal for us to visit the school together. As the date of the planned visitation drew near, my faculty mentor shared a bit of information to his friend that he had not previous disclosed—I was an American researcher. My invitation to the boarding class was immediately revoked, but I continued my research focusing on Uyghur graduates of the program.

I spoke with over sixty Uyghur graduates of the Xinjiang Class during the total research period. Despite my use of snowball sampling, a method in which the researcher relies on key contacts to meet others within the targeted group (Bernard 2006, 193), my informants are representative of the Xinjiang Class's student body (see Chapter 1). Participants included thirty-three women and thirty-one men who graduated from eleven of the original twelve cities hosting a Xinjiang Class. Also included in this study are individuals from the Xinjiang Class's first seven cohorts (2000–2006). The hometowns of my informants are equally representative of the Xinjiang Class's enrollment quotas. That is, 70 percent of my informants (forty-five out of sixty-four individuals) were raised in southern Xinjiang (e.g., Kashgar, Khotan, Aksu, and Atush) before enrolling in the boarding school program. This figure compares closely with the widely published requirement stipulating that 80 percent of all Xinjiang Class students should be from southern Xinjiang (see Chapter 1).

Through regular interactions with these young highly educated individuals, I sought to learn about their ethno-national identities, their personal commitments to Islam, and their abilities to navigate between two seemingly distinct sets of cultural practices—Uyghur and Han. The majority of data for this research was collected through participant observation of their post–boarding school lives and semistructured interviews. I conducted semistructured interviews in the language preferred by the informant. However, by October 2010, after completing an advanced intensive one-on-one Uyghur language course, I interviewed my interlocutors in Uyghur.

In some regards, my research methodology differed significantly from the majority of research conducted on minority minzu boarding schools and, more broadly, minority minzu education in China (Chen 2008; Hansen 1999; Yu 2010; Zhao 2010; Zhu 2007a, 2007b). To begin, my research includes only those students who graduated from the Xinjiang Class. Unable to gain access to a boarding school, I hinged my research on the participation of graduates, and my research was conducted outside the confines of a school. Although visitations to the boarding schools would have enriched this study, in other ways conducting research outside of the schools proved to be rewarding. School officials never monitored my activities (see, for example, Hansen 1999), and my informants could speak frankly about their experiences. Not confined to a campus or classroom, I met with individuals at coffee shops, soccer matches, informal language exchanges, Muslim restaurants and cafeterias, and celebrations organized by Uyghur university students.

This study is also longitudinal. As I stated earlier, I carried out my research between February 2006 and July 2017. On each "focused revisit"—a method valued because of its potential for applying new theories to the field as well as providing opportunities to record important historical changes (Burawoy 2003, 647; Foster et al. 1979)—I attempted to reconnect with my informants. I used follow-up interviews to gauge whether students' attitudes and opinions toward the Xinjiang Class and their ethno-national identities had changed. Although there are several individuals in this study with whom I spoke on only one occasion, I met with a majority of informants on multiple occasions over a span of several years.

During all components of the research program, my first priority was to protect the safety and anonymity of my interlocutors. Because of the political sensitivity associated with conducting research on the Uyghurs (see Smith Finley 2006), I only recorded handwritten notes of my interviews in a journal I kept with me at all times. Although I did not keep audio records of my interviews, I have strived to keep all quotes from my interlocutors as close to verbatim as possible.

Limitations

I have made every effort to conduct methodologically sound research. However, there are several limitations to this study that must be addressed. First, the majority of data have been collected from the responses of sixty-four graduates of the Xinjiang Class. Statistically speaking, this number, compared with the total number of Xinjiang Class students during its twenty-year history, is unimpressive. Nonetheless, I trust that the richness of these interactions can compensate for my inability to recruit more participants. Second, I recognize that my status as a foreign researcher may have elicited certain types of responses from my interlocutors. As later chapters will make clear, the individuals included in this study expressed strikingly different attitudes toward the CCP, Han people, and other matters, compared to individuals who were included in studies about minority minzu education in China that had been conducted by Han researchers (see, for example, Chen 2008; Yang 2017; Yu 2010; Zhao 2010; Zhu 2007). Recognizing that my own status may have influenced my informants' comments—as Han researchers' statuses may have affected what their respondents told them—I do not seek to discredit previous research but only hope readers will view my findings as an interesting counternarrative. Nevertheless, one can at least assert that a researcher not obviously identified with any group directly involved in a contentious situation is less likely to introduce a bias by evoking positive or negative group feelings in informants (Bernard 2006, 373; Starn 2011).

Structure of the Book

This book is organized into four main chapters and a conclusion. The first chapter introduces the institutional hallmarks of the Xinjiang Class. It carefully examines the CCP's current objectives for maintaining costly boarding schools for Uyghur students. It draws on documents drafted by China's Ministry of Education, Xinjiang's Department of Education, and individual schools hosting a Xinjiang Class, as well as oral histories, to paint a vivid picture of the daily lives of Xinjiang Class students. The chapter pays careful attention to the ways Xinjiang Class students both comply with and resist school policies.

Chapter 2 assesses the effectiveness of the program in meeting its political goals. It demonstrates the ways in which Xinjiang Class graduates embrace and assert an ethno-national identity that is sometimes in contradistinction to a corporate Chinese identity. This identity, expressed through renewed efforts to practice Islam, the insistence on speaking Uyghur, and the reluctance to befriend Han classmates, persists after graduation from the Xinjiang Class. Paradoxically, the performance of transregional and transnational identities is possible because these individuals participated in the boarding school program and embraced some elements of "Chinese" identity.

Chapter 3 reveals the tendency for Xinjiang Class graduates to seek opportunities abroad or in neidi instead of returning to Xinjiang. China's Ministry of Education and Xinjiang's provincial-level government place pressure on Xinjiang Class graduates to return after their formal education. Yet many delay their homecomings indefinitely. I interpret these students' decisions as a tacit expression of ethno-national identity and an unwillingness to pay back their "debt" to the party.

The final chapter follows Xinjiang Class graduates' return to the XUAR. Contrary to the political goals of the program, few of its graduates return to the region with the intention of serving the party, their country, or even their hometowns. More often, institutional restraints that cripple mobility in China, unrelenting pressure from family members, and inconveniences adhering to Islamic practices in neidi compel these individuals to return. The return, however, only marks the beginning of a sometimes-frustrating process of reintegration. The second part of this chapter describes how these young adults reacclimate to daily life in Xinjiang. I focus on the difficulties these individuals experience in their social and professional lives.

1
Incubating Loyalty (or Resistance) in Chinese Boarding Schools

> You can clearly tell the darker, skinnier students are those who have just begun their preparatory studies, and the whiter, taller, and stronger students are seniors.
>
> —Sun Qi, director, Xinjiang Class Office of Student Affairs

A Tried-and-Tested Method for Educating Young Uyghurs

The party announced the Xinjiang Class in a brief five hundred-character statement. A 1999 policy paper on "strengthening minority minzu education" (Ch. *jiaqiang shaoshu minzu jiaoyu*) drafted by the General Office of the State Council confirmed that a senior high school boarding program was scheduled to begin in fall 2000. The document indicated that one thousand students—80 percent of whom must be rural and nomadic minority minzu (Ch. *shaoshu minzu nongmu min zinü*)—would enroll in courses taught entirely in Chinese at one of twelve designated cities in neidi. Few additional details were provided at that time.

Party officials surely scrambled to fill the one thousand vacancies. In late January 2000 the CCP—recognizing the "time crunch" (Ch. *shijian jin*)—laid out very basic selection criteria: participation must be completely voluntary, and students must be junior high school graduates, be outstanding morally and in their studies (Ch. *pinxue jianyou*), and be in good health. Individuals accepted into the program would only be required to pay at most a RMB 900 (USD 135)[1] flat fee per year to cover tuition, room and board, medical treatment, and roundtrip train transportation from Xinjiang to neidi (Ministry of Education 2000).

In the final eight months leading up to the inaugural Xinjiang Class, the CCP drafted two key governing documents for its new boarding schools. The Ministry of Education's May 2000 "Summary of the Xinjiang Class Work Meeting" affirms the program's commitment to instilling socialist values in Xinjiang's youth. It also reveals the additional aim of improving Uyghur-Han relations. Article three explains:

---

1. All RMB-USD conversations were calculated using July 2018 exchange rates (RMB 1: USD 0.15).

> The Xinjiang Class will be established at schools in provinces (or municipalities) where Han people make up the majority. Doing so will help promote friendships between minority minzu and Han people from neidi . . . as well as help to establish a relationship of cooperation between neidi and Xinjiang. (Ministry of Education 2000)

Here the party evokes its strategy to encourage intermingling (Ch. *hunhe*) and amalgamation (Ch. *ronghe*) between minzu to weaken intense ethnic loyalties. Publicly, China's Communist leaders promote cultural and intellectual exchange between minzu groups in hopes they will gradually fuse into an all-inclusive Zhonghua minzu collectivity (Mackerras 1994, 8). In reality, the process is didactic and hegemonic (Hansen 1999; Harrell 1995; Smith Finley 2016); minority minzu are to become more like the Han.

The June 2000 "Administrative Procedures of the Xinjiang Class" (Ch. *neidi Xinjiang gaozhong ban guanli banfa*) established the program's guiding principles and bylaws in twenty-six articles. The document opens:

> The Xinjiang Class must fully carry out the national education policy and minzu policies, provide quality education, and always implement education's demands for the "three directions" and "four unifications" so that it can train qualified senior high school graduates from Xinjiang who support the Chinese Communist Party's leaders, love China, love socialism, defend the unity of China, [and] uphold [the principle of] "minzu unity" . . . and are determined to dedicate themselves to socialist modernization. (China Education and Research Network)[2]

Article 10 reiterates:

> Schools hosting a Xinjiang Class will adhere to the socialist direction for managing schools; [they will] emphasize moral education work, Marxism, Mao Zedong Thought, Deng Xiaoping Theory and the Party's minzu theory as guides. In accordance with the overall goals of moral education, the growth of students, as well as the [special] characteristics of minority minzu students, courses and teaching activities, in and out of the classroom, will be guided in the context of political and ideological work. In addition to requiring organized political thought classes . . . special attention will be placed on strengthening support for the Chinese Communist Party, on loving the socialist motherland, on upholding the unity of Chinese patriotic education, and on strengthening minzu unity—i.e., Han people are inseparable from minority minzu, minority minzu are inseparable from the

---

2. Deng Xiaoping formulated the "three directions" of Chinese education in 1983. Deng believed Chinese education should be geared towards "modernization" (Ch. *xiandai hua*), the "world" (Ch. *shijie*) and the "future" (Ch. *weilai*). During Peking University's 100-year anniversary celebration on May 4, 1998, Jiang Zemin proposed four criteria, the "four unifications" (Ch. *si ge tongyi*), for Chinese education. These are "the unification of studying science and culture along with strengthening ideological cultivation" (Ch. *xuexi kexue wenhua yu jiaqiang sixiang xiuyang*), "the unification of book knowledge with practical experience" (Ch. *shuben zhishi yu toushen shehui shijian*), "the unification of the realization of self-worth with service to the Chinese people" (Ch. *shixian zishen jiazhi yu fuwu zuguo renmin*); and "the unification of ambitious ideals with painstaking struggles" (Ch. *yuanda lixiang yu jinxing xianku fendou*).

Han, and every minority minzu is inseparable from each other. (China Education and Research Network 2000)

Details about the program's basic curriculum are buried deep beneath the boilerplate. The first year of coursework is to be devoted to "preparatory courses" (Ch. *yuke*) aimed at improving Chinese language skills and building strong foundations in mathematics and the physical sciences. Courses in classical Chinese (Ch. *guwen*)[3] and English are also to be taught during this intensive first year. Students who successfully complete their yearlong preparatory course are to study the local curriculum for the remaining three years of their schooling (China Education and Research Network 2000).

The CCP's intentions were clear from the beginning: the boarding schools were established to be insulated spaces for promoting party ideals. CCP officials and school administrators give primacy to political indoctrination before educational goals, which sets the Xinjiang Class apart from otherwise similar regional institutions attended by Han students (*Economist* 2017a), but ties it closely to the Tibetan boarding school program (Postiglione 2008; Yang 2017; Zhu 2007a). The CCP's "Grand Ethnic Experiment" (McKenzie 2014) to acculturate young Uyghurs to the Chinese mainstream through a boarding school experience in neidi was to begin in a matter of months.

Enrollment

Applications have poured into the Xinjiang Class Administration Office since 1999. The open-enrollment policy of the Xinjiang Class separates it from boarding schools for indigenous children in North America and Australia during the nineteenth and early twentieth centuries, when students were—at least initially—forcibly removed from their homes (Amir 2015; Jacobs 2006). During the Xinjiang Class's first admissions cycle, student applications exceeded vacancies by 20,000; in certain regions, applicants outnumbered available spots fifty to one (SEAC 2004). This trend has continued. During the 2015 admissions cycle, nearly 41,000 applicants vied for one of only 10,000 spots (New Oriental 2015); in 2017, 43,000 students applied for 9,880 openings (*Xinjiang Daily* 2017).

Officials have responded to the overflow of applicants by implementing an invasive admissions review process to ensure classrooms are filled with only top-performing students whose families' political dossiers are blemish-free. Recruitment cycles typically extend into six months from beginning to completion and require the coordination of the provincial, county, and village/township governments. For instance, in 2015 the recruitment cycle kicked off in March with a month devoted to

---

3. Although not a formal subject of the *gaokao* National Higher Education Entrance Examination, classical Chinese poetry is often included in the language arts section of the exam.

publicity work. March 7 was designated as the XUAR's region-wide Xinjiang Class Publicity Day (Ch. *Xuanchuan ri*) (Xinjiang Class 2015d).

Following publicity work, students may complete online registration forms. Before being tested in any academic subject, students wishing to enroll in the program undergo thorough political screening. The Xinjiang Class Administration Office, working in coordination with local and provincial-level education departments (Wu 2013, 41), evaluates potential students' and their families' commitments to upholding Deng Xiaoping's Four Cardinal Principles (Ch. *si xiang jiben yuanze*);[4] to loving the fatherland (Ch. *re ai zuguo*); to protecting minzu unity (Ch. *weihu minzu tuanjie*); and to abiding by Chinese law (Ch. *zunji shoufa*) (Bureau of Education of Turpan 2011b). As part of their political background checks, students must also complete a form in which they describe their religious beliefs (Ch. *youwu xinfeng zongjiao*), list the types of religious activities they (and their parents) have engaged in, and verify that neither they nor their families have ever violated the law (XUAR 2014).

After students are carefully vetted, they may participate in the Xinjiang Class entrance examination. Typically, students register for the examination through early April. Test takers pay a registration fee ranging from RMB 35 to RMB 42 (approximately USD 5–6), which is determined by annual household income (Bureau of Education of Ürümchi 2006). The entrance examination is uniformly administered in June, on dates roughly corresponding to the national high school entrance examination (Ch. *zhongkao*).[5] The three-day examination covers literature, mathematics, political ideology (Ch. *sixiang daode*), and history. Students are also tested in Chinese or English depending on their educational background (Bureau of Education of Turpan 2011a; Tianshan Net 2015b).[6]

Examination scores can be inflated by "bonus points" (Ch. *jiafen zhengce*). Since as early as 2007, top-performing Uyghur students in an annual "bilingual" (read: Putonghua) speech competition receive five to fifteen bonus points on their entrance examinations. Although its official name is the "Loving My Zhonghua Minzu Minority Minzu Student Bilingual Speech Competition" (Ch. *ai wo*

---

4. Deng Xiaoping announced the Four Cardinal Principles in 1979. According to Deng, the Four Cardinal Principles (i.e., keeping the socialist road, upholding the dictatorship of the proletariat, upholding the leadership of the Communist Party, and upholding Marxism-Leninism and Mao Zedong Thought) were fundamental for modernization. See Deng 1979.
5. Most cities in Xinjiang have at least one designated testing site, and many major cities have multiple testing sites. For example, there are three testing centers in Kashgar, two in Khotan, three in Ghulja, etc. Regardless of testing location, the number of examinees per room cannot exceed twenty-five (Bureau of Education of Turpan 2011a).
6. Here I am referring specifically to *minkaohan* and *minkaomin* backgrounds. Translated literally, *minkaohan* (民考汉) simply refers to minority minzu students who take their standardized tests, usually the college entrance examinations, using the Chinese language. *Minkaomin* (民考民), on the other hand, complete their exams in their minority minzu language. Although these designations refer to an individual's testing language, the vast majority of *minkaohan* students attend schools in which the dominant language of instruction has been Chinese, whereas *minkaomin* classes use a minority minzu language as the primary language of classroom instruction.

Zhonghua–shaoshu minzu xuesheng shuangyu kouyu dasai), the event showcases and rewards students who have obtained high levels of Putonghua. The "bilingual" aspect of the competition refers to participants' mother languages. The five-to-fifteen-point scale is determined as follows: students who place in the top three of their school's competition receive five points; students who place in the top three of their respective districts receive ten points; and students who place in the top three of the Xinjiang-wide competition receive fifteen points. These points, however, are not cumulative. For example, if an individual finishes in the top three of the Xinjiang-wide competition, that person is only granted fifteen (not thirty) points (Xinjiang Class Online 2011a). An additional five to ten points are awarded to students whose parents forgo a third birth (Tianshan Net 2007).[7]

The Xinjiang Class's bonus-point policy is yet another example of the CCP's carrot-and-stick approach to governing its ethnic borderlands (Leibold 2015); it provides an additional incentive for Uyghur families to comply with controversial policies in Xinjiang.[8] Families in violation of the law put their children at risk of being left out of the program.

Final admissions decisions are determined by a quota system that considers the applicant's minzu status, prior education, hometown, and financial background. As mentioned previously, admissions officers are required to recruit 80 percent of the program's students from impoverished families living in southern Xinjiang's rural areas—regions considered to be the Uyghur Islamic heartland (Rudelson 1997; Thum 2014; Wang 2016). Specifically targeting southern Xinjiang also ensures that Xinjiang Classes will be filled mostly with Uyghur students, and that they will be separated from their religious milieu. Meanwhile, this policy restricts the number of less "restive" Kazakhs, Hui, Mongols, and other minzu who primarily reside in northern and eastern Xinjiang (see Table 1.1).

---

7. Families who adhere to Xinjiang's family planning policies receive a "certificate of honor" (Ch. *guangrong zheng*). This certificate must be presented for a student to receive bonus points. For more on the CCP's incentive program to control Xinjiang's population, see CECC 2009b.

    The CCP has imposed a complex system of measures to control China's population growth. To begin, the CCP raised the national minimum age of marriage from eighteen to twenty years for women and from twenty to twenty-two for men. In Xinjiang, however, minority minzu women may marry at eighteen and men at twenty. The CCP also limits the number of children per couple. Until 2015, Han and Zhuang couples were only permitted to give birth to one child, while most minority minzu couples, including Uyghur, were permitted two to three children since their total population was less than ten million persons. Finally, couples were rewarded with payments from both their work units (Ch. *danwei*) and the government for abiding by family planning laws.

    The family planning law has undergone rapid modification since 2015. First, officials adjusted regulations to allow all Chinese couples to give birth to two or three children, depending on rural or urban status; nevertheless, officials still advocate for "fewer, higher quality births" (Ch. *shaosheng, yousheng*). In Xinjiang, authorities limited families to three children (*Global Times* 2015a). Then, in 2017 officials once again adjusted the policy to effectively remove "preferential" treatment for minority minzu in Xinjiang. Therefore, all urban couples can birth two children, and all rural couples can birth three children (Xinjiang Health Inspection 2017).
8. For example, Uyghur families in southern Xinjiang, who until recent times had very large families, have expressed abhorrence to contraception and limits to births (Smith Finley 2013, 143–44).

Uyghur students are overrepresented in the Xinjiang Class. According to the 2010 census, only 45.8 percent of Xinjiang's total 21.8 million permanent residents are Uyghur. Han people are the second largest group at 40.5 percent. However, sporadically released enrollment plans reveal that the boarding schools are primarily targeting young Uyghurs. According to enrollment figures from 2008, 3,310 (68 percent) of the Xinjiang Class's 4,850 total vacancies were reserved for Uyghur students. Uyghur students from Kashgar (757 students), Khotan (402 students), and Aksu (348 students) alone accounted for nearly one half of all incoming students during this recruitment cycle. The remaining spots were divvied out to Kazakhs, Hui, and Han, who respectively filled 506 (10 percent), 321 (6.6 percent), and 85 (1.8 percent) of the vacancies (Xinjiang Class Online 2008). This trend continued in 2012. That year, the number of Uyghur students increased slightly to 70 percent or 5,511 of the 8,030 total vacancies (China Testing Online 2012). Some officials have even indictated that in the near future at least 90 percent of all incoming students will be Uyghur (Xinhua 2011).

Table 1.1: Xinjiang Class enrollment plans by minzu, 2008 and 2012

Minzu / Year	Kashgar	Khotan	Aksu	Uyghur subtotal	Kazakh	Han	Other	Total
2008	757	402	348	3,310	506	85	949	4,850
2012	943	491	431	5,511	805	80	1,634	8,030

Although their numbers are small compared to Uyghurs, the inclusion of other minzu in Xinjiang serves important political aims. First, a multi-minzu student body reinforces the CCP's claim that Xinjiang is the historical home to thirteen minzu and does not belong solely to the Uyghurs (China State Council 2015; cf. Bovingdon 2010, 45–46). Second, a multilingual student body necessitates the use of Putonghua for communication among Xinjiang Class students. Similar to the use of English among pan-tribal boarding schools in the US (Child 2000, 73), Putonghua is the only shared language between Uyghurs, Hui, Tajik, Mongols, and the other minzu who make Xinjiang their home.

Once quotas are met and admission decisions are released, newly enrolled students must satisfactorily pass a physical examination. According to health standards established jointly by Xinjiang's Department of Education and the Department of Public Health, students must meet minimum height, weight, and vision requirements. Students are then screened for pre-existing medical conditions, many of which can preclude them from participating in the program (Tianshan Net 2005).[9]

---

9. Disqualifying medical conditions include heart disease, any type of mental illness, obesity, ringworm, vitiligo, psoriasis, and a history of major surgery.

Figure 1.1: Xinjiang Class enrollment and schools, 2000–2018

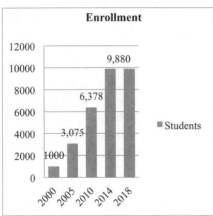
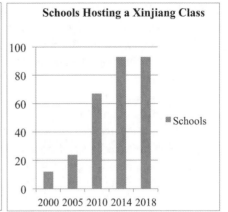

Despite its tedious and invasive application process, the Xinjiang Class has enticed young Uyghurs in droves to leave their homes and complete their formal schooling in neidi. From 2000 to 2014, yearly enrollment grew from 1,000 to over 9,000 students, with substantial increases before the 2005, 2010, 2012, and 2014 academic years. The dramatic increase before the 2010 school year was likely a response to the 2009 Ürümchi riots. The number of schools hosting a Xinjiang Class correspondingly increased from twelve to ninety-three, and these schools are spread across forty-five cities (Xinhua, 2013). Although there is little evidence suggesting a decline in applicants, officials have capped enrollment at 9,880 students for the foreseeable future (*People's Daily Online* 2015).

Certainly, the affordability of sending their children to boarding schools in neidi has helped garner support for the Xinjiang Class among Uyghur parents. Tuition is calculated on the basis of annual household income, and students are placed into one of three tuition brackets. Households in which at least one parent receives a government salary pay RMB 900 (USD 135); students raised in households in which both parents are farmers, or if one parent is unemployed, pay RMB 450 (USD 65); and families who experience extreme economic hardship are not required to pay tuition (Shanghai Songjiang No.1 High School 2010a). Several of my informants hinted that the low costs of the Xinjiang Class swayed their parents to send them to neidi. One male student from Kashgar whose father is an elementary school teacher and whose mother is a homemaker explained:

> At that time [when I was in middle school] the government promoted the affordability of the Xinjiang Class. Officials told my parents that they wouldn't have to worry about their own futures (Uy. *kelgusidin ensirmeysiler*) if they sent my siblings and me to study in neidi. So my father advised me [to enroll] (Uy. *bek nesihet qilatti*). Under pressure from my father, I agreed to attend the Xinjiang Class, a decision that pleased (Uy. *razi bolghan*) my parents. (field notes, June 30, 2012)

First, the influence of the young man's father is encoded in the phrase *bek nesihet qilish* (*very* strongly advise), which he used instead of *meslihet qilish* (suggest or advise). In other words, the young man probably had little choice in the matter. Second, the young man suggests that propaganda campaigns convinced his father of the Xinjiang Class's financial benefits; he would not have to worry about his son's future financial security nor would he have to worry about the immediate costs of his son's education.

Parents can avoid paying expensive school fees by enrolling their children in the Xinjiang Class. Before 2014—the year party officials in Xinjiang extended the otherwise nationwide policy to eliminate tuition and miscellaneous fees to Kashgar, Khotan, and Qizilsu (Xinhua 2014)—the costs of public education forced many Uyghur families to withdraw their children from school (Rehangu 2006; Xiao and Baihetiye'er 2004). Families in Pichan County (Ch. *Shanshan*) faced similar circumstances. According to my communication with a principal in Pichan, students paid upwards of RMB 1,000 (USD 150) for tuition, books, and supplies each semester (field notes, June 21, 2006). Although most schools have since eliminated these expenses, some urban schools still require students to pay tuition as high as RMB 900 (USD 135) per semester (Xinjiang Normal Middle School 2015) and may attach additional fees to textbooks and school uniforms. Although confounding, sending children to boarding schools several thousand miles away in neidi is often more affordable than sending children to local schools.

Indeed, the Xinjiang Class provides a viable option for a quality education that may otherwise be unavailable in Xinjiang. Many Uyghurs are frustrated with local schooling (Chen 2008, 70–71; Dwyer 2005; Grose 2010; Schluessel 2007). They often complain about the region's inadequately equipped schools and poorly trained teachers and begrudge urban Han for their access to state-of-the-art facilities. A female graduate of Hangzhou's Xinjiang Class remarked that "the Xinjiang Class is a good opportunity [for Uyghurs] because it provides ideal conditions for studying. Many schools in Xinjiang are still backward (Ch. *luohou*)" (field notes, August 5, 2011).

Xinjiang Class students study at some of China's prestigious "key" (Ch. *zhongdian*) senior high schools equipped with the latest technology. A promotional DVD produced by Shenzhen's Song Gang Middle School and distributed to its Xinjiang Class students highlights the perks of an education thousands of miles from Xinjiang. Set to a soundtrack that features Elmer Bernstein's *The Magnificent Seven* and John Williams's *Star Wars*, a booming voice promises that the school only staffs its faculty with first-class (Ch. *yiliu*) instructors who teach in state-of-the-art classrooms. Having described the apparent benefits of Song Gang's Xinjiang Class, the narrator assures that the school will "instill love for the fatherland and minzu unity into its minority minzu students." The twelve-minute video concludes with the school's principal, Luo Yuping, pledging, "Our school continues to make strides. Under the direction of our leaders, broad public support, and our faculty's arduous efforts, we have already taken the first step in realizing leap forward development (Ch. *kuayue shi*). We will continue to work tirelessly."

Acknowledging neidi's superior economic and educational development, an instructor at Qingdao's Laoshan No. 2 Middle School welcomes the opportunity to share the school's technology with Xinjiang Class students, many of whom, she claims, have never come in contact (Ch. *meiyou jiechu guo*) with a computer before arriving in Shandong. The teacher recalls becoming overwhelmed with nerves and breaking into song midsentence as she began to introduce her students to the school's computers. Believing her students, as minority minzu, possessed an innate appreciation of singing (Ch. *benlai jiu xihuan chang ge*)—a persistent stereotype in China (Gladney 1994; Harris 2008; Schein 2000)—she assumed they would enjoy hearing her rendition of the "ethnic tune," "Our Xinjiang Is a Good Place" (Ch. "Women Xinjiang hao difang")—even though it is always sung in Putonghua—instead of listening to her instructions (Laoshan No. 2 Middle School 2006). Clearly this particular teacher doubted she could acquaint Xinjiang's youth with "modernity" in one brief lecture.

Realizing the Xinjiang Class may be one of the few opportunities to gain a competitive edge over Han people in the job market, many young Uyghurs embrace the academic and social challenges of learning in a foreign environment. Alimjan, a 2010 graduate of a Xinjiang Class in Beijing who grew up in a poor farming community in Atush, accused the CCP of enforcing policies that marginalize minority minzu. He pointed to university preparatory classes, where Uyghurs educated in their native language in Xinjiang (i.e., *minkaomin*) must complete an intensive year of Chinese before officially matriculating at a neidi university, to support his claim: "The government seeks to guarantee (Ch. *baozheng*) Uyghur development will not surpass (Ch. *chaoguo*) the Han, so bright Uyghur students [who do not enroll in the Xinjiang Class] are forced into remedial classes ultimately delaying their graduation. By enrolling in the Xinjiang Class, I am able to graduate and enter the job market at the same age as my Han peers" (field notes, November 24, 2010).

Hasiyet, a 2007 graduate of Wuxi's Xinjiang Class, provides another illuminating glimpse into why some young Uyghurs are choosing the Xinjiang Class over local schools:

> I enrolled in the Xinjiang Class in order to receive a better education [than what was offered in Xinjiang]. Uyghur students in Xinjiang can't learn as [well] as Han students because the government puts fewer requirements [on] minority minzu; we almost have no pressure [to do well] in school. For example, if we [Uyghurs] take our college entrance exams in Chinese, we don't have to perform as well as Han students, yet we can go to the same college. The best universities [in China] won't accept students who take their examination in Uyghur. As a result, many students lack the motivation to study hard. (field notes, June 2, 2012)

According to Hasiyet, preferential policies (Ch. *youhui zhengce*)[10] in Xinjiang put Uyghur students at a distinct *disadvantage*, a sentiment shared by many Xinjiang Class graduates. These voices join the chorus of Han critics opposed to the party's current affirmative action policies in education (Leibold 2014a). The only way to break out of this "inequitable system" (Leibold 2014a, 300), according to these individuals, is to "play the Hans at their own game" (Smith 2000, 211). Whereas in the past this meant to be educated in one of Xinjiang's many Chinese-medium schools, now it requires Uyghurs to study alongside Han people in neidi.

The strategy may be paying dividends for young Uyghurs. Figures indicate that 90 percent of Xinjiang Class students attend either a four-year university or technical school in *neidi* (Tianshan Net 2009). Many young Uyghurs and their families consider the Xinjiang Class as the best, if not only, chance to enroll in a prominent Chinese university and eventually find stable employment.

Its ability to propel students into Chinese universities has certainly helped the Xinjiang Class earn a reputation for being an elite program reserved only for Xinjiang's brightest students. My informants remarked that their acceptance into the Xinjiang Class was a source of pride for their families. Rahile, a young woman from Aksu, was initially hesitant to attend school in neidi. However, Rahile's parents exerted pressure to convince her to enroll. They insisted that if she decided against participating, her extended family and close neighbors would think that the young girl was a poor student (field notes, November 2, 2010).

The CCP has worked hard to build a positive image for the Xinjiang Class. Riding a bus between Kashgar and Khotan in 2012, I observed many advertisements painted on brick walls lining rural communities promoting the benefits and affordability of sending children to study in neidi. To reach a broader audience, the state-run Uyghur language Xinjiang TV 5 regularly aired the program *Xinjiang Class Stories* (Uy. *Shinjang sinipi heqqide hékaye*) in 2013.[11] Catchy episode titles such as "The Outside World" (Uy. "Tashqi dunya"), "Where Dreams Begin" (Uy. "Arzuning bashlinish nuqtisi") and "Home Away from Home" (Uy. "Yiraqtiki yurt") attempted to draw the viewers to the minidocumentaries/infomercials. Each episode compresses student profiles, teacher introductions, and campus minitours into fifteen minutes of programming. If viewers—some of whom may be potential students—remain skeptical, the series's closing credits song reassures them: "You have a mother in Xinjiang, and you have a mother in neidi" (Uy. *Shinjangda bir ana, ichkiri ölkilerde bir ana*).[12]

Praise for the Xinjiang Class hit the silver screen in 2015 when the Ürümchi-based Tianshan Motion Picture Studio released the film *A Place Where the Dream*

---

10. As part of the central government's package of preferential policies (Ch. *youhui zhengce*) in education, minority minzu are evaluated differently than Han students on their college entrance examinations. In addition, minority minzu are awarded bonus points on their examinations. See Ma 2009, 243–49.
11. Xinjiang's Chinese and Kazakh language television channels also broadcast this program.
12. Some episodes have been uploaded for streaming on Xinjiang TV's official website. See http://www.xjtvs.com.cn/uyghur/record/list.shtml.

Begins (Ch. *Meng kaishi de difang*). Produced in commemoration of the XUAR's sixtieth anniversary, the film dramatized the lives of Xinjiang Class students and "vividly depicted the CCP's care of Xinjiang's minority minzu youth" (Ch. *shengdong zhanxian le dangzhongyang dui Xinjiang gezu qingshaonian de qinqie guanhuai*) (Tianshan Net 2015c). The film opens with a camera panning across Xinjiang's dramatic landscape—Turpan's fertile vineyards, Ili's lush grasslands, and Tashkurgan's rugged Pamir mountains. One by one, students rejoice as they receive their acceptance letters. Shortly thereafter, the film's protagonist, Aygül, describes the Xinjiang Class to the audience:

> The Xinjiang Class is a policy that benefits the people. It was established by the central government in order to develop education in Xinjiang. It allows the children of poor rural and nomadic families from remote areas in Xinjiang the opportunity to go to senior high school in developed cities in neidi.

While she studies in Shanghai, Aygül suffers from an eye disorder that had never been properly treated in Xinjiang and threatens her sight. As her vision deteriorates, Aygül confides her illness to a Han classmate who keeps the secret safe. Despite her worsening condition, Aygül makes several discoveries, none more important than an encyclopedia entry of a Han dynasty (206 BCE–220 CE) tapestry found in Khotan with the slogan "Five planets appear in the east indicating victory for China" (Ch. *wuxing chu dongfang li Zhongguo*) embroidered in the cloth. She associates the five planets with the five stars of the Chinese flag and realizes, perhaps for the first time in her life, that Xinjiang has been a part of China since ancient times. She graduates from senior high school, but her eyes do not properly heal until, several years after graduation, she returns to Shanghai to reunite with her Xinjiang Class schoolmates. During the reunion her beloved Han teacher arrives in a wheelchair. Debilitated by a stroke and unable to speak, the teacher prepared a letter for Aygül. In it, the teacher bequeaths her corneas to the young Uyghur woman. The political allegory is rather obvious: under the guidance of the party and Han people, Uyghurs too will someday have the correct worldview.

Carving Out an Uncontested Space in the Xinjiang Class

Strategies to supplant students' original support networks with a Han cultural milieu

Indeed, since the program's inception, officials have doubled down on the Xinjiang Class's political objectives. In 2005 Wang Lequan, then party secretary of the XUAR, announced that in order to more effectively counteract the "three evil forces" (Ch. *san gu shili*; Uy. *üch xil küch*), (i.e., terrorism, extremism, and separatism), threatening social stability in the region, ideological and political theory education (Ch. *sixiang zhengzhi lilun jiaoyu*) were to be placed at the "forefront" (Ch. *shouyao weizhi*) of the program (China Radio International 2005). The goal is for students to "skim the cream and remove the dregs" of their minority minzu culture (Leibold and Grose 2016, 15). During this transformative process, the boarding school will engineer a "modern ethnic" individual who is both "civilized and courteous" (Ch. *wenming limao*) (Leibold and Grose 2017, 6).

Educators and school officials go to great lengths to reorient the identities of Xinjiang Class students to align more closely with the party's values. Faculty—who receive regular training on the history, minzu groups, religious policy, and the nature of separatism in Xinjiang (Xinjiang Net 2016)—are instructed to "infiltrate" (Ch. *shentou*) their students' minds with the "four identities" (Ch. *si ge rentong*): identification with the fatherland (Ch. *zuguo*), the Zhonghua minzu, Chinese culture, and socialism with Chinese characteristics (Ch. *Zhongguo tese shehui zhuyi*) (Zhang 2010, 134). Tao Jiaqing and Yang Xiaohua (2010, 69)—who work at a Xinjiang Class in Jiangsu Province—confirm that, beyond providing classroom instruction, teachers "more importantly help [students] identify themselves with the culture of the Zhonghua minzu . . . and [help] enhance their awareness of national solidarity."

Teachers provide the party with an essential conduit for communicating politically correct thinking and Han-centric norms to students. They perform this task by assuming the role of parents. As such, Xinjiang Class teachers pledge to "love without suffocating, be strict and set boundaries; and be meticulous down to the minute" (Beijing No. 10 Middle School 2013). They are instructed to place high demands on student work and correct thinking, and must strictly monitor student behavior. Yet teachers should remain devoted to caring for students in their daily lives (Yao 2013, 21).

Unsurprisingly, some students develop close bonds with their teachers. Hasiyet, the young woman who acknowledged the advantages of a Xinjiang Class education, recalled her teachers being responsible (Uy. *tolimu mesuliyetchan*) and caring enormously for students (Uy. *bek köngül böletti*). Another young woman explained, "The teachers paid more attention to us than the Han students. They accompanied us on school trips, to hospitals when necessary, and visited our dormitories as much as possible. They cared about what we ate, what we wore, and how clean we kept our clothes."

Although the teacher-student bonds are strong, they are based on an especially unequal power relation. As Leibold and Grose (2019) have pointed out, Xinjiang Class teachers not only assume administrative power inside the classroom but also moral and cultural authority. They are expected to exemplify correct behavior, guiding minority minzu students in adopting Han cultural norms and correct political thinking. Tasked with these responsibilities, teachers must transition between dual personae: a moral and cultural beacon as well as a disciplinarian. Speaking about the authority of her teachers, Hasiyet added:

> When we made "mistakes," our teachers made it very clear that we were not appreciative of our "great" opportunities and [even suggested] we betrayed the

"unconditional" care they provided us. . . . As much as I appreciated my teachers, I felt uncomfortable having been constantly reminded of the good deeds that they did for us.

A similar disciplinary model was used throughout Native American boarding schools. Research on those student-teacher relationships suggests that some students obeyed school policy and their Caucasian teachers in public as a form of "introjection" (Colmant et al. 2004, 33–34). In other words, Native American students subconsciously yearned for praise from their authority figures, so they behaved to please them. We can aptly apply this analysis to the Xinjiang Class. Divorced from their families, minority minzu students may internalize the values promoted in boarding schools in order to gain the acceptance of their teachers and monitors, the few constant adult figures in their lives.

In an apparent attempt to reinforce the Han-centric values exemplified by Xinjiang Class teachers, students are educated on campuses and in cities where Han people are the overwhelming majority. As I noted above, authorities have predicted that a Xinjiang Class experience will strengthen relationships between Han and Uyghur students. However, local school officials have been instructed to patiently wait for "conditions to ripen" (Ch. *tiaojian chengshu hou*) before integrating classrooms (MOE 2000). Until then, school administrators are to exercise caution:

> The local education department, together with the school, will determine the form of the Xinjiang Class according to the abilities of the students, and [this policy] does not have to be implemented uniformly. Xinjiang Class students can be separated or mixed together; or students with outstanding grades can be selected to be integrated with local students. (MOE 2000)

Similar to the implementation of state programs in Xinjiang (Zhang and McGhee 2014; Cliff 2016), local Xinjiang Class officials act with some flexibility when carrying out the boarding school's policies. School administrators are, nevertheless, expected to create a "harmonious environment" (Ch. *hexie huanjing*) where Uyghur and Han students can study together. After these conditions are established, Xinjiang Class students will recognize "personality differences (Ch. *gexing de chayi*) [between Han and Uyghur] and will then be capable of accepting (Ch. *jiena*) them" (Dongguan Education Online 2012).

By placing Xinjiang Class schools in China's eastern and coastal cities, officials seek to sever students' intimate ties to their families and friends as well as Xinjiang itself. This strategy is similar to the one espoused in Native American boarding schools. As mentioned above, Richard H. Pratt predicted that removing native children from their families and educating them in schools built far from tribal lands would destroy tribal loyalties (Lomawaima 1994, 4; McBeth 1983, 119). We can descry common goals in the Xinjiang Class. Take, for example, Uyghur students from Khotan who are schooled in Guangzhou. The distance between the two cities is approximately 2,200 miles. Students must first travel by train to Ürümchi, which

Incubating Loyalty (or Resistance) in Chinese Boarding Schools 31

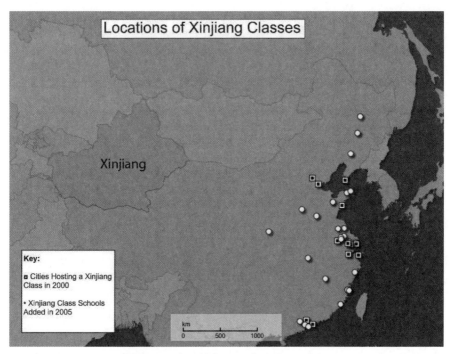

Figure 1.2: Locations of Xinjiang Classes, 2000 and 2005

can take nearly thirty-six hours. Once in Ürümchi, students commonly wait an additional day, sometimes even two days, before they can board a train to Guangzhou. Assuming there are no delays, the train to Guangzhou takes an additional fifty-two hours. The entire trip, then, can take up the better part of a week. Furthermore, students are only permitted to return home once per year—during summer recess. Visits home are often cut short of an entire summer, though. Students must travel between school and home at least twice each summer recess, once to arrive home and another to return to school. Therefore, students can spend two weeks out of their six- to eight-week recess traveling.

Contact between students and their parents is regulated and tightly monitored during the academic term. As I noted above, students are only permitted to return home during summer recess but must remain on campus for the monthlong winter break, which corresponds with the Lunar New Year. Although school administrators arrange sporadic "official" campus tours for a small number of parents (Tianshan Net 2011), they discourage parents and relatives from visiting Xinjiang Class campuses. In fact, a November 2005 article published in the *Xinjiang Daily* reports that a father who traveled to Beijing on business was only permitted to meet with his daughter at the school's work office (Ch. *zhiban shi*), and the entire visitation was supervised by an official (*Xinjiang Daily* 2005). Some schools require parents to sign waivers pledging not to "interfere" with their children's educations by visiting more than once each term, calling outside designated times, or sending more than four packages each year (Shanghai Songjiang No. 1 High School 2010b).

Separated from their parents and extended families, Xinjiang Class students suffer widespread homesickness. A male student from Kashgar remembered one occasion in particular:

> Since we were only fifteen and sixteen years old, we really missed our parents. There is one instance from my first year that really stands out (Uy. *hélimu éwimde*). My classmates and I began a countdown on the blackboard located in the back of our class of the number of days we had until we were able to return home. We counted down all the way from one hundred. (field notes, November 15, 2010)

Arzugül, a 2008 graduate of Wuxi's Xinjiang Class who was raised in Korla, found homesickness to be unbearable during her year of preparatory studies:

> The first year was the worst. I missed home very much. I couldn't bear it (Uy. *chidiyalmitim*). I called home every day to talk to my mother, sometimes two or three times a day. (field notes, November 12, 2010)

In October 2010, I enjoyed a chance encounter with first-year Xinjiang Class students from Beijing's Luhe School at the Mutianyu section of the Great Wall. The students made the two-hour trip as part of the school's weeklong recess for National Day (Ch. *Guoqing*). I introduced myself in Uyghur and asked if they were enjoying their first experiences in Beijing. The group of students shouted in unison, "We miss home!" One young girl, then, proceeded to describe her daily routine for calling her mother.

Removed from their families and communities where Central Asian and Islamic cultural norms pervade, Xinjiang Class students confront a type of "double exposure" to CCP ideology in the boarding schools. That is, these students are subjected to CCP values in the classroom and at "home" (i.e., the many other institutional spaces of the boarding school's campus).[13] Under a carefully regulated environment, students are introduced to new standards of appearance and discipline, which are meant to create an "ideal" Weiwu'er zu.

School regulations, codes of conduct, and discipline in the Xinjiang Class

Upon arriving at the boarding schools, Xinjiang Class students' personal identities are transformed in an attempt to disrupt their worldview. The first year is especially critical for correcting what the CCP considers "backward" behaviors. According to the director of the preparatory course curriculum at a Xinjiang Class in Guangzhou, newly arrived Uyghur students tend to be "conservative" (Ch. *baoshou*), the girls "timid" (Ch. *xiaodan haixiu*), and some students possess a "religious way of thinking

---

13. See also Jennifer Taynen's (2006, 48) discussion on the "double exposure's" effect on the identities and senses of belonging among young Uyghurs whose parents are government officials and party members.

and behaving" (Ch. *zongjiao sixiang he xingwei*). Some students will even continue to pray in secret (Ch. *toutou zuo libai*) and wear headscarves or embroidered *doppa* caps (Xinjiang Class Online 2015b).

The first step in changing these behaviors is to alter students' names. In accordance with the CCP's naming policies for government-issued documents (Sulayman 2007), the names of Xinjiang Class students are rendered into Chinese for the entirety of their boarding school education. For example, the common Uyghur male name Memet would be pronounced *Maimaiti* while the female name Gülzar would be changed to *Gulizha'er*. Rendering Uyghur names into Chinese serves functional and symbolic ends. Few Han people in Xinjiang, let alone in neidi, learn Uyghur (Grose 2012, 372–74; Yee 2003, 446). Even those who must study the Turkic language often find pronunciation to be difficult. It is also rare for Han Xinjiang Class teachers to learn Uyghur; in fact, they are only tasked with learning their students' Hanified names. Nevertheless, Xinjiang Class teachers often find the length of their students' names and the efforts required to memorize them problematic (Tao and Yang 2010, 66). One educator at a Xinjiang Class in Beijing recalled his reaction the first time he studied his class roster: "The names left me dumbfounded (Ch. *sha le yan*). The longest contained eleven characters" (*Phoenix Weekly* 2014).

Students responded to their Hanified names variously with feelings of confusion, ambivalence, disdain, or even joy. One graduate recalled the absurdity of the practice as sometimes the same Uyghur name is rendered differently into Chinese on official documents. She explained how her two classmates, both named Parida, did not share the same Chinese name. Reflecting the absence of a standard orthography for foreign names (Sulayman 2007), one was transliterated as *Paretanmu* while the other was *Palidan*. Mahmud, an otherwise outspoken critic of the program, did not feel wronged (Uy. *horluq hés qilghan ish bolmighan*) when he was called by his Hanified name, however. He analogized the practice to Chinese transliterations of the United States (Ch. *Meiguo*) and England (Ch. *Yingguo*). He added, "Although my people have been subjugated [by Chinese rule] (Uy. *munqerz bolghan millet*), they aren't disrespecting us [by using Hanified names]; they don't pronounce the names of any group correctly." One student even preferred his Hanified name, Salamu: "When I was a student, Daolang's [a Sichuanese rock star] hit "Salamu Maozhuxi" (Salaam Chairman Mao)[14] was very popular. I enjoyed having my name associated with the famous musician."

Notwithstanding the reactions of Xinjiang Class graduates, using only Hanified names is an inherently political act. Since 2015, officials in Xinjiang have "standardized" minority minzu names with an interpunct between Hanified family and given names (Allen 2016), which are typically longer than the two or three-syllable

---

14. Daolang's performance is a cover of Wang Luobin's—a Han musician both loved and loathed for singing and attempting to copyright music native to Xinjiang—song of the same title. For more on Wang Luobin, see Harris 2005. We can trace parallels between Daolang's cultural appropriation of Uyghur music and the Xinjiang Class as both seek to "modernize" and "civilize" the ethnic Other (Smith Finley 2016, 88–91).

construction of Han names. Meanwhile, "overtly Islamic" names are outlawed in Xinjiang (Radio Free Asia 2017a). The naming politics of the boarding school, similar to the production of Chinese-language-only maps of Xinjiang (Dautcher 2009, 56), purposely anchors Uyghurs to a Han-centric mainstream. Pronouncing Uyghur names with tonal syllables audibly dissociates them from their Central Asian and Islamic roots and harmonizes them with their Han brethren. The practice is reminiscent of providing "Christian" names to Native American boarding school students because their birth names were considered "unpronounceable and pagan" (Child 2000, 28).

Students' appearances are also standardized. According to the Xinjiang Class's dress code, students are required to wear "neatly kept" (Ch. *zhengjie*), "simple" (Ch. *pusu dafang*) clothing, and most Xinjiang Class schools require students to wear school uniforms, which usually consist of a single-colored track suit. Students' hair must also be kept clean, and it cannot be permed (Ch. *tangfa*). Male students are not permitted to grow their hair out long, and female students cannot apply cosmetics nor can they wear jewelry or high-heeled shoes (Xinjiang Department of Education 2011).

As is the case throughout schools in China, female Muslim students are also prohibited from veiling in the Xinjiang Class.[15] Muqeddes, a female graduate of the program's first cohort, vividly recalled her school's abrupt decision to ban headscarves (Uy. *yaghliq*), which are ubiquitous in rural Xinjiang. After their arrival at the Hangzhou Xinjiang Class, many Uyghur girls continued to cover their heads with colorful cloth. Unaware of the religious significance of headscarves, school officials initially permitted female students to wear them on campus. As the semester continued, however, school officials discovered that wearing headscarves served as a form of religious expression and banned the practice. Muqeddes and several of her classmates protested the decision. These students insisted on covering their heads because "we are Muslim." According to Muqeddes, one teacher retorted, "No, right now you are not Muslims; you are only students" (field notes, May 28, 2011). This particular teacher's statement is especially incisive; not only are Xinjiang Class students forbidden to act as Muslims, but they are being told they cannot even claim that identity while enrolled in the boarding school.

Indeed, quotidian religious practices are forbidden in the boarding schools. Even greeting each other by shaking hands and saying "essalamu eleykum" (peace be with you), as is customary among Uyghur men, breaches the Xinjiang Class's draconian policy on religious practice.[16] The disciplinary measures outlined in the

---

15. For the sake of clarity, I adopt the term "veil" to describe a wide range of specifically Islamic head, face, and body coverings. Here, I draw on Bucar's (2012, 5) definition of veiling as "a cluster of ideas, debates, and practices about modest Muslim dress that includes the covering of at least some head hair . . . but [can also include] everything from long tunics to bathing suits." However, the styles of veils worn by women and the meaning they attach to them are richly diverse (Leibold and Grose, 2016).
16. Schools are given some flexibility in enforcing Xinjiang Class policy. For example, in contrast to Chen's (2008, 132–34) observations of Uyghur handshaking, my male informants indicated that they were not allowed to

Xinjiang Class's student handbook (Ch. *xuesheng shouce*) identify five violations warranting immediate expulsion:

(1) Participating in any form of separatist activity or illegal religious activity
(2) Engaging in feudalistic superstitious activities (Ch. *fengjian mixin huodong*), religious activities (including prayer) (Ch. *libai*),[17] especially if the student has been reprimanded several times and has not changed the behavior (Ch. *lüjiao bugai*)
(3) Leaving campus without permission, staying off campus, missing over three days of class
(4) Instigating trouble or disturbing classroom order
(5) Stealing the property of others, smoking, drinking, and gambling (Xinjiang Class Online 2011b)

These rules are policed through self-monitoring and an intricate system of rewards and punishments. For example, administrators at Beijing's No. 10 Middle School assess students in standards such as personal appearance, hygiene, and discipline by tallying demerits for infractions (Beijing No. 10 Middle School 2013). Clowning around in class, receiving phone calls during quiet hours, sullying one's dorm room, and wearing headscarves warrant demerits. Distinctions like "five-star dorm room" (Ch. *wuxing qinshi*) similarly attempt to encourage correct behavior (Leibold and Grose 2019, 21). At a Xinjiang Class in Shanghai, if any individual dorm member engages in "superstitious activities, such as praying, wearing a headscarf, and the like inside one's room," the entire dorm will be denied five-star status (Shanghai Yucai Middle School 2016).[18] Incorrigible students face harsh repercussions. In July 2011 two male Uyghur Xinjiang Class students in Hangzhou were reportedly expelled for attending prayer at a local mosque (Radio Free Asia July 11, 2011).

Older students are often asked to report on the behaviors of their junior classmates. In the process, Xinjiang Class students establish codes of conduct. Senior students often deal with the deviations of their classmates by using corporal punishment; however, they often do so to avoid dealing with Han administrators. A Xinjiang Class graduate who studied in Dalian recalled his days as a dorm monitor:

> I rarely hit my classmates. They were so small. As long as they studied hard and didn't get into trouble, I was kind to them—well, as long as they referred to me as "older brother" (Uy. *aka*).

---

greet other Uyghur students in this manner. Only one individual, a male graduate of Dalian's Xinjiang Class, explained that he and his classmates were allowed to shake hands (field notes, May 28, 2011).

17. This document does not discern between Islam's obligatory prayers, which are normally performed five times a day (Uy. *namaz*) and prayers of supplication (Uy. *du'a*). According to my informants, students are forbidden to engage in any public prayer.
18. I am grateful to James Leibold for bringing these important documents to my attention.

In the Xinjiang Class, especially, older students demand respect from their junior classmates (Chen 2008, 104). Within these peer groups, hierarchies based on education background, rural-urban divides, and southern-northern origins may become volatile (Chen 2008, 106–11). However, Uyghur peer monitors prefer handling matters "in house" over the intervention of a Han teacher.

Evaluating the behaviors of dormmates and fellow classmates is reminiscent of the "civilized household" plaque system (Ch. *wenming hu xingjipai*) used throughout rural China but with added significance in Xinjiang. Government officials assess a family's adherence to ten state-defined values, including morals (Ch. *daode*), lawfulness (Ch. *shoufa*), family planning (Ch. *jisheng*), and unity (Ch. *tuanjie*). Upstanding households are presented with a ten-star plaque, which is hung outside the front door. Some county-level governments award citizens with up to RMB 1,000 (USD 150) and the honorary title "Most Outstanding Civilized Household" (Ch. *zuijia xingji wenming hu*) if they perform beyond expectations.

School regulations reflect more broadly the CCP's policy on religious practice. Although Chinese law guarantees its citizens the freedom to believe or not believe in religion, Article 8 of the 1995 "Education Law of the People's Republic of China" stipulates that "the state shall separate education from religion. Any organization or individual may not employ religion to obstruct activities of the state education system" (MOE 1995). Li Sheng, a senior research fellow at the Research Centre for China's Borderland History and Geography Studies, adds that regional laws further prevent the spread of religious ideas in schools:

> It is banned to preach religion or instill religious ideas into students, to force students to follow a religion, to suspend class for collective religious activities, to put religious teachings into the curriculum, to give religious lectures, or to use religion to interfere or disrupt normal teaching order in schools. (2005, 198)

As Bovingdon (2010, 69–70) has pointed out, these laws effectively limit students to the single freedom of *not* believing in religion while enrolled in state-sponsored schools. Since parents and grandparents, commonly the guardians of Islamic knowledge in Uyghur communities (Dautcher 2009; Smith Finley 2007a, 637–38), are not present, enforcing these policies in the Xinjiang Class effectively severs almost every channel from which students can cultivate religious piety.

Daily routines

Daily routines leave little time for students to ponder about Islam or engage in other inappropriate behaviors. Students spend the preponderance of their time in the boarding schools studying and communicating in Putonghua, their second language. They must maintain a tightly structured schedule of coursework and monitored self-study, which requires them to work up to fourteen hours a day, six days a week. A typical day follows this basic schedule:

6:30 a.m.: Wake up	5:00–6:00 p.m.: Self-study
6:45 a.m.: Morning exercises	6:00–6:30 p.m.: Dinner
7:00 a.m.: Breakfast	6:30–7:30 p.m.: Self-study
7:30 a.m.: Morning reading	7:30–7:50 p.m.: Watch national news broadcast
8:00–11:20 a.m.: Class	8:00–9:30 p.m.: Self-study
11:30 AM–1:00 p.m.: Lunch break	9:30 p.m.: Return to dormitory
1:00–5:00 p.m.: Class	10:10 p.m.: Lights out[19]

Daily schedules change slightly on weekends. Saturdays afternoons are sometimes set aside for arranged outings to local sites of interests, but students return in the evening for self-study sessions. Sundays are reserved for laundry and supplementary classes (Ch. *buke*).

Relief from this routine comes in the form of organized activities for Chinese holidays. Party officials have guided schools to celebrate every "traditional holiday of the Zhonghua minzu" (Ch. *Zhonghua minzu de chuantong jieri*), including Qing Ming, Mid-Autumn Festival (Ch. *Zhongqiu jie*), and Lunar New Year or Spring Festival (Ch. *Chun jie*) (Xinjiang Class Online 2012). While schools across the country close and many Han people reunite with family during the Lunar New Year period, Xinjiang Class students must remain on campus where they are immersed in Han-centric cultural practices. Although students do not attend regular classes during this multiweek recess, they are not afforded an extended vacation. Instead, students spend their time going on outings, learning Chinese folk crafts, and receiving supplementary Chinese language lessons. For example, Xinjiang Class students in Shenzhen spent the holiday composing New Year's couplets (Ch. *chunlian*), creating paper cuttings (Ch. *jianzhi*), and filling dumplings (Shenzhen No. 2 Vocational School of Technology 2005).[20] In addition to making dumplings, Xinjiang Class students in Zhejiang held a New Year's banquet and a dorm inspection contest (Ch. *qinshi neiwu piping*) (Xinjiang Class Online 2015c). According to official reports, students enjoy spending Lunar New Year at the boarding schools. "Gülzöhre," a student at Wuhan's Xinjiang Class, praised, "The school has arranged many activities for us, and we've happily celebrated the New Year with our teachers. We don't even really miss home" (Tianshan Net 2015a). One school official remarked: "Xinjiang Class students will feel the unity of the Zhonghua minzu and will strive for a better life by celebrating [New Year] in the festive atmosphere in neidi. This [experience] is important for Xinjiang Class students as they absorb (Ch. *xishou*) the significance of Chinese traditional culture" (Xinjiang Class Online 2013a).

---

19. Several of my informants reconstructed a typical day in their respective Xinjiang Classes. Although these individuals attended different schools, their daily schedules were remarkably uniform. For another example of a weekly schedule of Xinjiang Class students, see Chen 2008, 192–93.
20. To be sure, several types of dumplings (e.g., *manta*, *samsa*, *chöchüre*) are found in Uyghur cuisine. However, Uyghurs did not historically celebrate Lunar New Year, let alone celebrate the holiday by preparing dumplings.

To celebrate the Qing Ming Festival, Xinjiang Class students visit local Martyrs Parks (Ch. *lieshi lingyuan*) to tidy the graves of Chinese Communist revolutionaries (Jiangsu Ethnic Religions 2011).[21] According to the Xinjiang Class's official website, "grave sweeping" outings on Qing Ming teach students two important lessons. First, by visiting revolutionary heroes, students learn that "New China" would not exist without the Communist Party. Second, as the students sweep away rubbish that has collected around the tombs, the motion becomes symbolic of "beating away (Ch. *aida*) [their own] backwardness" (Xinjiang Class Online 2012). The five-year report (Ch. *gaikuang*) of a Xinjiang Class in Shanghai concludes that holiday celebrations strengthen minzu unity among students and allow them to "feel the loving care (Ch. *guanhuai*) of the government, the school, and party members" (Shanghai Fengxian Middle School 2006b).

The school's decision to require mass participation in Chinese holidays attempts to reorient Xinjiang Class students' organization of time away from the umma and toward a Han-centric culture. Eric Hobsbawm (1983) pointed out the importance public holidays play in the creation of national subjects and in the assimilation of diverse populations. Recently, Xi Jinping has called on all Chinese to celebrate specifically Chinese festivals over Western holidays in order to combat the incursion of Western values (*Economist* 2017b). Xi's imploration carries greater urgency for Uyghurs who historically did not observe Spring Festival, Mid-Autumn Festival, or Qing-Ming. Although the CCP has made New China; it still must make Chinese citizens out of young Uyghurs.[22]

Yet most days are spent in class. Invariably, Xinjiang Class graduates complained about their long, monotonous days in the boarding schools. Bahar, a native of Kashgar and graduate of the Xinjiang Class in Qingdao remarked:

> When I was studying at the Xinjiang Class, all of the students around me were very talented, so I felt a lot of pressure [to do well]. We woke up every morning at 6:00 a.m. and didn't go to bed until 11:30 p.m. At noon, we only had a one-hour break to nap. Our daily lives and coursework were really stressful (Uy. *jiddiy*), and competition (Uy. *riqabet*) between students was fierce (Uy. *kuchluk*). Nevertheless, we got along well with each other (Uy. *bek inaq ottettuq*).

A young woman from rural Khotan who studied in Wuxi recalled:

> Classes were too hard, especially Chinese language. My whole day was arranged from 7:00 a.m. until 10:00 p.m., and all I did outside of class was study. I didn't have hobbies or leisure activities. You know, I was a good student in Xinjiang, but in neidi I struggled in my classes, which made me feel very inferior (Ch. *zibei*) [to my classmates]. (field notes, September 30, 2010)

---

21. "Jiangsu Ethnic Religions" is the official English translation for *Jiangsu minzu zongjiao*.
22. Of course, here I have altered Massimo d'Azeglio's famous comment in 1861, "We have made Italy; now we must make Italians."

Hasiyet held especially bitter memories of her time in the Xinjiang Class:

> Those four years were the hardest of my life. First, I had to adapt to the really stressful education program. We [completed] all of the English classes, which take Chinese students six years to learn, in one year. We started to learn ancient Chinese literature, so I had to work very hard to not fall behind. I was the top student in class, so I always felt a lot of pressure. On top of that, there were tons of regulations we had to obey. We felt like we were in prison. (field notes, June 2, 2012)

Xinjiang Class graduates regularly compared their boarding school experiences to "prison" (Ch. *jianyu* or Uy. *türme*). When I shared this observation with three male graduates of the Hangzhou Xinjiang Class, one joked, "If the Xinjiang Class is like prison, then the Hangzhou Xinjiang Class is like Guantanamo Bay" (field notes, November 28, 2010), a reference to the controversial US detention center where over two dozen Uyghurs were unlawfully held (Wright 2005).

Finally, Ilham, a male student from Kashgar who also studied at the Xinjiang Class in Hangzhou, grumbled:

> The rules at the Xinjiang Class were very strict (Uy. *ching*), and we weren't allowed to leave the grounds of the school. It was like prison (Uy. *türme*). Every day was spent studying. A twenty-four-hour day for me at the Xinjiang Class consisted of studying, eating, and sleeping. You could say we were like robots (Uy. *mashina adem disemmu bolidu*). (field notes, July 1, 2012)

The discipline required of Xinjiang Class students is key to transforming them into instruments of government, or trained subjects capable of carrying out the state's projects (see Foucault 1984, 188). Under constant surveillance, a strict code of conduct, and a demanding academic schedule, Xinjiang Class students are induced to conform to a set of *correct* behaviors, as if they were "robots."

Meanwhile, teachers and administrators use every resource available in an attempt to program Xinjiang Class students to speak only in Putonghua, China's national language. Putonghua is the only language of classroom instruction, and students are required to speak Putonghua in most social situations. Points are deducted (Ch. *koufen*) for speaking Uyghur. According to the language policy of a Xinjiang Class in Shanghai, students must speak Putonghua during class and cocurricular activities, communicate only in Putonghua during organized outings, and are encouraged to use Putonghua for all social interaction (Shanghai Fengxian Middle School 2006a). A Xinjiang Class in Beijing even stipulated that phone calls home must be conducted in Putonghua if the student's parents were able to speak the language (Beijing No. 10 Middle School 2013).

Some of my interlocutors supported the boarding school program's language policy. Gülzar, a graduate of the Xinjiang Class in Hangzhou who was raised in Kashgar, defended her teachers who strictly enforced a Chinese-speaking environment:

> The teachers asked us to speak Chinese. At first I spoke in Uyghur, even in class, but then realized the teachers' requests were reasonable. Plus they were just doing their job. We had to improve our Chinese. If we didn't, we wouldn't have been able to keep up with our coursework. (field notes, June 13, 2011)

My informants found learning Chinese instrumental to their future success. They opined that Chinese is an important international language but craved learning about their own language as young adults.

Despite implementing a strict language policy on campuses, Xinjiang Class documents, in theory, leave room for Uyghur students to continue using their native language during designated times. Article sixteen of the "Administrative Procedures of the Xinjiang Class (trial)" stipulates:

> Xinjiang Class students will properly study their mother languages. [As such], schools will purchase books printed in relevant minority languages, provide students with time outside of class for self-study, and possibly organize lectures or other activities to allow students to properly study their [mother] tongue. (China Education and Research Network 2000)

This policy appears to be rarely enforced. I pointed out this clause to my informants. They scoffed at my gesture and invariably denied ever having Uyghur language reading materials provided to them.

The total absence of instruction in Uyghur reflects the hypocrisy of China's minority minzu language policy, at least how it has been implemented in Xinjiang. To be sure, both the Constitution of the People's Republic of China (1982) and the Law of Regional Ethnic Autonomy (1984) protect the rights of minority minzu to "use and develop" (Ch. *liyong he fazhan*) their native languages. However, the Uyghur language has steadily become subordinate to Putonghua, especially in the realm of state schooling.

This process began shortly after the CCP ratified the Law of Regional Ethnic Autonomy in 1984. It was also in 1984 when policymakers in Xinjiang extended formal instruction of Putonghua, which was originally introduced in the first year of junior high school, to the third year of primary school (Dwyer 2005, 36). This model, which remained in place until 1992, used minority minzu languages for classroom instruction in most subjects. Putonghua was typically taught for four to five hours per week (Simayi 2014, 144). Nevertheless, the decision to extend Putonghua instruction foreshadowed a new direction for "bilingual" education in the region, one that prioritized Putonghua learning. In 1992 "experimental bilingual classes" (Ch. *shiyan shuangyu ban*) were introduced wherein Putonghua is used for all mathematics and science-related courses. Although exact numbers are difficult to ascertain, it is clear that schools throughout Xinjiang are adopting the "experimental bilingual class" model at a rapid pace (Ma 2009, 210–12). In 2004 another mode of bilingual schooling was introduced in Ürümchi wherein Putonghua is the language of instruction for all classes. Currently this model of schooling predominates in

Xinjiang's developed cities such as Ürümchi, Shihezi, and Karamay (i.e., cities with substantial Han populations). However, policymakers hoped all primary schools in Xinjiang would adopt this model by the 2016 academic year (Simayi 2014, 147). For undisclosed reasons, reaching this goal has been delayed.

Stripped of the opportunity to formally learn their native languages, Xinjiang Class graduates found great joy in subverting the program's language policy. Yasmin, a young woman from Kashgar who graduated from the Hangzhou Xinjiang Class, explained:

> We spoke Uyghur with each other except if we were someplace where a teacher could hear us; then, we would speak Chinese. But of course, I would speak Uyghur because it is my mother tongue (Uy. *ana tilim*). (field notes, June 8, 2012)

Ilham, Yasmin's former classmate in Hangzhou, also originally from Kashgar, mocked:

> I always spoke Uyghur with my Uyghur classmates. If I spoke Chinese with them, it would feel really strange (Uy. *ghelitila tuyulidu*). Personally, I can't think of any two people from the same ethnic group (Uy. *millet*) who would speak in a language other than their mother language. (field notes, July 1, 2012)

As these statements suggest, Xinjiang Class graduates considered it an aberration to adopt Putonghua as the boarding school program's lingua franca. Some even dared to speak Uyghur inside the classroom. Ablimit proudly recalled an instance he and his classmates defied the school's language policy. The morning of the eve of Eid al-Adha (Uy. *Qurban Héyt*)—a major holiday celebrated by Muslims—Ablimit and his roommates were the first students to arrive to their morning classes. While waiting for their teacher and fellow classmates, the young men wrote "Happy Qurban Feast" in large Uyghur lettering (*Qurban héytinglargha mubarek bolsun*) on their classroom's blackboard. Upon entering the room and discovering the foreign script, the teacher demanded that the board be erased—in accordance with the regulation mandating that any calligraphy or wall posters must be written in Chinese, "so it is easy for teachers to understand their content and provide suitable interchange and guidance" (Beijing No. 10 Middle School 2013)—and interrogated the students about the meaning of the writing. After the students translated the phrase, the teacher offered a compromise: if the young men wanted to wish their classmates a happy holiday on the blackboard, they could do so in Chinese (Ch. *Gu'erbang Jie kuaile*). The students declined the offer and promptly erased their greeting (field notes, November 24, 2010).

Uyghur was so widely spoken that some individuals improved their own competencies. Malik, a graduate of the Xinjiang Class in Beijing, admitted to having a limited knowledge of Uyghur before arriving at the boarding school. Having been raised in a largely Han neighborhood in Ürümchi, Malik spoke Chinese at elementary and junior high school. In the Xinjiang Class, however, he was forced to speak to his classmates in Uyghur since many of them had not formally studied Chinese in the past. Reflecting on this experience, Malik was not only amazed by the large amount his Uyghur improved while studying in the Xinjiang Class but also felt fortunate to have become close friends with classmates from places like Kashgar and Khotan whom he never would have met in Ürümchi (field notes, February 15, 2013).

Segregated (dis)unity

Despite future plans to integrate classrooms, officials currently offer Xinjiang Class students few opportunities to mix with their local Han schoolmates. Xinjiang Class students attend classes in buildings separated from the rest of campus; they study and sleep in their own dormitories; and they eat meals in halal (Ch. *qingzhen*) cafeterias where Han students rarely visit (Chen 2008, 117). This practice seems counterintuitive considering one of the aims of the program is to strengthen minzu unity. Nevertheless, some of my informants could not remember meeting, let alone befriending, their Han schoolmates.

My informants' few encounters with Han students were often marred with misunderstanding. Raziye, a 2004 graduate of Beijing's Luhe Xinjiang Class, remembered her Han classmates' condescending questions: Had she even watched television? Are floors in Xinjiang made out of concrete? Did she and her family share a living space with farm animals? (field notes, February 21, 2008). Clearly these students knew little about Xinjiang. Raziye was raised in Korla—a well-developed city that has benefited from PetroChina-led oil explorations—which is predominantly populated by Han people. Similarly, Ekber, a graduate of a Shanghai Xinjiang Class, recalled several instances when Han students teasingly asked if he traveled by horse instead of by car (field notes, November 10, 2010).

Feeling belittled by their Han schoolmates, Xinjiang Class graduates sought to showcase their athletic prowess on the playground, one of the few shared spaces on campus. Mahmud, who graduated from a Xinjiang Class in Beijing, bragged:

> Before we arrived at the Xinjiang Class, we were the elite of our schools. After we came to neidi, though, we were no longer elite, so we loved comparing ourselves to local Han students. They thought we were fools and wanted to make us feel inferior to them. That's why we always competed with them in everything. We wanted to show them we wouldn't back down to anyone. (field notes, December 5, 2010)

In ways similar to tight communal spaces in Ürümchi (Smith 2002, 169–70), Xinjiang Class playgrounds are sometimes breeding grounds for conflict between Han and Uyghurs (Chen 2009, 9–10 and 116). According to one report from the same Beijing school, a friendly tug-of-war contest between local students and their Xinjiang Class schoolmates erupted into a fist fight (Ch. *dadachushou*). After reflecting on the incident, the school's administrators blamed the Xinjiang Class students for turning the friendly game into a contest between "Xinjiang" [Uyghurs] and "Beijing" [Han] (Zhang 2010, 127).

To be sure, a minority of my informants spoke of pleasant interactions with their Han peers. Ayjamal, a 2004 graduate of Guangzhou's Xinjiang Class, believed that the local Han students genuinely cared about their Xinjiang Class companions:

> For the most part, the Han students at our school respected (Ch. *zunzhong*) us [Uyghur students]. Sure, we had to obey what they said (Ch. *ting tamen de hua*). For example, a lot of the local Han students said there were certain places outside of the school that we weren't allowed to go to, like the Internet café, but I think they did this for our safety. (field notes, December 14, 2008)

Ayjamal's remarks provide insight into the amicable relationships sometimes reached between Han and Xinjiang Class students: the relationship assumes the subordination of Uyghurs. As has been written about previously (Gladney 1994; Harrell 1995), minority minzu in China are expected to look to their older (and more "advanced") Han brethren for instruction on how to act properly.

This discussion about turbulent encounters between Han and Uyghurs invokes Barth's (1969) widely cited commentary on ethnic boundary maintenance. Barth persuasively argued that ethnic boundaries are negotiated, drawn, and maintained through interactions between separate self-conscious groups. Inclusion is decided by choosing and practicing what group members deem are significant ethnic markers (e.g., language, religion, diet, and dress). Joanne Smith Finley (2013, 131–34) has skillfully applied Barth's theory to Han-Uyghur relations in Ürümchi. She concludes that the recent influx of Han migrants to Ürümchi has provoked Uyghurs to demarcate a rigid ethnic boundary maintained by the assertion and even "exaggeration" of linguistic, religious, and cultural difference. In other words, an essential element of Uyghur identity is the rejection of Han cultural norms.

A similar process unfolds in the Xinjiang Class. The spatial boundaries ostensibly dividing campuses into clearly defined "Han" and "Uyghur" spaces appear to reinforce ethnic boundaries. In some instances, interactions with Han schoolmates even activated previously latent ethno-national identities of Xinjiang Class students. A conversation I had with Dilber, a female graduate of Jiangsu's Xinjiang Class, illustrates this point:

> I grew up in a small village in Khotan where everyone around me was also Uyghur. [At that time], I never thought of myself as a minority (Uy. *azsanliq millet*). After coming to the Xinjiang Class, I was asked by some local Han students if I lived on a mountain, and many Han students thought we [Uyghurs] were all pickpockets (Uy. *yanchuqchilar*). These questions made me start thinking about what it means to be Uyghur. Then I realized [other] Uyghurs share the same religion, language, and ways of thinking (Ch. *sixiang*) [as myself], and these were different from the Han. (field notes, November 11, 2010)

Describing a remarkably similar process, Shérin, also a native of Khotan who attended a Xinjiang Class in Wuxi, discovered that Uyghur and Han possess different "modes of thinking" (Ch. *sixiang*):

> Our [Uyghurs'] mode of thinking (Ch. *sixiang*) is different from Han people. At school, the teacher required all students [both Xinjiang Class and local Han students] to take a certain path to the sports field. There were many paths leading to the sports field, some of which were even shorter than the one the teacher instructed us to take, but we were only allowed to take the one. My [Uyghur] classmates and I were upset by this rule, so we asked the local Han students why we had to take the designated path. They responded, "because those are the rules, so we have to obey them." I found it strange that the local Han students didn't even question the rule, and it was then I discovered there are real differences between Han and Uyghurs. (field notes, September 30, 2010)

Rashid, a graduate of the Hangzhou Xinjiang Class whom I first met in 2010, offered his own experience:

> During my first year in the Xinjiang Class, lights in our dormitories had to be shut off by 10 p.m. sharp. One night [after the lights had been turned off], I had to use the restroom. After getting out of bed, I turned on our light so I could see where I was going. The monitor assigned to our dormitory, a Han woman, asked why I turned on the lights after 10 p.m., and I tried to explain. Before I could finish explaining, she interrupted, "Why didn't you use the restroom before lights out?" The next day the dormitory monitor reported me to the principal who called me into his office. He scolded me and told me that I was selfish for turning on the lights as this would disturb my roommates.
>
> After being lectured, I asked some local Han students who also boarded at the school if they had to obey the same lights-out policy. Much to my surprise, they did. So then I questioned the importance of the rule and expressed to them that I thought the rule was stupid. The Han students were surprised at my anger, and told me the rule didn't bother them. They explained to me that all the rules of the school are important, so I should obey them. From this point on, I really began thinking about the differences between Han and Uyghurs. (field notes, June 26, 2012)

Although seemingly contrived, many of my informants, in fact, demarcated ethnic boundaries based on a perceived fundamental difference in the ways in which Uyghur and Han think. They evidenced their Han classmates' insistence on blindly complying with school policy as proof of unbridgeable chasms between Han and Uyghurs.

While "us-versus-them" ethnic dichotomies are sometimes created based on matters as abstract as modes of thinking, others claimed that differences between Uyghurs and Han are present in prosaic everyday life. Two young men who attended the Xinjiang Class in Dalian and Nanjing, respectively, shared with me the following vignette:

Murat: [During my time in the Xinjiang Class] I discovered that our [Uyghur and Han] languages, customs, and religions are different. However, there is much more to it.

Küresh, *quickly jumping into the conversation: Even* the way we dry our hands is different. After washing their hands, Han people do this [*Küresh quickly shook his hands up and down feigning a drying motion. Then, Murat and Küresh began laughing*]. Uyghurs never dry their hands like this.

You know, there were a few skirmishes between Han and Uyghur students that broke out at my school [in Nanjing], and some of them became serious, so Nur Bekri [the former Chairman of the XUAR] visited our school to help mediate. He tried to tell us the only difference between Uyghur and Han is the food we eat, so we [Uyghur and Han] should get along with each other. [*Both Murat and Küresh began laughing out loud.*] (Grose, field notes, May 28, 2011)[23]

In the company of my Uyghur informants, my actions were also judged within a rigid Uyghur-Han binary paradigm. While pouring tea for a group of friends, I lifted the pot away from the cup. Mid-pour, a young man shrieked: "Don't do it like a damned Han!" (Uy. *Xitaydek qilmang*). He then instructed me how to pour tea the "Uyghur way"—holding the pot with my right hand steadily above the cup.

These accounts animate Barth's theory as well as build on Smith Finley's observations in Ürümchi. In other words, Xinjiang Class students, similar to their peers in the XUAR, construct their ethno-national identity by defining who they are *not*. For Xinjiang Class students, an essential component of their Uyghur ethno-national identity is the (at least temporary) rejection of "Han-ness," an identity that can be expressed by speaking Putonghua, adhering to non-Islamic worldviews, or even by engaging in behaviors as mundane as obeying rules, drying one's hands, or pouring tea.

Sanctioned Space for Weiwu'er zu Culture

Similar to the Tibetan Class boarding schools (Postiglione 2008; Postiglione and Jiao 2009; Zhu 2007a), school officials provide Uyghur Xinjiang Class students limited space for state-sanctioned versions of their culture. In a largely token gesture, students are sometimes required to don ethnic costumes for formal photo ops. For example, a China National Radio (CNR) article describing how Xinjiang Class students spent their Spring Festival features several photographs of the activities. One photograph staged in front of Guangzhou's Guangya High School contains eight Uyghur girls wearing dresses made of *etles* fabric and *doppa* hats flanked on each side by three Uyghur boys, who are all donning embroidered shirts (Uy.

---

23. Individuals included in Joanne Smith Finley's study (2013, 106) similarly discussed their distaste for the ways Han people dry their hands. Although my informants never explained Uyghurs' preference to towel-dry their hands, Smith Finley indicates that shaking one's hands dry may fling dirty (and ritually impure) water on nearby people.

kanway köynek) and *doppa* (CNR 2015). When asked about similar colorful images of Xinjiang Class students, Alimjan dismissed the gesture: "The photographs are just advertisements. Once these kinds of pictures were taken, we had to put on our uniforms" (field notes, November 24, 2010).

In another display of cultural accommodation, Xinjiang Class officials honor students' dietary restrictions. Host schools are required to operate (and if necessary, build) a halal cafeteria—with the characters 清真 (*qingzhen*) visibly displayed—separate from the school's main dining hall. Ingredients must be purchased from government-approved "halal markets," and meals are prepared by local Hui chefs, or occasionally by Uyghur chefs hired from Xinjiang (General Office of the MOE and General Office of the SEAC 2011).

China's state media praises the cafeteria food. These reports are often written by students in letter form. In one such example, a female student enrolled in Beijing's Yangzhen Xinjiang Class, attempts to comfort her parents:

> The school has a large and clean halal cafeteria. I eat meat-filled dumplings every morning. Plus they serve mixed cold dishes, milk, yoghurt, eggs, fruit, *nan* flat bread, and several beverages. For lunch, we usually eat rice with stir-fried dishes. Sometimes they even prepare *dapanji*,[24] pilaf [Uy. *polu*], and pulled noodles [Uy. *lengmen*]. These dishes are all so delicious. They taste like home! Since coming to school [in Beijing], we've all become fatter and taller. (*Xinjiang Daily*, 2010)

The meals presume the power to positively transform the physical appearance of students. Commenting on the nutritional benefits of these meals, Sun Qi, the director of the Xinjiang Class's Office of Student Affairs, claims, "You can clearly tell the darker, skinnier students are those who have just begun their preparatory studies, and the whiter, taller, and stronger students are the senior students" (*People's Daily Online* 2011). Here Sun Qi implies that Uyghur students will "naturally" morph to conform to Han standards of beauty—fair skin and tall bodies (Thornham and Feng 2010, 203)—after living in the boarding schools for four years.[25]

My informants' opinions about the food were mixed. Ayjamal complained that the meals were bland. She recalled being served potatoes at every meal because the Hui chef mistakenly thought the starchy vegetable was a staple of Uyghur diets. It took weeks of student complaints to change the menu. Ilham could barely stomach the food served to him in Hangzhou:

> At first, I couldn't get used (Uy. *könelmigen*) to the school's food. Every day we had to eat either rice or *mantou* (Uy. *aq moma*); I really couldn't eat it. After a while, I had no choice (Uy. *amal yoq*) but to eat the food. (field notes, July 1, 2012)

---

24. Literally translated "big plate chicken," this popular dish contains large pieces of chicken, potatoes, leeks, and green peppers that have been flavored with chili peppers, star anise, cinnamon, garlic, and ginger. The dish is less commonly known by its Uyghur name *chong tehsilik tohu qorimisi*.
25. Graduates of the Tibetan Class also reported that they were judged by Han based on the complexion of their skin noting that Tibetan students with lighter skin, as opposed to those individuals with darker skin tones, were often more easily accepted by Han classmates. See M. Yang 2017, 186.

Other students found comfort in the cafeteria food. Nijat, a Turpan native and a 2007 graduate of Shenzhen's Xinjiang Class, fondly remembered her meals:

> The food was delicious. The halal cafeterias even served fresh fruit every day, and milk tea was available for breakfast. And, it was all free! The food they served to us was much better than the stuff I eat at my university's Muslim cafeteria. (field notes, February 23, 2008)

Regardless of the food's quality, allowing Uyghur students to adhere to Muslim dietary laws and providing these meals in a Han-dominated environment importantly serves the CCP's political aims. First, the CCP can claim to be upholding its commitment to respect minority minzu customs. Above all, by operating Muslim cafeterias at schools with large numbers of Han Chinese students, school officials create the impression that Han and Uyghur can and do coexist peacefully.

Yet some administrators and teachers desecrate halal eating spaces. At Shanghai's Jinshan High School, students learned to prepare fermented rice, a process that requires ample amounts of alcoholic rice wine (Ch. *mi jiu*). To be sure, Muslims debate over the permissibility of eating foods that contain cooking wines.[26] However, the Qur'an (5: 90–2) unequivocally condemns consuming intoxicating substances; therefore, many Muslims refrain from storing alcohol in halal spaces. The teachers celebrated the occasion nevertheless, announcing, "Steamed dumplings warm the heart while rice wine intoxicates it" (Ch. *baozi wennuan woxin, mijiu zuiren xintian*) (Shanghai Jin Shan High School 2011).

The teachers' and administrators' possible good intentions notwithstanding, the activity introduces students to alcohol, a substance authorities in Xinjiang are reportedly forcing Uyghur shopkeepers to sell. CCP officials claim that alcohol abstinence is a sign of "extremism" (Denyer 2015). Despite a long history of alcoholic beverages in China, Islamic dietary restrictions likely limited its consumption among Uyghurs, especially among the aristocracy (Bellér-Hann 2008, 313) until the Reform Era. When alcoholism spread in northern and eastern Xinjiang in the 1990s, Uyghur men responded by forming social clubs (Uy. *meshrep*), which banned drinking, and organizing a boycott of alcoholic beverages in Yining (Dautcher 2005, 282–88). Adding alcohol to food consumed by Xinjiang Class students may legitimize the unfounded yet powerful claim that alcohol and the social problems it can create were largely nonexistent among Uyghurs before Han people arrived (Rudelson 1997, 125–26).

Activities arranged in celebration of Eid al-Fitr (Uy. *Roza héyt*) and Eid al-Adha (Uy. *Qurban héyt*), excise Islam from the two most important feasts celebrated by Muslims worldwide. Unlike Muslim minzu students in Xinjiang, who receive three days of vacation for Eid al-Fitr and one day for Eid al-Adha, Xinjiang Class students are only granted one vacation day for each holiday (General Office of the MOE

---

26. See, for example, an online forum for Muslims entitled "Rice Wine," www.shiachat.com/forum/topic/75760-rice-wine.

2000). Moreover, these celebrations are entirely secular, usually consisting of song-and-dance performances. Given the state's perennial preference for secular material culture of minority minzu, it is evident that state promotions of Muslim minzu holidays are not intended to celebrate Islamic culture (Gillette 2000).

Some school officials even coerce students to attend class during the two major Muslim holidays. Graduates of the Wuxi Xinjiang Class recalled the "option" they were given to attend class during Roza. As one former student explained:

> All of us went to class on Roza. Even though we had the day off, the teachers still came in and taught class like normal. The pace by which things were taught at the Xinjiang Class was so fast we would be so far behind if we missed one class. Plus, the teachers wouldn't be willing to reteach a lesson. We would be crazy not to go to class. (field notes, June 1, 2012)

Xinjiang Class students are guaranteed the right to celebrate officially recognized "minzu holidays." However, students are only permitted to celebrate the Roza and Qurban holidays under the terms of the party and on the school's watch.

Xinjiang Class students at Wuhan No. 1 High School staged a variety show to celebrate the Qurban Feast. The program featured comedy sketches (Uy. *étot*), choreographed dances, and singing performances. To be sure, the event incorporated elements of Uyghur culture: *etles*, *doppa*, and Uyghur-inspired dance (Uy. *ussul*), and the highlight of the evening—measured in audience reaction—was a male student's rendition of "Kashgarian Girl" sung entirely in Uyghur. When the young man sang his first note in his mother tongue, he was greeted with resounding cheers from classmates in the audience. However, in order to ensure the celebration did not stray from the Xinjiang Class's language policies and political goals, an emcee introduced each act in Putonghua. At the conclusion of the event, which was marked by a group dance, the emcee returned to the stage to wish, in Putonghua, everyone a happy "Gu'erbang Jie."

By allowing Uyghur students to observe certain Muslim holidays in a Han-dominated environment, the CCP can publicly display its commitment to multiculturalism. We should not, however, misinterpret these compromises as avenues—consciously paved by the CCP—for young Uyghurs to engender an identity grounded in Islamic ethics and cultural norms. Quite the contrary—the party is engaging in "internal Orientalism" (Schein 1997). In other words, the party routinely selects certain elements of a minzu's culture and institutionalizes them as a "package of [traditional] 'customs and habits'" (Ch. *fengsu xiguan*) (Gillette 2000, 27). Expressing "Weiwu'er zu" identity—even through the Uyghur language—is sanctioned as long as it remains confined to song, dance, state-recognized minzu holidays, and other performances. Meanwhile, officially identifying and celebrating distinctly "minzu traditions" (Ch. *minzu xisu*)—which the CCP regards as remnants of the past—cements Xinjiang Class students behind the Han in the

Marxist-inspired hierarchy of ethno-social development and justifies the state's attempts to "modernize" these minority minzu youth in neidi.

Concluding Remarks

The political goals of the Xinjiang Class are evident. Party officials intend to instill Chinese patriotism, feelings of minzu unity, and the values of the CCP in young Uyghurs. To this end, the Xinjiang Class enforces a series of policies, from stringent restrictions on religious practices to a Chinese monolingual language policy that limits Uyghur students' use of their mother tongue, in an attempt to realign Uyghur identity to fit within the Zhonghua minzu. These policies are augmented by a learning environment in neidi that promotes Han cultural norms. Similar to the US government's goals for Native American boarding schools, the party hopes a boarding school experience will "mold a 'successful' student—obedient, hardworking . . . punctual, clean, and neatly groomed—who will become a 'successful' citizen with the same characteristics" (Lomawaima 1994, 129).

Students have responded with a mix of compliance and resistance. Few dared to challenge the school's policy on religious practice, yet most tested the limits of the program's language policy. The next chapter will begin to assess the effectiveness of the Xinjiang Class in molding "successful" minority minzu students by looking at the behaviors of these individuals after boarding school.

2

Asserting Uyghur Identity from China's "Central Plains"[1]

> Imagine two cups placed side by side with the edges touching. The two cups represent Han and Uyghur people. The point where the two cups meet represents common ground between the two.
>
> —Tursunjan, graduate of the Guangzhou Xinjiang Class
> (field notes, November 24, 2010)

On an unseasonably hot and humid afternoon in Beijing during spring 2011, I received a call from Murat, a Xinjiang Class graduate whom I had begun to meet with regularly throughout the previous year. Murat completed his primary education in Aksu and then attended a Xinjiang Class in Hangzhou. After graduating in 2007, he enrolled in a top-ranking university in the sprawling capital. In fall 2011 Murat entered his final year of coursework, and he planned to travel to Turkey to study immediately after commencement ceremonies. Murat's final examinations were quickly approaching, so he insisted we meet soon. He wanted to introduce me to three of his friends, all Xinjiang Class graduates. We gathered at a university located in northwest Beijing. After exchanging introductions, we found a shady spot to chat over tea and watermelon. Murat methodically sliced the melon into perfect wedges and proudly displayed them on the flimsy white plastic table ubiquitous to outdoor dining in China. "See, it's as if we were in Xinjiang," he joked.

The afternoon quickly gave way to evening, but our conversation did not fade with the daylight. Knowing that the nearby Uyghur-owned restaurant would soon open for dinner service, Murat suggested that we continue our discussion over a proper meal. While Murat cleared the watermelon rinds and the piles of seeds littering the table, he paused suddenly and asked his Uyghur companions, "Do we need to perform a *du'a*?" (Uy. *du'a qilishimiz kérekmu*), referring to the prayer of supplication or invocation recited by some Muslims after a meal.[2] "I don't know" (Uy. *Uqmaymen*), the others shrugged in unison. A debate ensued on whether eating watermelon is considered to be a meal and would, therefore, require a du'a.

---

1. Parts of this chapter were published in an article in the refereed *Journal of Contemporary China* (Grose 2015b).
2. There are several occasions deemed appropriate to recite du'a. Some scholars of Islam in Xinjiang, citing hadith, list ten, one of which is immediately after eating a meal (Ababekri Qari 2006).

To break the impasse, Murat suggested erring on the side of caution and offering the short prayer. Satisfied with the recommendation, the others joined Murat around the table, raised their open palms toward their faces, uttered "God is Great" (*Allahu ekber*),[3] and feigned wiping their faces, which signaled the completion of the invocation.[4]

This extended anecdote puts into focus the multivalent identities of Xinjiang Class graduates. These young Uyghurs, divorced from their parents' influence and educated in neidi where the CCP attempted to "interpellate" them as subjects of the state, sometimes hesitate over the religious rituals and social customs performed instinctually in many Uyghur communities. As illustrated in the above exchange, Xinjiang Class graduates often make impromptu decisions to express their ethnonational (and religious) identities. Nevertheless, the decision to perform du'a reflects the tendency for Xinjiang Class graduates to express themselves as Uyghurs, as well as Muslims, in ways forbidden in the boarding schools they attended. Therefore, the four individuals' simple act of performing du'a suggests an embrace of unsanctioned Uyghur culture and resistance to the interpellative ideologies promoted in their boarding schools. To be sure, assertions of this identity are not simply rejections of their Chineseness. Rather Xinjiang Class graduates exaggerate their ethnic markers (cf. Bateson 1958) to demarcate a more inclusive transregional Uyghur identity while they selectively embrace elements of their Chinese identity they regard as instrumental to establishing tangible connections to transnational and international communities, both Muslim and secular.

Han-Uyghur Interactions beyond the Xinjiang Class

Proponents of the Xinjiang Class tout the program's graduation and college admission rates. As pointed out in the last chapter, nearly all Xinjiang Class students take the national college entrance examination (Ch. *gaokao*). Reports indicate that over 90 percent of Xinjiang Class students attend either a four-year university or technical school in neidi (Tianshan Net 2009). Temporarily keeping Uyghurs in Han-dominated neidi for school and work programs has been integral in President Xi's strategy, introduced in 2014, to deepen "mutual understanding" between the two groups (Wang 2014).

However, the four years spent in neidi appear to fail at building camaraderie between Han and Uyghurs. As is the case in the boarding schools, Xinjiang Class

---

3. Before uttering "Allahu ekber," some of my informants quietly recited Surah Fatiha. Surah Fatiha is the first chapter of the Qur'an, and it is often spoken during namaz—or the ritualized prayers of Islam.
4. Debate within the broader Muslim community ensues over the necessity, and even the appropriateness, of symbolically wiping one's face after offering an invocation. However, scholars of Islam in Xinjiang, who generally adhere to the Hanafi school of Islamic jurisprudence (*fiqh*), have pointed to a hadith collected by Abu Dawud (d. 889 CE) in which the Prophet Muhammad (SAW) instructed his followers to wipe their faces after offering du'a (Uy. *du'adin parigh bolghan waqtinglarda qolunglarni yüzünglargha sürkenglar*) (Ababekri Qari 2006, 298–99).

graduates rarely mix with Han people on university campuses. Although the boarding school program's ostensible aim is to strengthen minzu unity, the previous chapter made clear that school experiences do not dramatically improve Uyghur-Han relations. On the contrary, Xinjiang Class policies appear to heighten Uyghur students' ethno-national identities and put them distinctly at odds with Han people. If Xinjiang Class students begin sketching ethnic boundaries in the boarding school program, they shade these lines more boldly as adults, in ways analogous to a "minkaohan" woman profiled by Smith Finley (2007b).

The organization of a recreational "Uyghur" soccer team at the University of International Business and Economics (UIBE) in Beijing demonstrates the reluctance of the two groups to cooperate. Soccer has stood apart as one of the most popular pastimes among young Uyghurs in Xinjiang since it was introduced by Hussein and Bawudun Musabayov as part of their school's secular curriculum in the late nineteenth century (Zhang 2014).[5] Some Uyghurs even claim the sport was invented in Kashgar (Rudelson 1997, 193). UIBE's intramural soccer league is one of the most anticipated extracurricular activities for male students. Team members purchase uniforms, arrange mandatory practices, and compete in a season of intramural soccer. The champions of the campus-wide competition earn a spot in a citywide inter-university tournament. Most academic departments organized their own teams. However, Muhtar and Bayram, two graduates of the Xinjiang Class, broke the common practice of joining their department's squad and formed what they called the "Uyghur team" (Uy. *Uyghur komandisi*). Citing their belief that Uyghurs were superior soccer players compared to Han people, my two friends bragged about the athleticism of their teammates, who included six Uyghurs (four of whom had graduated from a Xinjiang Class), a student from Kazakhstan and another from Sudan. I pointed out the obvious fact that two of their teammates were not Uyghur, and teased my friends about the inaccuracy of the team name. The two quipped, "At least they are both Muslim."

The two young men's response suggests the importance Xinjiang Class graduates place on cultural and religious bonds, especially those forged with foreign (i.e., non-Chinese) Muslims. Soccer provides a vehicle for forging transnational bonds. On the international stage, Uyghurs rooted for Turkey as they dominated China 3–0 in the 2002 World Cup in a benign assertion of pan-Turkic nationalism (Bovingdon 2010, 101–2). At a local level, Uyghurs strengthened transnational bonds based on a common creed within their own soccer squad. In other words, membership in the "Uyghur Team" was not determined by ethnicity. Rather, acceptance into the team, as well as by the group of young Uyghur men, was based at least partially on a shared Muslim identity.

Meanwhile the Uyghur Student Association at the same university left Han students off its events' guest lists. Each year the association, composed of approximately

---

5. For more on the Musabayov brothers and their Jadid-inspired schools in Xinjiang, see Schluessel 2010.

Asserting Uyghur Identity from China's "Central Plains"

fifty Uyghur students, holds celebrations for the Roza and Qurban feasts. I attended both evening parties in 2010. The events provided the university's Uyghur students an opportunity to share the important holidays with their close friends. The evening parties were open to anyone with an invitation, and I recognized some of the university's international students from India and Kazakhstan. Despite the otherwise inclusive nature of these celebrations, Uyghur students largely excluded the university's eight thousand Han students. I witnessed one Han couple walk timidly into the Roza celebration, however. Their host, a Xinjiang Class graduate, spotted them immediately, welcomed them to the party, and enthusiastically invited the two to join the rest of the attendees on the dance floor. Unintentionally reinforcing the Uyghur stereotype that Han people are "killjoys" (Smith Finley 2013, 98–100), the couple politely refused and found a seat in the corner of the room. They tiptoed out the door when they noticed that their host was caught up in *sama*, a rhythmic "folk" dance with its roots in Sufism once performed en masse by men outside Kashgar's famous Héytgah Mosque on major holidays (Brophy 2015).

Dormitories, however, force Han and Uyghur classmates to interact. Despite spending at least four years in neidi before entering university, Xinjiang Class graduates often found living under the same roof with their Han peers to be unpleasant at best and unbearable at worst. Raziye complained to me several times about living

Figure 2.1: Xinjiang Class graduates mingle with their Uyghur classmates at UIBE's Uyghur Student Association's Roza celebration

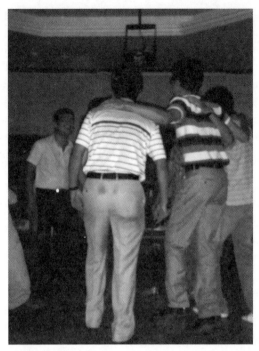

Figure 2.2: Uyghur Xinjiang Class graduates prepare to perform *sama* at the 2010 Roza celebration

in close quarters with her Han roommates, whom she claimed disrespected her religious beliefs. Her patience was stretched to the limits by her roommates' ignorance of Islamic dietary restrictions. Seething with anger, Raziye decried:

> My roommates regularly bring pork dishes into our room. I told them that, as a Muslim, I do not eat pork and find the sight of it to be offensive. I politely asked them to stop bringing food into our room. At first, they apologized and agreed to my request. Then, yesterday my roommates brought back pork blood soup (Ch. *zhuxuetang*) [a dish made from coagulated pig blood believed to benefit menstrual health] and left the container in our trashcan. Disgusted, I stormed out of the room. I can't stand those majority people [Han Chinese]! (field notes, January 19, 2008)

Raziye's relationship with her roommates deteriorated to the point that she sought alternative living arrangements. She requested, and was granted permission, to serve as a "Chinese" roommate to an American student in the international dormitory. To be sure, the Qur'an proscribes consuming "blood spilled out" and "the flesh of swine" (6:145). However, others have noted Uyghurs' preoccupation with pigs, pork, and ritually impure eating spaces (Cesàro 2000; Smith Finley 2013, 101–5 and 151–58). Similar to Hui Muslims (Gillette 2000), Uyghurs—my informants included—reify otherwise fluid food boundaries to mark a difference from Han people. While the strict adherence to dietary restrictions confirms their Muslim identity, my informants often enforced these restrictions situationally in order to also assert their Uyghur ethno-national identity (Cesàro 2000).

Ritualized purity also shapes Uyghur standards of cleanliness, which often differ from those of Han people. Rashid, a graduate of Hangzhou's Xinjiang Class introduced in the previous chapter, bridled at his Han roommate's apparent apathy toward hygiene. Following a confrontation over dirty laundry, which prompted him to bunk with four of his Uyghur classmates, Rashid complained:

> My Han roommate is very dirty (Uy. *meynet*). First, he washes his clothes, face, and food in the same water basin. We [Uyghurs] would never do that. On top of that, he leaves his smelly socks around our room. I warned him not to leave his dirty socks lying around, but he left them in our room anyway. So, I tossed them. I told him next time he leaves his socks out in our room I would beat him. (field notes, May 21, 2011)

As has been previously noted (Smith Finley 2013, 105–6), Uyghurs claim to be meticulous about cleanliness while they stereotype Han people for being "dirty." By invoking an us-versus-them dichotomy in his statement, Rashid suggests that his roommate's poor hygiene is not a personal matter but an attribute of Han ethnicity. Therefore, Uyghurs, similar to Hui (Gillette 2000), point out ethnic markers with origins in Islamic hygienic jurisprudence to demonstrate superiority over Han people.

Uyghur Language as Ethnic Marker

Uyghur language is often spoken as another assertion of ethno-national identity (Dwyer 2005, 6; Smith Finley 2013, 134–41), especially as Putonghua becomes the lingua franca for education, commerce, and law in Xinjiang. Scholarship once linked Xinjiang's "bilingual" education system to the erosion of a distinctly Uyghur ethno-national identity and culture (Dwyer 2005, 38; Kaltman 2007, 16–17; Rudelson 1997, 127–29; Smith 2002; Smith Finley 2007; Taynen 2006). That research focused on the increasing number of Uyghur senior high school students who took the gaokao in Chinese, the so-called *minkaohan*, in comparison to those who took the examination in Uyghur (Ch. *minkaomin*). These terms have been used descriptively and prescriptively. According to these studies, minkaohan were more culturally aligned with Han people (Smith 2002, 163; Smith Finley 2007b, 230; Rudelson 1997, 128; Taynen 2006), and they generally possessed a "weak command" of the Uyghur language (Smith Finley 2007, 226). Some researchers have even suggested that the first three generations of minkaohan Uyghurs have emerged as a "hybrid" minority (Rudelson 1997, 128; Smith Finley 2007).

On the contrary, my informants expressed concern over the survival of their native language. Their anxiety surely stemmed from current language policy in

Xinjiang as well as their own lack of formal instruction they, as Xinjiang Class students, received in senior high school. Some of my informants even grimly predicted that Uyghur children in the not-so-distant future will become monolingual *Chinese* speakers.

Xinjiang Class graduates protested against language policies in Xinjiang. Nijaz, who studied at the prestigious Tsinghua University after graduating from the Xinjiang Class, once implored: "Your mother tongue is English, so you will never have to worry about your language becoming extinct. There aren't many Uyghurs in the world, so it is possible that we could lose our language" (field notes, May 28, 2011). Rashid often spoke to me at length about minority minzu language policy. During two conversations in which he haphazardly switched between Uyghur, Chinese, and English, Rashid bemoaned:

> The government says it is giving [Uyghurs] an opportunity to learn another language, and we [Uyghurs] should be happy because learning languages is a good thing. [He paused.] What the fuck? That's not the point [learning languages is a good thing]. Of course I want to learn Chinese. Without it, I wouldn't be able to find a job. But I want to study my own language too . . . Chinese government officials say that they are providing bilingual education (Uy. *qosh tilliq ma'arip*), but in reality it is a monolingual [Chinese] education. The Chinese [government] is very smart. Officials know that in order to assimilate other minzu groups, they first need to eliminate their languages. They even have an idiom that states this very strategy: *yu wang qi zu, bi mie qi yu* (欲亡其族，必灭其语). (field notes, 11 and November 21, 2010)[6]

An Internet meme shared on many of my informants' social network pages captures the above sentiments. A muscular man standing below a caption in bold lettering reading "this year's most fashionable pledge" (Uy. *bu yilqi eng muda söz*) points to the viewer and commands, "Speak in your own language" (Uy. *öz tilingda sözle*).

The language preferences of Xinjiang Class graduates require us to reassess the deportments of young, bilingual Uyghurs. As described in the previous chapter, Xinjiang Class graduates have undergone an intensive, four-year education in which the only language of classroom instruction is Putonghua, and they have taken the gaokao in Chinese. In other words, Xinjiang Class graduates are, for all intents and purposes, minkaohan despite sometimes being treated as a separate category (Chen 2014; Ma 2009). Yet these individuals behaved much differently than the minkaohan described by other Uyghurs in 1990s and early 2000s Ürümchi who accused minkaohan of feeling more comfortable speaking Putonghua than their mother tongue—as well as possessing weak ethno-nationalism, being "brainwashed," and being less religiously devout (Smith Finley 2013, 366–75). Despite their own minkaohan status, however, my informants did not demonstrate a preference to speak

---

6. This idiom may be translated: "If you desire to eliminate a group of people, you must get rid of their language."

in Putonghua, nor did they appear uneasy about communicating orally in their native language. Resentful of mainstream Han society's acculturative pressures, my informants insisted on speaking Uyghur with other Xinjiang Class graduates, their non–Xinjiang Class Uyghur classmates, and me as a form of resistance. Therefore, Xinjiang Class graduates more accurately resemble Uyghur multilingual "world citizens" who navigate through competing cultural spheres (Smith Finley 2013, 380–93).

For electronic communication, however, my interlocutors used Chinese more often than either the Arabic-based or Latin-based Uyghur script. To quantify this tendency, I recorded the WeChat[7] moments (Ch. *pengyou quan*) of six Xinjiang Class contacts, three individuals who completed their formal schooling in Chinese-medium schools in Xinjiang (i.e., minkaohan), and three individuals who were educated in Uyghur (i.e., minkaomin), posted between January and June 2016. According to the results of this exercise, Xinjiang Class graduates used Chinese in nearly 75 percent of their posts, whereas minkaohan-educated Uyghurs used Chinese in 64 percent of their moments; minkaomin-educated Uyghurs composed less than 50 percent of their moments in Chinese. These numbers compare to similar studies on online language use conducted among Uyghurs in Ürümchi and Aksu between 2011 and 2013 (Hamut and Joniak-Lüthi 2015). Likewise, Elterish (2015, 84) reports Uyghurs use Uyghur, Chinese, and a mix of Uyghur and Chinese 25.8 percent, 40.7 percent, and 33.5 percent of the time, respectively, when using the Internet and 24.2 percent, 56.7 percent, and 33.5 percent when sending text messages.

Table 2.1: Language preference for WeChat moments among Xinjiang Class, Minkaohan, and Minkaomin Uyghurs

Education Background	Chinese	Latin-based Uyghur	Arabic-based Uyghur	Latin-based Uyghur and Chinese	Arabic-based Uyghur and Chinese	English	Chinese and English
Xinjiang Class (n=6)	472	30	63	5	9	44	10
Minkaohan (n=3)	55	0	26	0	1	4	0
Minkaomin (n=3)	102	2	99	1	1	0	0

The decision to adopt a certain script is complex and situational. For some, the adoption of Chinese may reflect individual deficiencies in their native written

---

7. WeChat is a wildly popular social-networking app created in China in 2011.

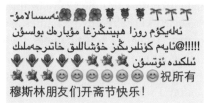 

Message 1: Uy. Peace Be Upon You. Have a blessed Roza Festival [Eid al-Fitr]. Wishing that your holiday is full of joy and peace; Ch. Wishing all of my Muslim friends a Happy Eid.

Message 2: Uy. Intirnatsi'onalizimlaxturalaywatqanliqimizdinmikintang Ch. Let me know if you can pronounce this word.

Figure 2.3: Hierarchy of languages used in bilingual WeChat moments

language (Elterish 2015, 82). For others, especially those who opened their own businesses (which was the case for two Xinjiang Class graduates), Chinese-language posts are valuable marketing tools as they can reach a broader customer base. Some individuals likely hope to accumulate "praises" (Ch. *zan*) by composing their WeChat moments in a mix of Uyghur and Chinese. Other Uyghurs prefer composing text messages in Chinese because inadequate software makes typing in Arabic Uyghur script on mobile phones difficult (Elterish 2015, 85).

Xinjiang Class graduates do not see a contradiction in posting in a mix of Uyghur and Chinese. Muradil, a graduate of Qingdao's Xinjiang Class, regularly composes bilingual posts on his WeChat profile. He sees little problem with using Chinese in some situations. In fact, he disagrees with those Uyghurs who refuse to learn Chinese altogether. Similar to most Xinjiang Class graduates with whom I spoke, the young man expressed concern about the current education system wherein Uyghur students spend more time formally studying Chinese than their native language. However, he hoped that other Uyghurs would regard this situation as an opportunity: "Chinese is knowledge (Uy. *bilim*) too, right? We should all try to increase our knowledge" (field notes, July 18, 2016).

Some individuals demonstrated their language preference in a hierarchical ordering of bilingual posts in which Uyghur is placed above Chinese. Xinjiang Class graduates regularly favored the Arabic-based script over the Latin-based when composing text messages and social media posts.

Chinese-language posts become useful when combating discrimination and Islamophobia, which have been on the rise since 2009 (Al Jazeera 2017; Erie 2016). During the 2010 Qurban Feast, Han students at Beijing Normal University (BNU) became angry when they learned that their Muslim classmates received meal vouchers worth RMB 50 (USD 7) and free fruit. Several Han students voiced their complaints on BNU's intranet message board, which Alimjan brought to my attention. Alimjan sifted through the eleven pages of posts to point out those he found particularly offensive. Assuming all Muslims at BNU were Hui, one student netizen remarked, "Wow. Even schools in northern China [regions dominated by Han] are stressing the importance of minority folk customs (Ch. *minsu chuantong*). I bet Hui students don't even know about this holiday." Another remarked, "Why do minority minzu believe they can resort (Ch. *pingjie*) to using their minzu identity to stake claim (Ch. *zhanyouquan*) to social resources (Ch. *shehui ziyuan*)? Alimjan then proudly read to me his replies:

> Do you [Han classmates] think the Qurban Feast is about receiving 50 kuai (RMB) meal vouchers? How about you? You are able to return home during winter break to celebrate Lunar New Year. Are you willing to celebrate it at school? If you don't know what you're talking about, buzz off (Ch. *piaoguo*)!

In one heated exchange, Alimjan emphasized the religious importance of Qurban to Muslims. Then, he issued a stern warning:

> The Qurban Feast isn't a minority minzu festival, it is a holy day celebrated worldwide by the over 1.5 billion Muslims. This isn't about minzu identity; it's about religion. If you believed in Islam, Qurban would be your holiday too. . . . This is your way of thinking? Acting like this causes good people to become extremists (Ch. *jiduan fenzi*). If this is the outcome you want, I'll be here waiting (Ch. *wo lai gen ni wan*).

With slightly more anonymity online, Uyghurs in neidi can use cyberspace to draw ethnic boundaries and establish transnational networks (Clothey and Koku 2016; Harris 2012; Leibold 2010; Leibold 2014; NurMuhammad et al. 2016). Paradoxically, Alimjan employed Chinese—not Uyghur or Arabic—to assert a transnational Muslim identity, which even welcomed a hypothetical Han convert.

Xinjiang Class graduates have responded to systematic attempts to weaken their native language by using Uyghur in otherwise Chinese-speaking environments. These individuals spoke in their mother language at every opportunity, and this practice continued outside the boarding school. Therefore, we should not misinterpret their preference to communicate with each other in Uyghur as a matter of convenience (Chen 2008, 125–26); rather, they consider the Uyghur language to be central to their ethno-national identity.

Dating: "Our Future Spouse Must Be Uyghur"

Apparent irreconcilable differences in religion, diet, lifestyle, and language contribute to Xinjiang Class graduates' aversion to romantic relationships with Han partners. When asked about future spouses, my informants often repeated that their significant other "must be Uyghur" (Uy. *choqum Uyghur*). Tursunjan, a native of Kashgar and a graduate of Guangzhou's Xinjiang Class, illustrated this point with the following improvisation:

> Imagine two cups placed side by side with the edges touching. The two cups represent Han and Uyghur people. The point where the two cups meet represents common ground between the two. Although we share some similarities with Han

people, there are many, many more differences, as you see with the amount of the cups' edges that do not touch. Sure we can get along during everyday interactions, but not in marriage. (field notes, November 24, 2010)

Objections to interethnic relationships are unsurprising given Uyghur taboos against exogamy (Rudelson 1997, 155; Smith Finley 2013, 297–347). Yet, my informants' intolerance must unnerve party officials, who continue to gauge integration and assimilation from rates of interethnic marriage, which remain very low among Uyghurs (Leibold 2016a; Smith Finley 2013; Yang 2006; Yee 2003).

The few individuals who challenged the taboo on interethnic relationships were stigmatized. Originally from Turpan, Bayram graduated at the top of Shenzhen's Xinjiang Class in 2007 and enrolled in UIBE. During the last week of Ramadan in 2010, Bayram invited me to the Uyghur Student Association's Roza celebration. He called me on the day of the event to suggest meeting at the venue later that evening. But, first, he needed to attend the communal prayer at the Madian Mosque (马甸清真寺), the closest mosque to his university, and join his classmates for dinner. We eventually met outside the large hall and entered the party together. During a pause in the music, Bayram, reeking of *erguotou*—an inexpensive but potent liquor made from sorghum—sat down beside me and slurred that he had a girlfriend. I congratulated him and requested an introduction. Lowering his voice to a whisper, Bayram continued, "She's not here. You don't understand. She is Han. I haven't told very many people yet." Unsure how to properly respond, I tried to offer words of encouragement. Bayram appeared skeptical but nodded in agreement anyway and stumbled back to the dance floor.

Rumors about Bayram's relationship slowly spread among his Uyghur classmates. The news was not received warmly. Aynur, a university classmate of Bayram's who spent her childhood in Kamul (Ch. *Hami*) and attended a Xinjiang Class in Wuxi, shared her opinion with me one afternoon:

I can't accept it [the two being together] (Uy. *chidayalmaymen*). Bayram is a good guy (Uy. *yaxshi bala*); he is very smart and kind. There aren't many Uyghur guys like Bayram. And did you know that there are more Uyghur girls than guys? So, Bayram should really date a Uyghur girl. (field notes, June 19, 2011)

While not as candid as Aynur, Bayram's closest friend, Muhtar, expressed his own reservations about the relationship. Muhtar graduated from the Dalian Xinjiang Class in 2007 and served as a cocaptain of the Uyghur intramural soccer team with Bayram. Knowing that I had recently shared dinner with the couple, Muhtar arranged for us to meet for coffee. He wasted little time before sharing his impressions of the young woman:

It's a little strange when we are all together because Bayram wants us to speak in Chinese, so his girlfriend can understand what we are saying. We [Muhtar and his Uyghur classmates] are Uyghur and like speaking Uyghur with each other. Maybe it would be OK if Bayram's girlfriend would learn Uyghur, but I don't think she wants to learn. (field notes, June 4, 2011)

Perhaps owing to his close friendship with Bayram, Muhtar at least entertained the possibility of accepting the relationship. But his acceptance had conditions: Bayram's girlfriend must learn to speak Uyghur. Put another way, although the young woman could not change her minzu category, she was expected to at least perform some markers of this ethno-national identity (see Butler 1990) before she would be welcomed by Bayram's Uyghur peers.

Bayram grew increasingly sensitive about his classmates' disapproval of his relationship. Over the course of a year, he withdrew from his Uyghur social circles to shield himself from their snickering. He continued to participate in the soccer league but no longer spoke about his girlfriend with his teammates. In the middle of the soccer season, Bayram and his girlfriend invited me to dinner. As was the case when the three of us met the previous year, our conversation was conducted in Putonghua. At the end of the meal, Bayram seized an opportunity to switch to Uyghur when his girlfriend was occupied with settling the bill. "I feel embarrassed (Uy. *xijil bolimen*) about having a Han girlfriend," he acknowledged, "Especially since many of my [Uyghur] friends do not support this relationship." He added that his parents, whom he finally told after hiding his relationship for nearly a year, were vehemently opposed to his decision to date a Han girl. Bayram sighed, "My mom fears that if I marry my girlfriend, our children won't be able to speak Uyghur" (field notes, May 27, 2012). Her disapproval is not surprising; many Uyghurs oppose Uyghur-Han intermarriage (Smith Finley 2013, 302–5; Yee 2003, 437).

Parental approval is still essential before marriage. Ablimit, a Xinjiang Class graduate from Kashgar, referred to the following well-known idiom: "Misfortune will come to marriages that do not receive blessings from parents" (Uy. *ata-anining raziliqsiz bolghan toy bextsiz qilidu*) (field notes, June 27, 2012). Without his parents' blessing, Bayram had little choice but to end the relationship. But not before he resisted their authority. Bayram remained in Beijing for an additional two and a half years after his graduation to earn a master's degree and to continue his relationship. Despite his efforts, however, Bayram was unable to change his parents' views of his Han girlfriend. Rather than protracting his four-year estrangement from his parents, Bayram returned to Ürümchi in late 2014. In May 2016, he married in Turpan, his hometown, to a Uyghur woman.

Forging Transnational Islamic Bonds

Although they remained insular in their attitudes about mixing with Han people, Xinjiang Class graduates actively stepped outward into a transnational Muslim community. Muradil, the individual who defended his bilingual social media posts, worked as a chemical engineer for Sinopec in Beijing after graduating from university. He found the work uninspiring and left his job to open a small *polu* (Central Asian pilaf) restaurant. Between the busy lunch and dinner services, Muradil chose to read from a small collection of Uyghur-language books to pass the time. On a hot July afternoon, he pulled out a Uyghur translation of Aatish Taseer's *Stranger to History: A Son's Journey through Islamic Lands*, which is known in Uyghur by the title, *My Muslim Father* (Uy. *Méning Musulman dadam*). The book details the author's travels through Muslim-majority countries in South Asia and the Middle East as he seeks to understand more about his father's past. Muradil looked up from the book and said, "I'm not really interested in the story about this guy's father and his military service. I'm reading it for the parts about the author traveling to Muslim countries. For now, reading books like this helps me to learn how Muslims in different countries live" (field notes, July 18, 2016).

We can draw another important parallel between Muradil's own experiences and those of the author Aatish Taseer. Both young Muslim men spent their formative years in non-Muslim-majority countries: Muradil in China where religious activities are monitored and controlled; Aatish in Leeds, where Islamophobia reared its ugly head after authorities discovered that three perpetrators in the July 7, 2005, London Underground bombing hailed from the West Yorkshire city (*Yorkshire Evening Post* 2015). These two young men's upbringings as Muslim minorities have produced a yearning to know more about Islam and to seek membership in a transnational Muslim community.

Indeed, many Xinjiang Class graduates seek to deepen their knowledge of Islam after leaving the boarding school. Although the harsh punishments for openly practicing Islam compelled my informants to obey the Xinjiang Class's policy on religion, graduates of the program use the relatively relaxed political climates of neidi's large cities to cultivate personal piety and connect with other Muslims. In neidi, Xinjiang Class graduates do not risk serious repercussions for attending prayers at mosques; they can surf a less-regulated Internet, which provides access to Islamic websites operated outside China; and they can meet the growing number of foreign Muslim residents in China.

Qur'an: Reciting Piety

Even those individuals who initially did not impress me as devout committed themselves to Islam to varying degrees. Aynur, the young woman who disapproved of Bayram's relationship, rarely spoke about religion during the first two years of our friendship, which began in 2010. By 2012, however, Aynur's attitudes toward Islam had changed. Aynur and I agreed to meet at a campus coffee shop, a popular hangout and the spot we had designated for our language practice. Normally punctual, Aynur did not arrive on time. I waited a few minutes hoping she did not forget about our plans. My phone vibrated violently on the wobbly table. It was a text message from Aynur apologizing that she could not chat for very long. Several minutes later Aynur rushed into the café appearing more formal than usual. The young woman's regular ensemble of a T-shirt, blue jeans, and a ponytail had been replaced with a long dress and straightened hair. I asked about her formal attire, to which she proudly replied:

> Today, I am going to the Saudi Arabian Embassy to receive a Uyghur-language Qur'an. You know the versions of the Qur'an available in Xinjiang aren't good because the government has translated them incorrectly. The Qur'ans at the Saudi Embassy are "real." As long as I present my passport at the embassy, and they see that I am a Uyghur, they will give me a Qur'an. I am going to get two—one for my parents and one for me. Since I am a college senior and do not have much coursework, I finally have time to start reading the Qur'an. (field notes, May 24, 2012)

Aynur learned from a university classmate in Beijing, also a graduate of the Xinjiang Class, that the Saudi Embassy supplied copies of the Qur'an to Muslims. Fully aware of the CCP's tight control of religious publications,[8] I asked Aynur if she had to obtain special permission to receive a Qur'an. She confidently replied, "No, but I am not going to tell anyone about this either" (field notes, May 24, 2012).

Aynur's trip to the Saudi Embassy is significant. After four years of carefully planned translation work supervised by the China Islamic Association and the Islamic Institute of Xinjiang, authorities published a highly anticipated new Uyghur translation of the Qur'an in August 2012 (Tianshan Net 2013).[9] Although the editors insist the work accurately renders the 2008 Qur'an printed by the King Fahd Complex for the Printing of the Holy Qur'an (*Qur'an Kerim* 2012, 66), Uyghur netizens have criticized the translation for altering the holy text's sacred meaning.[10] Despite the political risks associated with owning unsanctioned religious texts, Aynur chose to retrieve copies of the Qur'an from the Saudi Embassy instead of waiting for the state-approved version to roll out in bookstores. This decision suggests Aynur attaches more authenticity to copies of the Qur'an produced outside China than those printed by state publishers. By extension, we can assume that Aynur, similar to many young Uyghurs, looks past the CCP's "approved" version of Islam in her pursuit of faith in its "purest" form (Smith Finley 2013, 245–55) and seeks membership in a global community of Muslims over sinicized Islam (Liu 2017).

---

8. Printing or disseminating religious materials is one of the original twenty-three identified illegal religious activities (Ch. *Feifa zongjiao huodong*; Uy. *Qanunsiz dini pa'aliyetliri*) in Xinjiang.
9. The previous Uyghur translation of the Qur'an was finished by Muhemmet Salih and published in the mid-1980s.
10. For instance, netizens complained about the replacement of Arabic loan words with Turkic synonyms. In Surah 113 of the 2012 (604) Uyghur translation, for example, the Arabic loan *sherridin* is replaced with *yamanliqdin*. Although both terms denote "evil," some Uyghurs claim that the removal of Arabic, the original language of the Qur'an, aims to prevent Uyghurs from better understanding God's message. See, for example, discussions on the Meripet forum: http://meripet.biz/bbs/forum.php?mod=viewthread&tid=3525 [URL no longer active].

While some young Uyghurs were content to read the Qur'an in translation, others aspired to recite the holy text in Arabic. According to Muslims, the Arabic Qur'an is the literal word of God as it was transmitted to the Prophet Muhammad by the angel Gabriel. Since translations of the Qur'an are often regarded by believers as imperfect, many Muslims insist on learning Arabic (Hughes 2013, 71). During the 2010 fall semester, news about Beijing Foreign Studies University's free public Arabic classes quickly spread to Uyghur students at the nearby Beijing Normal University (BNU). A group of five female Xinjiang Class graduates from BNU, who all had spent their early childhoods in either Kashgar or Khotan, regularly participated in the program. Unlike many university students in Beijing who used their weekends to find relief from full course loads, these young women elected to study another foreign language during their leisure time.

Over lunch, I asked about their motivations for studying Arabic. They told me that they hoped the weekend classes would provide the necessary foundation required for pronouncing Qur'anic verses (*ayat*) correctly. The group of women then promptly reminded me that the Qur'an was originally revealed to the Prophet Muhammad in Arabic (field notes, November 20, 2010).

Raziye, the young woman who could not tolerate her Han roommates, also began to study the Qur'an in Arabic. Instead of enrolling in Arabic classes, Raziye—who married a Muslim foreign national—studied under the tutelage of her mother-in-law—a native Urdu speaker who is also proficient in Arabic. Raziye enthusiastically shared her experiences reading the Qur'an with her mother-in-law:

> While I was visiting family in [South Asia], my mother-in-law began to teach me how to read the Qur'an in Arabic. I would never have been able to do this so openly in Xinjiang. [Studying the Qur'an] also showed me how closely related Arabic is to the Uyghur language. So many words are the same. Reading the Qur'an made me feel close to my husband's family; even though it was hard to communicate with them, we shared being Muslim. (field notes, June 20, 2011)

Of course, it is possible that Raziye's apparent enthusiasm for reading the Qur'an was insincere and derived from familial pressure. Nevertheless, Raziye insisted she would continue studying the Qur'an with her husband after returning to China. More important, reading the Qur'an strengthens the potentially fragile bond between Raziye and her non-Uyghur, non-Chinese mother-in-law.

Reading the Qur'an also provides a sacred bond between these Uyghur women and Muslim women living elsewhere. Recent studies have shown that young, often highly-educated, Muslim women in Central Asia, South Asia, and the Middle East form reading groups to study Islamic texts (mainly the Qur'an and hadith) in their leisure time. In addition to providing an outlet for religious expression, communal readings of sacred texts help build a sense of solidarity among Muslim women (Huq 2008; Raudvere 2002; Schwab 2012), and—through activism—these groups help to pave avenues for political and social change (van Doorn-Harder 2006). Although the formal reading groups that were the focus of the aforementioned research are distinct from the informal reading groups organized by my informants, they are nonetheless related: not only do communal readings of Islamic texts strengthen religious ties and social relationships, the practice often connects Muslim women to a transnational or even global Muslim community (Schwab 2012; van Doorn-Harder 2006).[11] Finally, through the discovery of many Arabic loan words in their native language, these Uyghur women strengthen imagined (Anderson 1991) cultural ties with Arabic-speaking Muslims.

"She's the One That Veils"

Some women began veiling after the Xinjiang Class (see also Chapter 4). Rena, a 2010 Beijing Xinjiang Class graduate originally from Khotan, completely covered her hair with a hijab, a style virtually unseen among Uyghur university students in Beijing. Rena told me she "accepted" (Uy. *qobul qildim*) her veil after returning to China from a summer in Egypt. She explained:

> Veiling is an important part of my religion. When I cover my head others will know my religious beliefs. Furthermore, Islam teaches women to cover their heads and wear modest clothing. By dressing in this manner, we [Muslim women] can prevent men from gazing at or harming us. I feel very happy every time I put on my veil; when it is on, I'm reminded of my religion, my faith, and God. (field notes, June 10, 2013)

Rena's veil serves as a visible assertion of her Muslim and Uyghur identity, and this particular style of head covering signifies her consumption of global Islamic fashion trends. Veiling also provides Rena with a habitual act to cultivate specifically Muslim-defined pulchritude and femininity, especially modesty and "shyness." Her remarks about the male gaze recall Richard Antoun's (1968) concept of the "modesty code," in which he recasts analytical inquiries on veiling from narrow discussions about garments to include idealized feminine virtues (especially humility, docility, and shyness) and social institutions including marriage and honor.

But some of Rena's peers rejected her views on veiling. On my way to meet Rena, I was surprised by her classmates' disparaging remarks. "Rena?" one woman asked, which prompted her friend to gesture an outline of a hijab. Another young woman looked at her friends and giggled, "She once asked me why I didn't cover my head and insisted that Muslim women are required to wear veils. I told her that Allah also created our hair to be beautiful, so he wouldn't want us [Muslim women] to cover our heads. We got into an argument. Now we won't discuss veiling

---

11. In his comparison of the Piety Movement and the Ata Zholy—two socioreligious groups in Kazakhstan—Schwab (2012) reveals that Kazakhs—especially those associated with the Ata Zholy movement—are defining a distinctly "Kazakh" way of being Muslim by promoting certain interpretations of the Qur'an and hadith over others.

anymore." In her justification for not veiling, Rena's acquaintance demonstrates the flexibility by which Islamic modesty standards are interpreted within a community. She even challenges Rena's knowledge of sacred texts with her allusion to a popular hadith, or saying of the Prophet Muhammad, that proclaims Allah's love for beauty (Ahmad ibn Muhammad ibn Hanbal IV, 133–34, cited in Lings 1983, 70).

Rena continued to veil despite pushback from her peers. She explained, "My hijab is fashionable. Sure, at first I was influenced by Arabic styles [when I was in Egypt]. But then I began to combine my own culture and fashion. Now, the style of hijab I wear changes according to the occasion." Rena's response does not suggest that her decision to veil is in defiance of her Chinese identity or in protest of Xinjiang's ban on veiling (cf. Leibold and Grose 2016). Quite the contrary; it reflects an individualized way to navigate her multilayered identity. In fact, after returning from a study abroad experience the next year, Rena shared how she embraced her Chineseness while living in Canada:

> I enjoyed my life in Canada. I befriended Muslim students from around the world. It's funny—some people have never heard of Uyghurs. My classmates and professors often asked me where I am from. I say, "China." They were surprised by my answer because I don't appear [Han] Chinese. But I am Chinese. Yes, I'm Uyghur, but I'm from China. I don't want to be someone without a country. I don't understand why, but some Uyghurs living abroad say they are from Turkey or East Turkestan. We are from China.

My encounters with Rena highlight the various and situational ways by which Xinjiang Class graduates embrace Chinese and Uyghur identities yet express transnational Muslim cosmopolitanism through multilingualism, consumerism, and renewed religiosity (Erkin 2009; Smith Finley 2013, 380–93).

Time for Prayer

Male graduates of the Xinjiang Class similarly practiced some tenets of Islam as university students. These young men put forth a faithful effort to perform Islam's obligatory five daily prayers (Uy. *besh waq namaz*) despite hectic class schedules. Adil, a native of Kashgar and a graduate of Guangzhou's Xinjiang Class, stood out as one of my most devout interlocutors. Although Adil's father worked as a police officer in Xinjiang, and thus was forbidden from openly practicing Islam,[12] Adil learned at a young age how to perform namaz from his grandfather. After graduating from the Xinjiang Class, Adil recommitted himself to the five daily prayers. If his class schedule conflicted with one of the prescribed prayer times, he simply prayed immediately after his class. In another example of Adil's commitment to

---

12. According to the "Regulations on Routine Service" document, which outlines the rules for individuals serving in the People's Liberation Army, servicemen, including police officers, "may not take part in religious or superstitious activities." See DOS 2004.

prayer, he attended the weekly *jüme* Friday communal prayer at a mosque forty minutes away by public bus (field notes, June 3, 2012).

Murat, the devout young man who planned to study in Turkey, followed the same prayer schedule. He set aside space in his dormitory room, which was large enough to allow several individuals to simultaneously perform the ritual prostrations (Uy. *reket*). Several vibrantly colored prayer rugs (Uy. *jaynamaz*) demarcated the makeshift *musalla* prayer room and infused life into the otherwise drab concrete living space. On the west-facing wall (i.e., the direction facing Mecca), Murat had hung a large poster depicting hajj pilgrims circumambulating the Kaaba in Mecca. Several embroidered *doppa* caps, which Murat would wear while praying, and a set of *teswi* (prayer beads) draped from several hooks fastened below the poster of Mecca. Viewed from the perspective of a non-Muslim, Murat flawlessly executed the prayers. However, he doubted his ability to correctly perform the prescribed postures and recitations. In an attempt to perfect his practice, Murat routinely consulted online step-by-step prayer manuals available on a multilingual website hosted in Turkey.[13] Exhibiting great exactitude, Murat adjusted his postures to more closely resemble those featured in the manuals.

To be sure, these two young men belong to a small group of my informants who prayed five times daily. Most prayed once a day, in the early morning (Uy. *bamdat namazi*), and only attended mosque on major holidays, a routine typical among young men in some regions of Xinjiang (Bellér-Hann 2008, 311; Dautcher 2009, 259). Others, citing a lack of time or conflicts in their daily schedules, admitted they rarely, if ever, perform namaz. Bayram, the individual once romantically involved with a Han woman, criticized his own religious laxity. At one point he even doubted being a "real Muslim" (Uy. *heqiqiy Musulman*), though he quickly justified his lifestyle: "I have no choice (Uy. *amal yoq*). I'm not allowed to pray in Xinjiang, and there is nowhere for me to pray in Beijing" (field notes, May 27, 2012). Erkin, a native of Kashgar who graduated from the Xinjiang Class in Nanjing, also expressed guilt for not praying. When asked if he ever prayed, Erkin sighed, "It's a shame that I don't, but believing is just as important" (Uy. *epsus, bularni qilip kételmidim, lékin, étiqadi bolush muhimdur*) (*field notes*, June 1, 2012). The two young men's inability or unwillingness to pray notwithstanding, their justifications for religious laxity reveal an identity crisis: they recognize Islam as an essential element of Uyghurness, despite their atheist boarding school education. If these young men internalized the state-defined "Weiwu'er zu" identity over a Uyghur identity that is grounded in Islam, their casual commitment to religious practice would be an unlikely source of guilt.

---

13. For one example of these websites, see www.dewr.org/kutuphana/?namaz/namaz.sureleri [URL no longer active]. Dewr—the name of the site, which means "a period of time"—in addition to containing instructions for performing namaz, complete with pictures, contains links to downloadable Uyghur fables (Uy. *mesel*), Uyghur translations of hadith, elementary Turkish language textbooks, and audio recordings of the Qur'an in Uyghur and Arabic.

To a certain extent, my informants expressed themselves as Muslims (and Uyghurs) through gendered religious practices. Reading the Qur'an, a devotion primarily undertaken by my female informants, and the adherence to Islamic prayers maintained by many of my male informants attests to this point. The existence of gender-specific forms of devotion is certainly not unique to Xinjiang Class graduates but in fact mirrors many Muslims communities (Dautcher 2009; Jaschok and Shui 2000; Raudvere 2002; Tapper and Tapper 1987).

Other forms of devotion, however, blur gender divisions in religious practice. The recitation of post-meal du'a (or *chay du'asi*), described at the beginning of this chapter, provides one such example. In the company of other Uyghurs, my informants recited these quick prayers of supplication after every meal, and—as shown in the introduction to this chapter—sometimes even after eating snacks.[14] Remarkably, the recitation of du'a—in at least some Uyghur communities—is largely determined by gender, with men less likely to engage in the practice (Dautcher 2009, 262).[15] During my research in Beijing, however, I commonly witnessed groups of my informants—comprising both men and women—performing du'a at school cafeterias and in restaurants.

Several factors may account for why du'a is practiced differently outside the XUAR. On strictly a practical level, performing du'a requires little commitment or formal instruction. Although the majority of my informants did not attend religious schools as children in Xinjiang, they learned how to perform du'a from their parents or grandparents. If one did not learn as a child, one could easily mimic one's peers. Even I quickly learned the required hand movements and proper utterances. We also cannot overlook the influence of community and peer pressure on Uyghur Islamic practice (Bellér-Hann 2008; Smith Finley 2013, 244–45). In other words, because of its simplicity, du'a provides an opportunity for otherwise unreligious individuals to publicly reaffirm their commitment to Islam and assert their ethno-religious identity in the company of other Uyghurs. Failure to participate in du'a is a social risk and may come at the expense of criticism from peers.

We may also understand the performance of du'a as another form of "symbolic" boundary maintenance (Smith Finley 2013). In Ürümchi—although it is certainly not uncommon for Han to eat at Uyghur-owned restaurants—the patronage of certain restaurants, especially those located in non-tourist-friendly Uyghur enclaves, is almost exclusively Uyghur. Moreover, most university cafeterias in the provincial capital are segregated (Smith 2002, 166). In Beijing, however, Uyghur-owned "Xinjiang-style" restaurants attract a mostly Han clientele, especially those upscale establishments offering song-and-dance performances (Baranovitch 2003).

---

14. I documented the instances in which my informants did not perform du'a. In most cases, my informants did not offer the prayer when eating alone or when eating only with me. The recitation of du'a was more consistent when several Uyghur students shared a meal.
15. Although we can assume that some men in Xinjiang routinely recite du'a after a meal, there are no systematic studies available on this practice to compare with Dautcher's account.

Han students also frequent university halal cafeterias. Having, in a sense, become a minority of their own food culture in Beijing, Xinjiang Class graduates must rely on strategies to reclaim "their" cuisine and ritually pure eating spaces. Apart from generally receiving better service from Uyghur staff,[16] which in itself suggests a degree of transregional solidarity among Uyghurs, Xinjiang Class graduates can reinforce ethnic boundaries vis-à-vis Han patrons through the performance of du'a.

Unlike their non–Xinjiang Class peers in Beijing (Grose 2013), however, my informants exhibited laxity during Ramadan's thirty-day fast (Uy. *roza tutush*). In 2010 the holy month overlapped with the academic year. I asked my informants about their views on fasting. No one observed the entire thirty-day fast,[17] and only a group of four men fasted at all—on the last day of Ramadan.

Several circumstances prevented Xinjiang Class graduates from fasting. They pointed to the inconvenience of dormitory life, which did not afford the space or appliances to prepare the hearty predawn meal (Uy. *zoluq*). Some individuals worried that fasting would inhibit their studies. Others still questioned the necessity of the practice. When I asked Aynur, the young woman who received a copy of the Qur'an from the Saudi Embassy, about her reasons for not fasting, she dismissed the injunction to do so:

> My parents are teachers and are not permitted to fast, so I never fasted as a child. It's not like it used to be in Xinjiang, and women commonly work outside the home. I also want to work and go abroad to study, so I have to study hard. If I fast, I won't be able to concentrate in class. But being Muslim isn't about how many times a day I pray or about fasting. Being Muslim is a feeling in your heart and is about how you treat other people. (field notes, September 8, 2010)

Aynur's response helps to summarize one of the prevailing arguments of this chapter. Although Islam continues to be an essential element of Uyghur identity among Xinjiang Class graduates, its expressions are not confined to a single set of practices. Rather, Xinjiang Class graduates communicate the Islamic components of their identity in several ways and to varying degrees—from reading the Qur'an, praying, or even an action as simple as professing their faith. Indeed, Xinjiang Class graduates assert a distinct (yet fluid) "Uyghur" identity wherein Islam continues to play a significant role.

Transnational Yet Mono-minzu Islam

Uyghur Xinjiang Class graduates' visions of a transnational Islamic community largely excluded Hui Muslims. Similar to Uyghurs in Xinjiang (Cesàro 2000, 230;

---

16. At several Uyghur-owned restaurants in Beijing, large parties of Uyghur students commonly received significant discounts on their bills.
17. Although the verb *tutmaq* may be translated most accurately as "holding," I commonly refer to "observing" the Ramadan fast for sake of convenience. For an interesting discussion on this topic, see Dautcher 2009, 285.

Han 2010; Smith 2002, 161–66), Xinjiang Class graduates in neidi distrusted their Hui coreligionists. The tensions were palpable when Xinjiang Class graduates and their Uyghur classmates at UIBE boycotted a nearby Hui-owned restaurant. Uyghur university students in Beijing have few halal options outside halal *qingzhen* (清真)[18] cafeterias, but those attending UIBE patronized Master Ma's (Ch. *Ma Shifu*), a long-established qingzhen restaurant owned by a Hui family from Lanzhou, Gansu that serves several Uyghur-style dishes. During the fall 2010 semester, a new Hui-owned eatery opened just doors down from Master Ma's, despite an unwritten agreement among Hui restaurateurs to refrain from opening competing businesses within 400 meters of each other (*Global Times* 2015b). Desiring variety in my lunch routine, I tried the new restaurant and was pleasantly surprised by the food's quality. After lunch I met with Aynur for our language exchange and excitedly asked if she had tried the new restaurant. "Don't go back there," she insisted. "The owners and chef are not *real* Hui; they are from Sichuan. My friend ate there earlier this week and became ill. My [Uyghur] friends won't eat there anymore." The business closed within months, perhaps because it could not attract a Uyghur clientele.

The informal boycott reflects Uyghur distrust toward Hui, deep sentiments not erased by a Xinjiang Class education. Although the CCP recognizes both groups as Muslim minzu, Uyghurs question Hui piety and commonly regard the group as "newcomers" to Xinjiang who share physical features and political loyalties with Han people (Côté 2015, 145–46). In fact, Uyghurs teasingly refer to Hui as *tawuz* (watermelon) because they are green (i.e., Muslim) on the surface but red (i.e., communist) at the core (Côté 2015, 145; Rudelson and Jankowiak 2004, 311). Aynur's jibe about "fake" Hui from Sichuan signals the belief that pious, and therefore "acceptable," Hui live in concentrated communities in Gansu, Ningxia, Qinghai, and Xinjiang; religiously lax Hui, on the other hand, are scattered throughout the rest of China (cf. Gladney 1991).

Concluding Remarks

The identities of Xinjiang Class graduates have not been fixed by their boarding school experiences. This chapter has demonstrated that the demarcation of spatial boundaries, the preference to speak Uyghur over Putonghua, and renewed interests in Islam—the very deeply rooted practices the CCP attempts to undermine and "re-engineer" (Byler 2017)—evidence a strengthened Uyghur ethno-national identity as well as a transnational Islamic identity. This is not to say that Xinjiang Class graduates are more religious or prone to conflict with Han people than their non–Xinjiang Class peers. However, the boarding schools have not successfully co-opted all young Uyghurs as compliant members of the Zhonghua minzu. Conversely, the

---

18. Literally meaning "pure and true" and applied similarly to the concept halal, qingzhen refers to ethnic and religious categories of permissible behaviors, especially consumption (Gladney 1991; Gillette 2000).

Xinjiang Class has led—or at least allowed—a group of highly educated, socially conscious individuals to develop a spirit of "everyday resistance" (Scott 1989). Xinjiang Class graduates are drawn to Uyghur culture, membership to the umma, and even secular cosmopolitanism, but do not squeeze themselves into the state-defined "Weiwu'er zu" category.

Figure 2.4: The "Uyghur" Team squeezes tightly in a huddle before a match

3

Ignoring CCP Calls to Return to Xinjiang[1]

> Upon Returning to Xinjiang, these minority minzu students, having been educated for a long period of time in neidi, will sense a call of duty to propagate Chinese culture.
>
> —Zhao Jie, Peking University

Although the last chapter demonstrated that Xinjiang Class graduates reshape and contest their state-ascribed identities as university students, they are always considered to be already "interpellated" as "Weiwu'er zu" minorities and contributing members of the Zhonghua minzu in the eyes of CCP officials. Therefore, the CCP expects Xinjiang Class Uyghurs to embody this role throughout their adult lives. As such, a Uyghur-Chinese bilingual "minzu unity reader" provides subliminal yet important reminders for Uyghurs post-Xinjiang Class; they are to return to Xinjiang after their formal education to help develop the northwest region.[2] One chapter, composed in letter form by the presumably fictitious Qurban Nisa—soon-to-be graduate of the program—to Ismail Tiliwaldi—former Chairman of the XUAR and current member of the Standing Committee of the National People's Congress—enumerates the benefits of the boarding school education. After he cheerfully describes his four years at a Xinjiang Class in Beijing and admiringly recalls the selfless acts of the school's Han teachers, Qurban reassures the official that he is ready to repay the party:

> As you know, our country has increased its investment in Xinjiang's education. This act clearly proves that our country emphasizes education in the region. Surely, I will not disappoint the party or our country. More especially, I will not let you [Ismail Tiliwaldi] down. I will study hard and continue to master even more scientific knowledge. I will diligently repay our great motherland and build a beautiful Xinjiang. (Tang 2011, 130)

---

1. Parts of this chapter were published in a chapter (Grose 2015a) contained in Joanne Smith Finley and Zang Xiaowei's (2015) volume, *Language, Education, and Uyghur Identity in Urban Xinjiang*.
2. In 2010, several state publishers began printing bilingual minzu unity readers that presented the "official" history, minzu customs, and minzu policies of Xinjiang to children and young adults. In addition to the book discussed above, titles of this genre include *Minzu Unity Education Youth Reader* (Uy. *Milletler ittipaqi terbiyesi yashlar oqushluqi*) and *Minzu Unity Stories* (*Milletler ittipaqi heqqide hékaye*).

Drawing on Emily Yeh's (2013) astute insights into state development in Tibet, we can interpret the Xinjiang Class as a neatly packaged gift—an affordable boarding school education in neidi—prepared by the CCP and offered to young Uyghurs and their guardians. By accepting this gift, however, Uyghurs consensually enter into a relationship of servitude. That is, participation in a national boarding school program reifies CCP authority and reaffirms the party's dictum that Xinjiang is an inalienable part of China. Why else would the party expend resources, energy, and care to the region and its people? Furthermore, since gift giving in China is wrapped within the dynamics of *guanxi*—interpersonal relationships forged from the potential of future social benefits and nurtured through reciprocal favors (Yang 1994)— the CCP expects these students to give something in return: their faithful service.

Indeed, the CCP regards Xinjiang Class graduates as instrumental agents to stability in the region. This model should sound familiar; it was imposed elsewhere. Benedict Anderson (1991, 126) reminds us that the education policy of colonial France attempted to create "a politically reliable, grateful, and acculturated indigenous elite, filling the subordinate echelons of the colony's bureaucracy and larger commercial enterprises." Similarly, the party must convince these young educated Uyghurs to return to Xinjiang and serve as conduits between the party, the growing number of Han residents, and those Uyghurs who still refuse to integrate into mainstream society.

This chapter examines the choices Xinjiang Class graduates face upon completing their studies in neidi. As participants of the boarding schools, these individuals exemplify both model students and upstanding Chinese citizens by studying in predominantly Han schools, disavowing religious devotions (at least as senior high school students), improving Putonghua competencies, and continuing their formal education at Chinese universities. After graduating from university, however, Xinjiang Class graduates often defer their "debt" to the party. Citing disadvantages in the job market and tightened restrictions on religious practice in Xinjiang, as well as greater freedom in neidi or in foreign countries, Xinjiang Class graduates often decide to postpone their homecomings indefinitely. This decision is significant and sheds light on the ways in which young Uyghurs interpret and challenge state-ascribed identities. Yet they do not completely reject their "Chineseness." Paradoxically, mobility within China and the chance to travel overseas is largely contingent upon temporarily *subscribing* to the Zhonghua minzu identity through participating and excelling in state schools.

Herding Xinjiang Class Graduates back to Xinjiang

Party officials appeared unprepared for the long-term effects of educating large numbers of minority minzu students in neidi. Caught off guard, the CCP addressed its first serious problem in 2008, the year the program's inaugural cohort of students would graduate from university: What was to be done with them after their formal schooling? The matter required immediate attention. On May 12, 2008, approximately one month before universities throughout China would hold commencement ceremonies, the General Office of China's Ministry of Education, the State Ethnic Affairs Commission, the Ministry of Public Security, and the People's Government of the XUAR jointly issued general guidelines on the issue. According to the document, employment for Xinjiang Class graduates is "a serious concern for society as a whole" (Ch. *shehui gejie guanzhu de wenti*). The document stipulated that graduates should be "encouraged to return to Xinjiang" but are "allowed to remain in neidi" if they so wish (Ch. *guli huixiang; chongxu liu neidi*) (General Office of the MOE 2008).

Policymakers undoubtedly intend for the program's graduates to return to, and find employment in, Xinjiang itself. Indeed, the CCP urges Xinjiang Class graduates to pursue certain professions in the region:

> Xinjiang Class students should be encouraged to return to Xinjiang for employment . . . in order to strengthen the Communist Party's work at the grass roots level. Xinjiang Class students should be guided to be employed at basic level public service institutions in order to fully utilize [these students'] professional skills and expertise in order to meet the needs of education, health care, family planning, agricultural technology, and other areas that have a high demand for professionals. (General Office of the MOE 2008)

According to the same document, Xinjiang Class graduates possess the skills and traits valued by CCP leaders and potential employers alike: they have "mastered both Uyghur and Chinese" (Ch. *minhan jiantong*); they have been trained in neidi for eight years; and they "generally are of relatively good quality" (Ch. *yiban juyou jiaohao de suzhi*).[3] Having equipped young Uyghurs with these new tools, CCP leaders can now showcase them as sufficiently worthy and reliable to participate in Xinjiang's social and economic development programs.

Meanwhile, some Han intellectuals confidently dismiss the possibility of large numbers of Xinjiang Class graduates remaining in neidi. Their boarding school education was to "interpellate" them to proceed otherwise. Zhao Jie (2007, 134), the noted Peking University professor who has published extensively on contemporary majority-minority minzu relations, writes:

> Xinjiang Class students are imperceptibly (Ch. *qianyimohua*) trained in the culture of the Central Plains (Ch. *zhongyuan wenhua*) so that they will develop an attachment (Ch. *yiliangan*) toward the Zhonghua minzu and steadily deepen their sense of patriotism. Upon returning to Xinjiang, these minority minzu students, having

---

3. The term *suzhi* refers to the "quality" of an individual. Those individuals possessing superior quality (Ch. *suzhi gao*) are generally considered to be educated, clean, economically stable, etc. The term has entered into Chinese state discourse concerning development, and its usage distinguishes between practices and modes of thinking advocated by the state and those considered "backward" (Ch. *luohou*). For more on this topic, see Jacka 2009.

been educated for a long period of time in neidi, will sense a call of duty (Ch. *shi minggan*) to propagate Chinese culture, and will be a great spiritual force (Ch. *jingshen liliang*) to consolidate minzu unity, oppose foreign hostile forces, and reject separatist activities.

Echoing sentiments of the Confucian concept "come [to the center of Chinese civilization] and be transformed" (Ch. *laihua*), which essentially paved a path for non-Chinese "barbarians" to become "civilized" (Ch. *shufan*) through a proper Confucian education and by adopting acceptable "modes of livelihood," Zhao's statement intimates that the Xinjiang Class is an important institution in the CCP's current iteration of China's "civilizing project" (Harrell 1995). Having anointed Xinjiang Class graduates as torchbearers of the party-state, the CCP expects that Xinjiang, too, will one day be "enlightened" by Chinese culture.

Party officials paint a similarly optimistic picture. During an interview with the Ürümchi-based *Xinjiang Daily* (Ch. *Xinjiang ribao*), the XUAR's most widely circulated newspaper, Sun Qi, Director of the Xinjiang Class Office of Student Affairs (Ch. *Neidi Xinjiang xuesheng gongzuo bangongshi*), was asked if graduates return to the region and stay there permanently. While Sun conceded that some have remained in neidi, he maintained that the "majority" (Ch. *da bufen*) return to Xinjiang to find employment. According to Sun, these young individuals have already emerged as the "new force" (Ch. *yi zhi xinsheng liliang*) behind Xinjiang's rapid economic and social development (*Xinjiang Daily* 2012).

A recent study published in mainland China ostensibly supports Sun's assertion. Drawing on figures published by a Tianjin Xinjiang Class and open-ended interviews with graduates who have already returned to Xinjiang, this investigation claims that "most" find their way back to the region and have found employment as teachers, police officers, doctors, or civil servants (Oudengcaowa 2014, 70). However, the primary investigator fails to explain that one-fourth of her study's participants—those employed as teachers—were likely bound by contract to return, a topic thoroughly discussed below. Another one-fourth of her informants remained in neidi for up to one year before personal and family matters compelled them to return. Above all, the study does not address the important reasons behind the highly personal decision to return.

In reality, Xinjiang Class graduates rarely choose Xinjiang when they are provided an alternative. In fact, one rarely published statistic indicates that nearly 50 percent of the program's graduates do not return (Xinjiang TV, 10 March 2012);[4] my research suggests a potentially higher percentage do not fulfill this duty. Among the fifty-five individuals who were not contractually bound to serve as school teachers

---

4. According to the numbers provided in this report, only 2280 Xinjiang Class graduates who have completed a four-year university program, out of 4,200, have returned to Xinjiang to find employment.

in Xinjiang,[5] thirty-six did not plan to return, were enrolled in a graduate program in Beijing, intended to move abroad, or had already emigrated. In other words, if given a choice, three-fifths of my informants pursued opportunities outside the region. Although this study focuses on a small number of individuals, there is little reason to doubt that these attitudes toward returning are not also shared by other Xinjiang Class graduates. In fact, virtually all my informants spoke of a Xinjiang Class acquaintance who either worked in neidi or relocated abroad. Similarly, Oudengcaowa's (2014, 66–68) informants knew several classmates, some dozens, who now live outside China.

Return to Xinjiang?

The blogosphere erupted in debate over the issue of returning to Xinjiang years before the program's first cohort graduated from university. These exchanges often became passionate. A student intent on returning to Xinjiang exclaimed:

> No matter what, after I graduate, I am returning home! For the service of my hometown! Because I love my home! My family and friends are there [Xinjiang]. (Baidu posts, December 14, 2005)

Another student identified by the alias "ali2001_2005" implored others to do the same—albeit for a very different reason:

> I hope that everyone does not forget the homeland [Xinjiang] in which they were raised. Do not forget your roots (Ch. *gen*)! In some respects, neidi is an opportunity; in some respects neidi will [provide us] with a good salary. However, these things are all material. The most important thing is our spirit (Ch. *jingshen*)... Since the country [China] and Xinjiang have trained us, we should develop the west; if not, there are those Khitay [Xitay] ... [ellipsis in the original][6] I would like to ask you, haven't you stayed in neidi long enough? Don't you want your home to catch up with neidi? (Baidu posts, January 1, 2006)

In a final excerpt from this debate, an unidentified, though presumably Uyghur, poster doubts whether the party will welcome Xinjiang Class graduates:

> The crucial question is whether or not "they" [Han CCP officials] will use you if you return. In "their" eyes, we [Uyghurs] are not regarded as talented and qualified individuals. (Baidu posts, January 4, 2008)

---

5. Nine of my informants chose to enroll in one of China's pedagogical universities (Ch. *shifan daxue* or *shifan xueyuan*) and participate in these universities' teacher-training programs. As I discuss below, Xinjiang Class graduates who become teachers receive a free university education. All nine of these students spent their early childhoods in southern Xinjiang (especially Kashgar, Khotan, or Aksu), and their parents were either farmers or common laborers. For families in southern Xinjiang who rely primarily on agricultural production for their often-modest annual incomes, the Xinjiang Class provides the most feasible option for children from these impoverished areas to receive senior high and university educations.
6. *Xitay* is a Uyghur pejorative for Han people.

As the above vignettes suggest, Xinjiang Class students are divided over returning. To be sure, some appear genuinely eager to leave neidi behind them, a sentiment expressed in the first post and a subject to be discussed in Chapter 4. However, as the second poster indicates, the decision is sometimes fueled by resentment toward Xinjiang's growing Han population. Others still remain unconvinced by the CCP's pledge to place Xinjiang Class graduates at the forefront of state-led projects in the region.

In light of this debate among Uyghurs, it is unsurprising that the CCP keeps close tabs on individuals once they graduate. Upon completing their university degrees, Xinjiang Class graduates must register with the boarding school program at its official website (www.xjban.com) and provide a contact number, employment status, and, if applicable, proof of employment. Individuals who return to Xinjiang are expected to register with the Xinjiang Class Work Office (Ch. *Neidi Xinjiang xuesheng gonzuo bangong shi*) in Ürümchi (Xinjiang Class Online 2015a).

Those planning to remain in neidi must receive official approval. First, individuals must file a written request (Ch. *shumian shenqing*) with the Department of Education of the XUAR (Ch. *Xinjiang Weiwu'er zizhi qu jiaoyu ting*). The request form, which explicitly reminds individuals that they are encouraged to return to Xinjiang, also asks for several supporting documents, such as copies of identification cards (Ch. *shenfen zheng*), student IDs (Ch. *xuesheng zheng*), and employment contracts (Xinjiang Class Online 2015a). Requests are said to be processed within two business days of their receipt (Xinjiang Class Online 2013b).

With much at stake, the XUAR government, local officials, and university administrators militate against Xinjiang Class graduates remaining in neidi. Those wishing to work outside Xinjiang must clear a discouraging series of bureaucratic hurdles, in addition to filing the necessary paperwork. Ayjamal, a young woman from Qumul (Ch. *Hami*) who attended university in Beijing, stumbled over these obstacles. In December 2007 Ayjamal was offered full-time employment at a business firm in Beijing. Before accepting this job, Ayjamal, in accordance with official policy, submitted her formal request to the Department of Education of the XUAR. After a lengthy delay, officials finally granted Ayjamal permission to accept the offer. However, unbeknownst to Ayjamal at the time, her university in Beijing had yet to revise its policy to conform with that of the Department of Education. The university's outdated policy stipulated that "upon graduating [Xinjiang Class graduates] must return [to Xinjiang] for employment" (Ch. *biye hou hui yuanji jiuye*) (UIBE n.d.). As such, university officials nullified the Department of Education's approval letter without explanation. Entangled in bureaucratic red tape and uncertain about her future, Ayjamal postponed her graduation and her inevitable return to Xinjiang by accepting an internship in India (field notes, December 14, 2007).

Despite these difficulties and the frustrations they create, many Xinjiang Class graduates aspire to a life beyond their hometowns. Below I present some of the reasons why these academically successful individuals, trained by the resources of the state and expected to serve their fatherland, are reluctant (or refuse) to return to Xinjiang.

"I will not be treated as a second-class citizen in my homeland"

Modern Uyghur ethno-nationalism is partly predicated on claims of indigeneity to the oases of the Tarim and Junggar Basins. Now enclosed within modern administrative borders, the XUAR—formally established in 1955—has provided the Uyghurs with a "convenient frame to Uyghur political imaginings" (Bovingdon 2004, 4). However, similar to other ethnic autonomous regions in China,[7] the Uyghurs are slowly becoming a minority in their own homeland. The shift in Xinjiang's demographics has strained Uyghur-Han relations. Stories of Han mistreatment of Uyghurs are widespread (Bovingdon 2010; Caprioni 2011; Kaltman 2007; Mackerras 2001; Millward 2007; Rudelson 1997; Smith 2000; Zhang and McGhee 2014), and Han disrespect for Uyghur culture has exacerbated Uyghur discontent (Smith 2000, 2002).

The discrimination experienced directly by my informants has left them feeling bitter. Aynur's decision to emigrate provides a case in point. She enrolled in a Beijing university to study business English. During her third year of courses, Aynur planned her next step—she would study overseas. At first glance, her plan appeared logical enough since she studied English as her university major. However, Aynur's decision to live abroad had little to do with furthering her studies. Instead, Aynur cited what she perceived as political injustices as the main reason for wanting to relocate. The young woman was dissatisfied with the CCP, despite both of her parents' status as party members; she described them as "supportive of the government and its policies." When asked why she would not return, she answered with two stories. I paraphrase below:

> During National Holiday,[8] I traveled to Dalian with four other Uyghur girls to visit my sister, who is currently enrolled at the Xinjiang Class there. Before we boarded the ferry [which carries passengers to Dalian from Tianjin], the armed police (Ch. *wujing*) came up to us, pointed their guns, and demanded to see our identification cards. I thought I was going to die. We didn't do anything wrong. The only reason they stopped us was because we were Uyghur.
>
> Then, in Qumul [her hometown], right before the Olympics [summer 2008] guards checked our purses as we boarded buses, and if [Uyghur] passengers carried drinks, they had to take a sip in front of the guards. I do not want to return to a place where I am treated like this. (field notes, September 10, 2010)

---

7. According to the 2010 national census, Hui accounted for 38 percent of Ningxia Hui Autonomous Region's population; Mongols in the Inner Mongolia Autonomous Region accounted for 17 percent of the population.
8. The PRC was established on October 1, 1949. Currently, PRC citizens are given a weeklong break to commemorate the founding of the New China. Similar to China's Spring Festival period, this holiday is a time for many Chinese citizens to travel.

Aynur's experiences are reminiscent of the "stop and search" and "stop and frisk" policies once practiced unchecked in London and New York, respectively. In the case of New York, federal judges ruled that the city's police unfairly targeted young black and Hispanic men, and that their actions constituted an obvious violation of their constitutional rights (Usborne 2013). To be sure, stop-and-search procedures have been implemented throughout China, even in Han-dominated cities. During summer research in Beijing in 2016 and 2017, young male subway passengers who appeared to be migrant workers were often stopped by local police, pulled aside, and interrogated. However, these measures are enforced more harshly in Xinjiang (Schmitz 2017). After attending a wedding in Kashgar in 2013, a Uyghur friend and I hired a cab home. As we were driven toward the Héytgah Mosque, we noticed a police checkpoint in the distance. The driver slowly pulled up to the armed personnel who ordered my friend and the driver, also Uyghur, to exit the vehicle and have their identification cards scanned. At gas stations, passengers were required to wait at a designated area while drivers refueled. By 2017, Uyghurs in Ürümchi were subject to random inspections of their mobile phones and personal computers. Customers at Nanmen's Xinhua bookstore had to swipe their identification cards before entering the store.

My informants view Xinjiang's enhanced security measures as forms of discrimination directed primarily at Uyghurs. Ilham, a graduate of Hangzhou's Xinjiang Class who emigrated to the Netherlands, explained:

> At first, I thought I would return to Xinjiang to work because [Xinjiang] is my home (Uy. *ana yurtum*). But as a Uyghur, I could have only found work as a government official or as a teacher. There aren't many other options. Also, I pray every day. If I had returned to Xinjiang to work, I wouldn't have been able to pray because it is forbidden (Uy. *cheklinidu*) for professional workers to pray. All I want is to be able to pray, do my job well, and make an honest living. I don't have any other intentions, but if I work in Xinjiang, I would be unable to do these things. So, I decided not to return to Xinjiang. (field notes, July 1, 2012)

In fact, several of my informants cited their desire to freely practice Islam as their main reason for not returning to Xinjiang. Adil, the graduate of the 2008 Guangzhou Xinjiang Class from Kashgar whom I introduced in the previous chapter, was accepted into a master's degree program at a university in Beijing. When asked why he would not immediately return to Xinjiang after graduating from university, Adil was adamant:

> Beijing is free (Uy. *erkin*) compared to Xinjiang. There are ridiculous restrictions (Uy. *chekler*) in Xinjiang about how long men can grow their beards and about going to mosque. I didn't notice [these forms of restrictions] until I had lived in Beijing for a couple of years, and would return home [in Xinjiang]. In Beijing, I go to mosque every Friday, and my school doesn't have a problem with it. (field notes, June 3, 2012)

Adil stood apart from other informants as being especially devout. As a practicing Muslim, Adil did not want to face the strong likelihood that, if he returned to Xinjiang, he would not be allowed to attend Friday prayers at mosques. Thus, Adil welcomed the comparatively relaxed political climate in Beijing.

Fewer than two decades after Deng Xiaoping announced China's economic opening and called for a general relaxation of the party's minzu policies, CCP officials are once again attempting to curtail Islam's influence on the Uyghurs. The shift in policy came after a string of violent events: the 1990 uprising in Baren, bombings that occurred in 1992–1993, and the 1997 Ghulja incident (Millward 2004, viii). The CCP responded to the unrest by launching several "Strike Hard" (Ch. *yanda*; Uy. *qattiq zerbe bérish heriketliri*) campaigns (Smith 2000), which aimed to eradicate "terrorism" (Ch. *kongbuzhuyi*; Uy. *terrorchiliq*), "separatism" (Ch. *fenliezhuyi*; Uy. *bölgünchilik*), and [religious] "extremism" (Ch. *jiduanzhuyi*; Uy. *ékstrimizm*)—the so-called "three evil forces" (Ch. *san gu shili*; Uy. *üch xil küch*) (Bovingdon 2010, 54). Anti-"extremism" campaigns intensified after the September 11, 2001, attacks on New York and Washington, DC. Shortly thereafter, the United States identified the East Turkestan Islamic Movement (ETIM) as a Uyghur "terrorist" organization, a decision that opened a window of opportunity for the CCP to impose sanctions on religious practice in the name of fighting global terrorism (Millward 2004; Shichor 2005).

These measures have become even more severe since the July 2009 Ürümchi riots. During Ramadan, officials forbid party members, state employees, and students from fasting (AFP 2012; BBC 2014). Reports claim that restaurants in the region were forced to remain open during daylight hours (Al Jazeera 2015)—though from 2012 to 2015 I observed many Uyghur-owned eateries in Ürümchi that were closed for lunch and did not reopen until sunset. In addition, officials continue to step up mosque surveillance. Some local governments require the faithful to scan their identification cards before entering mosques (Al Jazeera 2015; Radio Free Asia 2017b). By 2014 authorities throughout Xinjiang began enforcing a ban on the "five types of people" (Ch. *wu lei renyuan*)—those adorned with full veils, jilbab, hijab, crescent-moon-and-star clothing, and abnormally long beards—from public spaces (Leibold and Grose 2016).

Some devout Xinjiang Class graduates will not return to the region if they believe it will compromise their piety. Murat, the young man who emigrated to Turkey, plans to remain there until restrictions on religious practice are loosened. Through continued email correspondence, he explained his decision:

> My parents, sister, and closest friends all live in Xinjiang, so of course I really want to return, but as you know things aren't normal there. There are restrictions on the clothes [Uyghurs] wear and on how we grow our beards. And, in our schools, we can't even use our mother language. God willing, I will return one day. For now, though, I will study hard. If God wills it, I will help our people (Uy. *obdan oquwélip, helqimizge menpe'et yetküzgidek bolghanda, Allah nisip qilsun*).

Strict policies on religious expression in Xinjiang infringe upon the daily lives of Uyghurs, sometimes to the point that they feel as if they are being treated as second-class citizens (Bovingdon 2010; Fuller and Lipman 2004; Smith Finley 2007a). Their religious convictions unwelcomed by CCP officials, some Xinjiang Class graduates—like Ilham and Murat—seek belonging in a transnational Muslim community by traveling abroad and remaining there.

"There are no suitable jobs for me in Xinjiang"

Uyghurs also face employment discrimination, especially during the hiring process. As mentioned above, the population of Xinjiang's registered Han residents has ballooned over the last sixty years from roughly 200,000 in 1949 (Toops 2004, 245–46) to nearly 8.4 million in 2010 (SBX 2010, cited in Howell and Fan 2011, 123). In addition to activating ethnic boundaries between Han and Uyghurs on the basis of cultural, religious, and linguistic differences (Bellér-Hann 2002; Cesàro 2000; Mackerras 2001; Smith 2002; Smith Finley 2013), consecutive waves of Han migrants strain Xinjiang's fragile labor market by securing a disproportionately high number of jobs in the manufacturing, professional, clerical, and government sectors of the region's labor force (COX 2002, 572–79, cited in Ma 2008, 362; Mackerras 2001).

Cognizant of hiring practices in the region that unequivocally favor Han people, my informants doubted the likelihood of finding jobs suited to their educational levels and abilities. Raziye, the young woman who studied the Qur'an with her mother-in-law, anxiously contemplated returning to Xinjiang. A near-native English speaker with a diploma from a prestigious Beijing university, Raziye believed her education would be "wasted" in Xinjiang. She insisted that she would have to settle for work as a high school teacher in Kashgar or Khotan if she did not find work in the capital. Raziye complained that she had attended university in order to become a successful business person, not to become a teacher, and therefore Beijing would be an ideal city in which to gain work experience (field notes, December 7, 2007).

Indeed, Xinjiang Class graduates are highly sought-after candidates for teaching in rural Xinjiang. Prestigious universities in neidi offer all-inclusive teacher-training programs. In exchange for tuition waivers, subsidized room and board, and a modest living stipend, these teachers-in-training agree to serve in Xinjiang, particularly in understaffed and poorly equipped schools in Kashgar and Khotan's surrounding rural areas, for five to ten years.[9] The CCP accomplishes two tasks if Xinjiang Class graduates agree to serve as teachers: it provides stable jobs to young Uyghurs and can begin to relieve the shortage of well-trained bilingual teachers in Xinjiang (Grose 2016b). However, Raziye's response is indicative of party officials'

---

9. In fact, according to the 2007 recruitment plan for universities in neidi that enroll graduates of the Xinjiang Class, Beijing Normal University had seventeen places open to Xinjiang Class graduates, one of the highest numbers among such universities in Beijing (Xinjiang Department of Education 2007).

failure to convince Xinjiang Class graduates to serve as teachers. In September 2017, the XUAR government announced it would send 5,000 bilingual teachers annually to Xinjiang, particularly schools in Kashgar, Khotan, Aksu, and Qizilsu (*China Daily* 2017). This directive suggests Xinjiang Class graduates have not alleviated the region's bilingual teacher shortage.

Unwilling to return to Xinjiang, Raziye found stable work at an international business firm in Beijing after searching for several months. Shortly thereafter, she started a family with her husband who was earning a postgraduate degree in physics at a Beijing university. Raziye and I reconnected in Beijing in June 2011. Since our previous meeting in 2008, she and her husband had welcomed the birth of their first child, and the three of them had just returned to Beijing after a several months' stay at her in-laws' home in South Asia. Raziye and her husband were optimistic about job prospects in the United States or the Middle East once Raziye's husband had completed his doctoral dissertation. I questioned the necessity of working abroad, but Raziye, who had changed jobs and was then working as an English teacher at a Chinese preschool, retorted that neither she nor her husband would be able to earn enough money to properly care for their child (field notes, June 20, 2011). Even though Raziye did not work in a business firm, as she had hoped so desperately in 2007, she was satisfied in the knowledge that she made more money working part-time in Beijing than she would working full-time in Xinjiang.

I frequently visited the couple in 2012. They filled me in with the details of their last two years. Raziye's husband finished his degree, and the two moved to a small, mostly Hui community located in the southeastern outskirts of Beijing. She had more exciting news to share: she had recently been invited by one of Xinjiang's central television stations to be featured in a taping of its popular current events series *Today's Interview* (Ch. *Jinri fangtan*), which was profiling "success stories" of the Xinjiang Class. For the taping of that particular episode, Raziye was to appear alongside Dilmurat Ibrahim, a representative of the National People's Congress, and the two were to promote the benefits of the Xinjiang Class program. I was curious about the producer's decision to select Raziye to be on the program. When I asked her, she burst into laughter. Apparently, Raziye had been recommended for the show by the principal of her former school because she was one of the few members of her cohort "who is married, is not unemployed in Xinjiang, and is not living abroad" (field notes, June 29, 2012).

However, from the perspective of the CCP, Raziye's biography was missing one important point to truly be regarded as a success story—she had not returned to Xinjiang. Certainly, the CCP has been explicit about its expectations for Xinjiang Class graduates: after completing university, they should return to Xinjiang and find employment in basic-level units (Ch. *jiceng danwei*) of the region's workforce, ideally in rural primary and junior high schools. In an apparent attempt to align Raziye's biography and pending plans to relocate abroad more closely with the political goals of the Xinjiang Class, the show's producer and Dilmurat Ibrahim instructed Raziye to fabricate a story. When I later viewed the interview together with Raziye, she pointed out this moment in the taping. As the reporter begins to probe Raziye about her intentions to move to another country, the viewer can distinctly hear where the taping had been cut. The interview resumes after Raziye had been properly coached:

> Raziye: I should be able to do something [*break in tape*]. Eventually I really want to return to Xinjiang and open my own school. I am in Beijing because I still want to train myself further. I feel I still need to get better.
>
> Reporter: So the time still isn't right [for you to return to Xinjiang].
>
> Raziye: Right, I am still unable to make a significant contribution [to Xinjiang]. If, well, I feel as if there is a chance to meet with foreign scholars who are interested in education, and if we can work together [it will be good for me]. [And with this experience], I really hope to return to Xinjiang in the future and run my own school.[10]

Raziye's biography has been overlaid with a thick varnish. The final edit of the interview omits many details about Raziye's personal life—there is no mention of Raziye's non-Chinese Muslim husband, their child, or the several months she stayed with her husband's family—that may detract from the CCP's intended goals of the Xinjiang Class. Instead, the interview concludes with Raziye's insincere pledge to return to Xinjiang and open her own language school.

Some of my informants pointedly blamed Han migrants for the scarcity of jobs. Nazaket, a young woman from Aksu who graduated from Hangzhou's Xinjiang Class in 2008, voiced her concerns about job prospects in her hometown. When she and I first met, Nazaket was entering into her third year of university and preparing for graduate school examinations. She aspired to study in Germany and hoped her test scores would be high enough to earn a scholarship. I asked Nazaket why she wanted to study in Germany, and whether she would return to Xinjiang. Pondering over my questions for a moment, Nazaket replied:

> I study German, and I want to improve it. Studying at a German university will help me achieve this goal. I don't know if I will come back, though. If I can't find a job in Germany, then maybe I will come back to Xinjiang. But, you know, finding a good job in Xinjiang is difficult. I know firsthand. My mother had a good job working in a government-owned cotton factory. Eventually, the factory was privatized, and for no reason all of the Uyghur workers were laid off and Han Chinese migrants were hired to replace the Uyghurs. It is like this all over Xinjiang. (field notes, November 4, 2010)

---

10. 热孜亚：我应该能做一点儿什么 [*break in tape*] 以后我很想回到新疆自己开自己的学校。我在北京是因为我想更多的去深造自己。我觉得我还不够好。

   记者：还不是时候……

   热孜亚：对，我不够好去做一个更大的贡献。如果我觉得我要能够有机会跟国外的教育方面的这些学者有一个交流有跟他们有一个合作的话，我真的希望就是以后在新疆做一个自己的一个学校。

Murad, a male Xinjiang Class student from Kashgar who studied in Qingdao, became so frustrated with hiring practices in Xinjiang, which he claimed overwhelmingly favor Han applicants, that he emigrated to Italy. Writing from his new home, Murad protested:

> Currently in Xinjiang, people are openly discriminated against (Uy. *ochuqtin ochuq kemsitidu*) [by the CCP]. Although government agencies need new employees, they clearly write that they are only hiring Han (Uy. *éniq Xenzula élimiz dep yazidu*). There's simply no solution [for me in Xinjiang], so I found my own path elsewhere, and I didn't return to my motherland (Uy. *wetenge qaytmidim*). (field notes, June 30, 2011)

Mahmud, a 2005 graduate of a Xinjiang Class in Beijing and a native of Kashgar who left China to conduct doctoral research in the United States, voiced his discontent over hiring practices in Xinjiang even more forcefully:

> Every time I returned to East Turkestan, or "Xinjiang" as you [the author] call it, I hoped to have a great time with my family and friends. But every time I returned home, and saw how the Han were treating my people, how my friends who graduated from college could not find a job, and how Han who had only graduated from high school were bossing around Uyghurs, I felt as if someone was stabbing me in the heart. (field notes, December 5, 2010)

Although it is difficult to verify these claims, they nonetheless add to the growing volume of anecdotes contending that the Han people occupy Xinjiang's best-paying and most prestigious jobs, especially in the oil industry, in high-level government positions, and in the private sector (Benson 2004, 214; Dautcher 2009, 223–27; Kaltman 2007, 29–39 and 100–107; Liu Y. 2010).[11] Considering this imbalance, the noted demographer Stanley Toops agrees, "To get a good job is not easy in Xinjiang [for young Uyghurs], to do so one needs connections or *guanxi*" (2004, 24). Even for those Uyghurs who have been educated at senior high schools and universities located in neidi, employment in Xinjiang is by no means guaranteed.

Some graduates genuinely desire to find meaningful work in Xinjiang. I met Rabigül when she was a second-year university student in Beijing. Upon the completion of her undergraduate studies, she pursued a degree in England. She returned to China in 2016 when she was unable to find permanent employment in Europe. After marrying her longtime boyfriend, she found a position in a large international marketing company with branches in Beijing and Shanghai. At the time of our reunion, Rabigül had only been back for three months; however, she already felt misplaced in China's large cities. She explained:

---

11. Within Xinjiang's energy sector, which accounts for 57 percent of the autonomous region's GDP, only 1 percent of its employees are Uyghur. The average income for a worker in the oil industry is RMB 60,000 (approximately USD 9,000), which is twenty times the income a Uyghur farmer can make (Liu 2010, 29).

It is not ideal to work in Beijing. I will always feel as if I'm a guest in this city if I don't buy a home, but we cannot afford one. Really, I'd like to return to Xinjiang. If only one large international company opened there, I would return. But all of the brightest Uyghurs returning to the region are becoming civil servants or bank clerks. How can we develop Xinjiang if the brightest minds are working in positions where they cannot be creative? (field notes, July 14, 2016)

For individuals like Rabigül, the inability to succeed professionally and economically in China is certainly not a side effect of an identity crisis—that is, not feeling fully Uyghur or Chinese—that leaves them feeling suspended between two socio-ethnic groups. Rather, they struggle because they are overqualified for types of jobs available to them in Xinjiang; yet, as is the case for recent graduates throughout East Asia (Allison 2013; Song 2014; Yuen 2013), they are grossly underpaid in cities like Beijing and Shanghai to live comfortable lives.

"Maybe one day I will go back"

In contrast to the more jarring testimonies presented above, some Xinjiang Class graduates were ambivalent about returning. Many wished to first pursue employment or advanced degrees in neidi. Hesen, a male student from Kashgar who completed his senior high schooling in the Nanjing Xinjiang Class in 2007, provides a response largely representative of those individuals who ultimately planned on returning to Xinjiang. Hesen studied English at a university in Beijing and aspired to start a media company there. After developing his company in Beijing, a strategy he thought would be more lucrative than if he started a similar company in Xinjiang, he would return to Kashgar and settle. With a hint of regret in his voice, Hesen described the importance of raising his future children near his family and in a community bound by Uyghur cultural norms, an experience he did not enjoy as a student of the Xinjiang Class (field notes, September 2, 2010).

Xinjiang Class graduates consider their families when planning for the future. Amangül, a female university student in Beijing who graduated from Guangzhou's Xinjiang Class in 2008, insisted she would return even if she was not obliged by her contract to serve ten years as a teacher in rural Xinjiang. On the contrary, Amangül welcomed her reunion with family and friends. Moreover, her birthplace, Kashgar, was a source of pride for the young woman. She admitted that "although Xinjiang may not be developed (Uy. *tereqiy bolmisa*), I love my home (Uy. *yurtum*) anyway" (field notes, November 20, 2010). Distance and time strain family bonds. Many Xinjiang Class graduates expressed regret for missing weddings, births, and funerals while they lived in neidi. Therefore, some graduates eagerly await reunions with family and close friends.

Escaping Inseparability?

Assertions of ethno-nationalism are not limited to the maintenance of common ethnic markers (e.g., language, religion, and customs). Rather, expressions of ethno-national identity are situational, involve many nuances, and can take the form of resistance to political culture. To be sure, resistance does not always manifest itself in public protests and violent uprisings. Gardner Bovingdon (2002), building on the works of Michel Foucault (1990) and James Scott (1990), has persuasively demonstrated the necessity for Uyghurs to engage in "covert," rather than overt, forms of resistance. In other words, Uyghur resistance to CCP hegemony regularly takes subtle forms, such as stories, songs, and jokes—media that cannot be easily controlled by the state (Dautcher 2000; Smith Finley 2007c, 2013)—because they face strong repercussions from the state for engaging in public demonstrations.

When Uyghur Xinjiang Class graduates choose against returning, they tacitly renegotiate their belonging to the Zhonghua minzu. If Xinjiang Class students had fully embraced their corporate Chinese identity—as has been claimed in other studies on minority minzu boarding schools (Zhu 2007)—they would likely consent to return in service of the Zhonghua minzu. Closely connected to this point, the decision not to return subverts the party-state's power. It "exposes the gap between the state's vision of the Uyghurs as PRC citizens and the Uyghurs' understanding of themselves as first and foremost Uyghurs" (Bovingdon 2002, 44).

We can stretch Bovingdon's argument one step further. Bovingdon remarks that Uyghurs "cannot directly resist the form of social and political life into which they are born, so they resist its representation" (2002, 46). Yet Xinjiang Class students create new forms of political life for themselves: first by leaving Xinjiang as senior high school students and then staying away as adults. My assertion rings especially true for those individuals who emigrated. As the Xinjiang Class employment policy I have outlined above indicates, there are only two officially approved options for Xinjiang Class graduates: return to Xinjiang or remain in neidi. The document does not entertain a potential third option of going abroad, even if the relocation is only temporary.

Nevertheless, Xinjiang Class graduates often seek to continue their lives in other countries. Despite widespread reports citing the difficulties surrounding, or even the impossibility of, Uyghurs obtaining a Chinese passport (see, for example, Radio Free Asia 2007, 2012),[12] Xinjiang Class graduates can largely circumvent these obstacles. Like all college students in China, Xinjiang Class graduates are provided with a "student group residency permit" (Ch. *daxuesheng jiti hukou*) upon enrolling in a university. With this official document, Xinjiang Class graduates can apply for

---

12. My own informants, especially those Uyghurs living in Xinjiang, regularly shared stories with me about unsuccessful attempts to obtain Chinese passports. They claimed that the fees required for Uyghurs to successfully apply for a passport, including "official" fees and bribes, exceed RMB 50,000 (approximately USD 7,500). Others spoke of an endless string of requests from passport officers, who make spontaneous demands for documents from an individual's university, employer, bank, etc.

a passport at the nearest Entry-Exit Administration Bureau (Ch. *churu jing guanli-chu*), the office responsible for handling and processing passport applications. For academically successful and often trilingual graduates of the Xinjiang Class, there is little keeping them from starting a new life abroad once their Chinese passport is in hand.

Evidence from my research suggests that those Xinjiang Class graduates who apply for their passports in neidi have enjoyed much higher success rates than those who applied for them in Xinjiang. Hasiyet successfully obtained her passport in neidi. A graduate of Wuxi's Xinjiang Class who finished her bachelor's degree at a university in Harbin, Hasiyet exploited the *jiti hukou* loophole to obtain her passport, which she needed for a summer internship in the United States. Her university classmate and fellow Xinjiang Class graduate, on the other hand, had not opted to change her temporary residency status. When this young woman received an offer for the same summer internship Hasiyet would attend, she had to return to Xinjiang to apply for a passport. After several delays, her application was rejected, and she was unable to participate in the international program (field notes, June 26, 2012). Nadire, a 2004 graduate of the Xinjiang Class in Hangzhou who finished her university degree in 2008, experienced similar problems. She first returned to Xinjiang to look for employment. Unable to find work, she began studying for her postgraduate entrance exams at her home in Turpan. Her diligence paid off, and she was accepted into an Australian university. At the time of my visit, Nadire had already waited six months for her passport. She spent her days helping her mother with housework, tutoring her younger siblings, and anxiously checking the daily mail. Assuming she would eventually obtain her passport, I asked her if she planned on returning to Xinjiang once she had earned her degree. She looked at me sternly and intoned, "No, I will never come back" (field notes, September 22, 2010).

Despite the difficulties and costs required to leave China, some Xinjiang Class graduates firmly cling to the belief that pursuing an education abroad (while optimistically waiting for reform of the CCP's policies, or its decline) is the best way to help other Uyghurs in the long term. Later in our conversation, Mahmud, the Xinjiang Class graduate currently studying in the United States, proclaimed:

> First, I purely wanted to go abroad to get an education, and [I planned] to go back to my country and change it into a better place like the United States or European countries. As long as China becomes more and more powerful, I honestly cannot see any bright future [for me in Xinjiang], or a chance to build [a better Xinjiang]. After completing my PhD in engineering, I want to make money, and I want to inspire my people [Uyghurs]. I'll do what I can do to save my people. (field notes, December 5, 2010)

Mahmud's decision is significant on two levels. First, it implies that Xinjiang Class graduates are not responding to the CCP's interpellative attempts to mold Uyghurs into "Weiwu'er zu" subjects who will eventually develop Xinjiang for the benefit of the rest of China. Second, the decision suggests that some Xinjiang Class Uyghurs are responding to ideologies that compete with those promoted by the state (cf. Pêcheux 1982, 99–102): in this case, Murad is inspired to encourage other Uyghurs to embrace a specifically non-Chinese collectivity.

Indeed, Xinjiang Class graduates living outside China often become indefatigable advocates of Uyghur human rights. Through social media networks they raise political awareness of the reported injustices occurring in Xinjiang. For example, Mahmud posted a JustPaste.it link to Abdugheni Sabit's "A Brief History of East Turkestan and Chinese Occupation," which describes CCP rule as "the darkest chapters in the history of Uyghurs" and claims that "the Chinese Communist government has been carrying out a vicious campaign against Uyghurs . . . in order to permanently annex the lands of East Turkestan." Hajigül, a female graduate of the Xinjiang Class in Hangzhou who completed a graduate degree in the Netherlands, mocked the XUAR's beard ban by posting a *Shanghaiist* article with a caption warning her European friends that they may end up in prison if they visit her hometown with facial hair.

These examples provide insight into why many Xinjiang Class graduates are not returning in service of their hometowns and minzu as have other minority minzu (Harrell 2001; Litzinger 2000; Postiglione and Jiao 2009, 909–12; Yang 2017, 198–200). One may reasonably predict that if the Xinjiang Class strengthens Uyghurs' resistance to Han hegemony and their suspicion of state discourse, graduates would want to return to the region and serve their communities. However, these posts, and many others of similar tone, suggest that the situation for Uyghurs in Xinjiang is more dire now than ever. As the trial and imprisonment of the Uyghur scholar Ilham Tohti has shown (Millward 2014), the CCP is intent on intimidating and silencing even moderate oppositional voices. Engaging in political activism and demanding change in Xinjiang is perilous for Uyghurs. Although these activities are becoming dangerous abroad as well (Rajagopalan 2018), many of my informants have been willing to take this risk.

Concluding Remarks

Hand-picked by XUAR officials and trained with the resources provided by the central government, Xinjiang Class graduates are predicted to become the "new force" driving CCP-led development projects in the XUAR. Equally as important, they have been entrusted with providing a stabilizing, pro-CCP element in the region. However, the CCP's investment appears to have been miscalculated, as many Uyghurs decide against returning to Xinjiang.

Instead, many Uyghur Xinjiang Class graduates, citing discrimination in their daily lives and in their careers, decide to pursue opportunities in neidi and abroad. These individuals reject the status quo in Xinjiang where Uyghurs are routinely treated as "second-class citizens." Some readers may be left unconvinced that decisions against returning are expressions of meaningful resistance and assertions of a non-Chinese, specifically Uyghur ethno-national identity. At the very least, however, by relocating abroad or remaining in neidi, a significant number of Xinjiang Class graduates are breaching two important terms in their implicit contract with the CCP: "developing" the region and stabilizing its deteriorating minzu relations.

4
The Disappointing Road Home[1]

> I don't think I belong [in Xinjiang]; not because I hate my hometown, but because I disagree with so many policies here.
>
> —Adalet, graduate of Shenzhen's Xinjiang Class
> (field notes, June 8, 2012)

The previous chapter demonstrated that Xinjiang Class graduates favored the loosened political climates of neidi or foreign countries over their own homeland. Certainly, few intended to repay their "debt" by serving the party in Xinjiang. Yet some Xinjiang Class graduates returned to the XUAR. This chapter will describe the realities—crippling institutional restraints on migration, unrelenting pressure from parents, the inconvenience of practicing Islam in neidi, and economic insecurity—that induced Xinjiang Class graduates to return as the CCP intended. Their physical homecomings only marked the beginning of an often-frustrating process of reintegration, and the second part of this chapter describes the strategies Uyghur returnees adopted as they reacclimated to daily life in Xinjiang. After an initial period of readjustment, most of my interlocutors reestablished a genuine sense of belonging by embracing embodied Islamic practices, starting families, and focusing on careers. Some Uyghur women—confronted by strict gender roles—found their homecomings discouraging.

Reasons to Return

Recent research on international, domestic, and return migration introduces a rethinking of planned human movement. In particular, this literature posits that migration often lacks design. Viewed in this light, homecomings are identified as but one stage of an uneven process instead of the end to a neatly plotted cyclical pattern (de Bree, Davids, and de Haas 2010; Pessar 1997). To be sure, Xinjiang Class graduates do not fit perfectly within the broader conceptual framework of migration studies, or of migrant labor in China for that matter. Nevertheless, theories

---

1. Parts of this chapter were published in a chapter (Grose 2016a) contained in Anna Hayes and Michael Clarke's (2016) volume *Inside Xinjiang: Space, Place and Power in China's Muslim Far Northwest*.

on migration can be aptly applied to this study: others have convincingly shown that Uyghur experiences in neidi—where they face discrimination because of their outsider (Ch. *waidi*) as well as their minority minzu statuses (Hoy and Ren 2003; Iredale, Bilik, and Wang 2001, 221–27; Iredale and Guo 2003, 29; Zhang and McGhee 2014, 148–50)—are reminiscent of international migrants (Dong 2010; Hansen 2005) and "exiles" (Baranovitch 2007). Following the line of inquiry established in return migration studies (Cassarino 2004; Dumont and Spielvogel 2008; Şenyürekli and Menjívar 2012; Teo 2011; Wang and Fan 2006), this chapter uncovers the complex motivations (e.g., socioeconomic, familial, and religious) behind my informants' homecomings.

Dragging Their Feet back to Xinjiang

As university students, my informants rarely envisaged returning to Xinjiang immediately after graduation. They aspired to professional success in large cities. In some respects, Xinjiang Class graduates have heeded Xi Jinping's directive on integrated cities—that is, minority minzu are encouraged to work alongside Han people in neidi (Xinhua 2014; cf. Leibold 2014b). Yet, neither academic degrees, diligence, nor even President Xi's call for ethnic cooperation can always surmount the obstacles minority minzu face in neidi; therefore, some Xinjiang Class graduates have few options except returning.

Similar to the experiences of Han migrant workers in southeastern China (Gaetano 2015), Xinjiang Class graduates are subject to rigid policies that restrict their settlement in neidi. For example, China's household registration, or *hukou*, system continues to limit rural-to-urban migration. Although relaxed at the turn of the twenty-first century (Wang 2004), the hukou system continues to monitor the so-called targeted population (Ch. *zhongdian renkou*)—a social classification determined by eight physical, personal, and sociopolitical categories—and "high-risk" individuals (Wang 2004, 124–29). To be sure, the hukou system does not single out minority minzu: regardless of minzu background, an individual who does not possess a local hukou may be ineligible for important entitlements—including subsidized housing, free public education, and access to certain health care benefits—and employment opportunities (Martines 2016). Individuals cut off from these services find it nearly impossible to remain in a city long term.

Xinjiang Class graduates can temporarily circumvent institutional barriers such as the hukou system. As explained in the previous chapter, students may register for a group hukou—a certificate that functions as a residency permit—upon matriculating in a four-year university. This document allows Xinjiang Class graduates to live in the city where their university is located, and it remains valid as long as they are enrolled as students. However, when institutional affiliation is forfeited upon completing a degree, Xinjiang Class graduates who wish to delay their homecomings are left with only three realistic options: enrolling in postgraduate courses, finding permanent employment, or moving abroad.

Many Xinjiang Class graduates struggle to prolong their stays in neidi, often to no avail. Arzugül's experience provides a case in point. She graduated from Shenzhen's Xinjiang Class in 2006, and attended one of Beijing's medical colleges. By pursuing a six-year Chinese medicine degree, Arzugül had already extended her time in neidi longer than most of her Uyghur classmates who pursued four-year degrees. Nevertheless, she protested over returning:

> In Xinjiang, living conditions are poor, [economic] development is poor, and policies are bad [*Shara'it yaxshi emes; tereqqiyat yaxshi emes; siyasetler yaxshi emes*]. (field notes, June 5, 2011)

Arzugül hoped to delay her return indefinitely by studying in Sweden, where she planned to open her own clinic. Regardless of her diligence, Arzugül's career goals were never met. Her IELTS scores—an English examination required for postgraduate study in Europe—did not meet the specifications required by Swedish universities. Although disappointed, Arzugül took some solace in the possibility of continuing her studies in Beijing. Clinging to this hope, she devoted her summer to preparing for China's national graduate examination. Despite two attempts, she did not pass the exam and was resigned to returning to the XUAR. She sighed, "There's nothing I can do. It was God's will for me to return to Xinjiang [Uy. *Amal yoq. Xuda buyrup, Shinjanggha qaytimen*] (field notes, June 26, 2012).

Arzugül's response demonstrates the resilience of faith among Xinjiang Class graduates. Similar to other young Uyghurs' reactions to disappointment (Smith Finley 2013, 352 and 371), Arzugül coped with her failures within an Islamic worldview. More specifically, considered through the lens of *qadar*—predestination or God's "creative power" (Murata and Chittick 1994, 104–5)—Arzugül did not narrowly interpret her inability to pass her exam as failure; it was part of a divine plan.

For others, discriminatory hiring practices impede access to full-time employment, which provides documentation required for remaining in neidi. Reportedly, some employers discard the résumés of applicants whose names are discernibly "ethnic" (*Economist* 2015). But sometimes, employers do not discover the minority minzu status of applicants until they meet in person. Dawut spent weeks submitting online applications for positions in Beijing before he secured a phone interview. During the call, Dawut impressed the recruiter, who proceeded to invite him for an on-site interview. Capable of speaking Putonghua with pristine intonations, Dawut would not have necessarily divulged his minority minzu status over the phone.[2] However, when Dawut arrived at the company, the Han hiring manager realized that his candidate was Uyghur. According to Dawut, the Han man immediately became uninterested in the company's minority minzu applicant and abruptly

---

2. Nevertheless, one could assume that Dawut's name rendered into Chinese would have provided clues to his minzu background.

ended the interview (field notes, June 3, 2012). In an attempt to comfort Dawut, I reassured him of opportunities waiting in Xinjiang, but he insisted that this option would come at the expense of his "freedom" (Uy. *erkinlik*). I pressed him to be more specific. He interjected, "In Beijing no one asks if I have fasted, visited a mosque, or prayed" (field notes, June 6, 2011).

After a string of rejected applications and unsuccessful interviews, Dawut's only option was to return to the XUAR. In 2012 I attempted to reconnect with him, but he had changed his mobile number. One of Dawut's closest Uyghur companions, who had remained in Beijing as a graduate student, confirmed that the young man became a police officer in his hometown, Aksu. Dawut's friend then pulled out his smartphone and scrolled through photographs recently sent by Dawut: his wavy hair had been shaved, his urban-chic clothing style had been replaced by the black uniform worn by Xinjiang's paramilitary personnel (Ch. *wujing*), and his light-hearted smile had been transformed into a sullen glare. There is some irony in the fact that Dawut became a police officer: in all likelihood, he enforces the religious policies he so adamantly condemned.

Parental pressure

Persistent pressure from parents can also impede Xinjiang Class graduates' career plans, sometimes more so than government policies. Because parents risk losing an essential source of economic security if their children do not return, many parents have responded to this precariousness by asserting their authority from afar.

As was the case at the turn of the twentieth century (Béller-Hann 2008, 237–39), marriage continues to be a "normative expectation" in Uyghur communities. Young educated Uyghur women may compromise their allure if they become too career oriented. Although senior high school and university degrees from neidi institutions can afford Uyghur women professional opportunities, these certifications do not shield them from the social pressures of marriage and family responsibilities, which are still valued in Xinjiang. Indeed, Uyghur women who delay marriage often endure a form of stigmatization experienced by "leftover women" (Ch. *sheng nü*)—namely, unmarried, over twenty-seven years old, and accused of being too picky and assertive—in Han society (Fincher 2014; Luo and Sun 2015).

These expectations weigh heavily on young Uyghur women. Adalet graduated from Shenzhen's Xinjiang Class in 2004 and then studied accounting at a university in Beijing. During the final semester of her university course in spring 2008, Adalet was offered full-time employment at a multinational accounting firm in Beijing, and she proudly accepted the lucrative offer. Her parents, however, did not celebrate their daughter's success and expressed their disapproval during daily phone conversations. They pleaded with her to reject the offer and come home. Adalet initially ignored her parents' demands and started working in August 2008. I lost communication with her for nearly four years and assumed her demanding work schedule afforded little time for emails. Then, in spring 2012, six weeks before I returned to China, Adalet sent a detailed update on her life. After working for two years in Beijing, she left her career behind, moved in with her parents in their Ürümchi home, and started working for a small NGO. Adalet's homecoming was not a joyful occasion, however, and in her email the young professional blamed her mother for interfering in her personal life:

> Today, Uyghurs normally graduate from university at the age of twenty-three or twenty-four. Once Uyghur women begin working, their parents start arranging blind dates. I am kind of leftovers, because I am twenty-eight and haven't married. We are like some kind of freaks in other people's eyes. I received an offer from a university in Australia, but my whole family is opposed to me going. Do you know why? Because I am not young, I should get married as soon as possible and have babies. Honestly, I want that too; I want to start my own family, I want to be a mom, but it's not the timing yet. My mother cries all the time [when] we talk about these issues; I don't know what to say to her. (field notes, March 8, 2012)

By the time I reconnected with Adalet in person in Ürümchi in June 2012, her circumstances had changed again: Adalet's parents would permit their daughter to study in Australia if she agreed to marry before she left. Desperate, she became engaged to a former boyfriend from the Xinjiang Class whom her parents disliked.

Intense parental pressure dissuaded Méhrigül, a 2009 graduate of Shenzhen's Xinjiang Class, from settling in neidi. As a university student, Méhrigül charted a career path that would lead her to Turkey. During the summer preceding her final year of university, she even participated in a volunteer project in Istanbul where she began establishing a network of friends. However, her plans changed suddenly in May 2013—two months before she was to graduate—when her application to a Turkish university was rejected. Surprisingly to me, she shrugged off the disappointment; instead, she enthusiastically spoke about a job offer from a development company headquartered in Beijing. I was stunned again a few weeks later when she told me she declined the offer. Méhrigül's parents insisted that working in Beijing would offer few long-term benefits. Over several phone conversations, her father argued that living in the capital was an economically unfeasible plan and calculated the number of years—too many—it would take his daughter to afford a flat there. Meanwhile, Méhrigül's mother warned about the difficulties of finding a Uyghur husband in the Han-dominated capital (field notes, June 1, 2013).

Méhrigül begrudgingly followed her parents' advice and returned to Ürümchi to work as a bank clerk. Her parents rewarded their daughter's acquiescence: Méhrigül's father arranged a weeklong holiday in Singapore, and when she returned from the trip, a newly remodeled home waited for her near Döngköwrük (Ch. *Erdaoqiao*), a district of the city especially popular among Uyghurs. I asked Méhrigül if she was content with her decision. She replied, "I am going to try it out. If I don't like my job, I will reapply for the Turkish government scholarship" (field notes, July 1, 2013).

The Disappointing Road Home   95

The humdrum routine of bank telling left Méhrigül craving a more challenging career. Within a year, she quit her job, forwent the stable paycheck it provided, and enrolled in a graduate program in journalism at Xinjiang University. This degree would help Méhrigül follow in the footsteps of her father and become an investigative journalist.

I later discovered that Méhrigül's career leap may not have been possible without first gaining her husband's approval. She married in early 2015 to a successful marketing manager. The young Uyghur man purchased a newly built apartment located in a middle-class residential compound (Ch. *xiaoqu*) on the outskirts of Ürümchi before the couple married. Having moved in with her husband, Méhrigül's daily commute exceeded an hour, a trip that became too tiring to maintain. Having resigned from the bank, she devoted a year to studying for the graduate school entrance examination. Her husband supported this decision. At their home, he added, "Working fifty hours is stressful (Uy. *bésimi chong bolidu*) for women" (field notes, June 22, 2015).

My married female informants deferred to their husbands and in-laws. Sumbul, a 2004 graduate of Hangzhou's Xinjiang Class, embarked on postgraduate study in Shanghai while her longtime boyfriend—a Xinjiang Class classmate—returned to Ürümchi to work for Arman, a Uyghur-owned supermarket chain. The couple maintained a long-distance relationship and held their *toy* wedding celebration in Ürümchi in 2012 during Sumbul's winter recess. After a brief honeymoon, Sumbul returned to Shanghai for her last semester. Shortly after she resumed coursework, an international cosmetics company—where she had interned the previous summer—unexpectedly offered Sumbul a full-time position. Clearly confident in Sumbul's work ethic, the hiring manager stuffed the contract with benefits: she would earn a comfortable RMB 10,000 (USD 1,500) monthly salary, be eligible for a promotion after one year, and undergo intensive English training. Excited over this career opportunity but nervous about her family's reactions, Sumbul carefully broached the topic of settling in Shanghai to her husband. He dismissed the idea as impractical, despite (or because of) the fact that Sumbul would earn more than him. Meanwhile, Sumbul's in-laws protested that their son's education would be wasted if the young couple relocated. Unable to persuade her husband and in-laws, Sumbul returned to Xinjiang in January 2013 and became a substitute teacher. Sumbul still had not found full-time employment when she and I reconnected in July 2013. She confessed that her skills were underutilized in Ürümchi and conceded, "I guess sometimes a wife has to make sacrifices" (field notes, July 17, 2013).

Leyla, a 2008 graduate of Hangzhou's Xinjiang Class who spent her early childhood in rural Turpan, refused to accept her parents' terms for marriage. Before being formally introduced to Leyla—then a university student in Beijing—I was cautioned by another Xinjiang Class graduate that she was a "victim" of the boarding school. When I asked for clarification, the individual replied, "You will see yourself." Although I never observed signs of "victimhood" in Leyla (admittedly, I did not know what I should have been looking for), she behaved curiously around her Uyghur peers. Unlike other Xinjiang Class graduates, Leyla, with whom I met regularly over six years, rarely participated in the activities organized by her Uyghur classmates. Regardless of whether the gathering was large—such as a party organized for the Roza and Qurban feasts—or a small dinner, Leyla often found excuses not to attend.

Normally reticent about her personal life, Leyla opened up about the difficulties she experienced socializing with both Han and Uyghurs. The conversation began with Leyla's exciting announcement of her upcoming visit home. Clearly, Leyla, who sorely missed her parents, anticipated a joyous homecoming. However, she also expressed anxiety over her trip:

> Sometimes I feel as if I don't belong in Xinjiang. It's as if I'm not quite Uyghur, and I'm not quite [Han] Chinese. I'm kind of in the middle of both of them. It's as if our [Uyghur] parents tell us to study hard, so we can have a good future and then when we graduate, they want us [young single Uyghur women] to marry and take care of our children. I think this [lifestyle] is a waste of our education. (field notes, July 25, 2013)

From her statement, we learn that Leyla simplifies her identity by bifurcating its markers. On one end, Leyla pairs her "Uyghur" identity with "traditional" responsibilities of women—more specifically, marriage and parenting. On the other end, she couples her "Chinese" identity with formal education, secular modernity, and socioeconomic success. I interpret Leyla's response to mean that Uyghur parents only superficially encourage their children to pursue higher education—that is, to compete with Han at their own game (Rudelson 1997, 127–29). From her remarks about marriage and child-rearing, we can further surmise that Leyla believes the pursuit of higher education and respect for some Uyghur social norms are mutually exclusive paths.

She attempted to reconcile these tensions (or avoid them altogether) by spending little time in Xinjiang. Instead, Leyla coped with these frustrations by working at an international firm in Beijing. At an office where foreign and Han colleagues spoke a mix of English and Putonghua, Leyla was simply an inconspicuous "Chinese" coworker—neither a marginalized minority minzu nor a Uyghur who "sold out" and posed as a Han—determined to get ahead in a global workforce. Furthermore, the distance between Beijing and Xinjiang softened her parents' demands for an immediate marriage. Over dinner in 2016, I teasingly asked Leyla in Uyghur when she was going to marry. As she always did, she responded to my question in English, "Don't ask!" she snapped with a smile. She continued, "Things are much better now. My parents visited this past spring. It was their first time in Beijing, and they really enjoyed it. I think they finally understand why I don't want to return. At least they haven't raised the issue [marriage] in a while" (field notes, July 8, 2016).

To be sure, young men are not immune to their parents' authority or the expectation to marry. Diyanet, a 2004 graduate of a Xinjiang Class in Beijing, returned to his hometown, Khotan, to appease his parents. After graduating from Beijing Normal University in 2008, Diyanet remained in the capital where he worked for two years. However, his parents pestered him daily to return to Khotan and marry. Diyanet eventually agreed, and similar to Méhrigül, was rewarded with a new apartment. He quickly secured work as a receptionist for a government office. Diyanet did not rush into matrimony despite possessing all the attributes of an eligible bachelor—such as education, employment, and home ownership (Lim 2013; Pierson 2010). Instead, Diyanet leveraged his "worth" on the marriage market for an opportunity to study in Istanbul under the auspices of a Turkish government scholarship. Anticipating his parents' disproval, he proposed a compromise—he would marry before leaving, but his wife would remain in Khotan. His parents agreed, and Diyanet arranged to marry his childhood sweetheart. In fact, at the time of our meeting, Diyanet was a mere two weeks away from his wedding day (field notes, June 13, 2012).

Marriage is often the price extracted by the parents of Xinjiang Class graduates who wish to remain in neidi or go abroad. Parents' interference in their children's romantic lives—also shown in the story of Bayram and his parents in Chapter 2—underscores the communal nature of marriages in Uyghur societies (Béller-Hann 2008, 235–60). Uyghur parents continue to play important roles in determining the choice of their children's spouses and the timing of their weddings (cf., Smith Finley 2013, 300–305).

Responding to Islam

Piety pulled a small number of my informants back to Xinjiang. This rationale is slightly counterintuitive: religious practice is more scrutinized and strictly controlled in Xinjiang than it is in neidi. Nevertheless, concerns over adhering to Islamic dietary laws in neidi—where halal food can be monotonous and scarce—weighed particularly heavily on these individuals' minds. Pahliwan, a graduate of the Xinjiang Class in Dalian, carefully considered the practicability of maintaining a halal diet in Beijing when he decided to accept a position in Xinjiang. Seated around a neatly spread *dastixan* tablecloth with his parents at their home in Atush, Pahliwan listed his reasons for returning:

> I am tired of studying, so I did not want to attend graduate school. I want to get a job and make money, but life in Beijing is too expensive. Plus it is difficult to find halal food in Beijing. If you are not a university student, you might not live close to a Muslim restaurant, and many of the Xinjiang[-style] restaurants are very expensive. (field notes, June 9, 2012)

To be sure, Pahliwan considered many factors in his choice between neidi and Xinjiang, but his strict abidance to Islamic dietary laws posed an immediate problem. Recently graduated, Pahliwan was no longer permitted to dine at the university's halal cafeteria. As such, he would need to regularly dine in a halal restaurant or cook for himself.

Commitment to Islamic dietary laws does not waver easily, even if it invites unpleasant social consequences. Trained as an engineer, Eziz, a 2008 graduate of the Xinjiang Class in Dalian, aspired to work for the China State Construction Engineering Corporation (CSCEC; Ch. *Zhongguo jianzhu*), China's largest construction and real estate conglomerate. After several rejected applications, Eziz was finally offered a position, provided he complied with one important condition; he must eat food contaminated with pork. The hiring manager explained that since the majority of employees at CSCEC were Han and often eat communally at canteens located on-site, CSCEC could not provide special halal meals for its workers.

Faced with the difficult decision to work for CSCEC at the expense of his religious observances, Eziz declined the offer and returned to Kashgar and began working at a local government office. Eziz reflected on his decision:

> I could have said yes [and accepted the offer], and then just not eat at work, but everyone around me would wonder why I wasn't eating. More important, though, if I worked there, I would not only represent other Uyghurs but I'd represent all Muslims. If I ate pork, my Han colleagues would think that all Uyghurs will eat pork under the right circumstances. Then, all Han people will think that abstaining from pork really isn't important to us [Uyghurs and Muslims]. Since my childhood, I've feared God (Uy. *Xudadin qorqtim*), but Han people have no fears (Uy. *Héchnémidin qorqmaydu*) [presumably because many Han people are atheist], so they don't understand these things. I guess, I probably could have found better-paying work in Ürümchi, but there are too many Han people there. (field notes, June 12, 2012)

Eziz's piety extends beyond eating halal food. At the risk of being dismissed from his job, Eziz attends weekend prayers at a local mosque. In order to sidestep the Comprehensive Law Enforcement (Ch. *Zonghe zhifa*) officials who monitor mosque attendees, Eziz slips in and out of the mosque using a small side entrance.

Economic stability

The Xinjiang Class provides a practical path to upward socioeconomic mobility for some. Alimjan—the young man who actively posted on his university's message board—was raised by poor parents. His father, a common laborer, and mother, a homemaker, had little extra income to spend on Alimjan's education. Therefore, participating in the Xinjiang Class was a practical and appealing option for the young man and his parents. He also took advantage of the tuition-free teacher-training program offered to Xinjiang Class graduates (see Chapter 3) and enrolled in Beijing Normal University. Two days before he departed for Xinjiang to teach math, Alimjan assessed his career choice:

> To tell you the truth, I'm excited about teaching. My parents don't have a lot of money, but the Xinjiang Class allowed me to attend a good school for free. I really wanted to go to a university in Beijing, so I decided to become a teacher. Initially [some officials] told me I only had to serve for five years as a teacher, but now I hear it is ten. That is a long time, but I did attend university for free too, and the government will help me find a job. It is really hard to find a job in Xinjiang, you know, but I'm guaranteed one. Since my family's financial situation isn't good, having a job is really important to me. I even hear that I can make RMB 10,000 (USD 1,500) a year as a teacher. On top of that, I will return to Beijing Normal for three consecutive summers and eventually earn my master's degree in education. It won't be so bad to teach in Xinjiang. Plus my family and girlfriend are there.

Alimjan's remarks demonstrate how financial pressures may compel some Xinjiang Class students to become teachers in Xinjiang, where schools are facing a severe shortage of bilingual instructors (Xinhua 2015). When confronted with a volatile job market, some Xinjiang Class graduates occasionally choose economic stability above everything else.

Economic stability can even change the tunes of Xinjiang Class graduates who second-guess their decisions to attend the boarding school program and complain about its policies. After graduating from a university in Shandong in 2012 with a law degree, Mehrem returned to Xinjiang to reconnect with family whom she missed dearly. She took the civil service (Ch. *gongwuyuan*) examination but did not score high enough for a job in the judicial system. Her friend recommended Mehrem to join her at a state-owned factory that manufactures military supplies. With no other leads, Mehrem settled for the position, which she found to be menial. She complained, "All day long, I check serial numbers on a computer. I hate it. Participating in the Xinjiang Class wasn't worth it; even a child could do my work." Mehrem accepted the job because, according to her, few places willingly hired Uyghurs, especially Uyghur women. Her claim suggests that the steady reduction in urban labor participation among Uyghurs of both genders that began in the 1990s (Maurer-Fazio, Hughes, and Zhang 2007) continues in the twenty-first century.

Mehrem was also dissatisfied with restrictions on religious practice. During *iptar*—the evening breaking of the fast during Ramadan—she expressed a desire to embody her faith in daily practice:

> My work unit [a state-owned factory] forbids me to veil and fast [however, she waited until iptar to eat dinner]. I'm a Muslim, so I must respect Islamic law. In addition to praying, fasting, and making the pilgrimage to Mecca, I need to cover my head, arms, and legs. [But] if I veil or fast, I will lose my job. (field notes, July 13, 2013)

Mehrem's employer foreshadowed a broader ban on religious practices among party officials and government employees in Xinjiang that was introduced during Ramadan the following year: believing in religion, fasting, and offering namaz prayer became forbidden (*Guanchazhe* 2014). Under this policy, Uyghurs are often forced to choose between material comforts and their religious beliefs.

By 2017, it was clear that Mehrem chose material comforts. In the four years that had passed, she married her longtime boyfriend (a non–Xinjiang Class Uyghur), gave birth to their first child, and found work as a spokeswoman for a Communist women's organization. In a radio interview, she praised the 19th National Congress of the Communist Party of China, which was held October 18–24, 2017, in Beijing:

> We are all excited (Uy. *hayajlinip torduq*) for the official opening of the 19th National Congress. When we hear Chairman Xi speak of the beautiful and magnificent future of our country, our confidence swells with pride (Uy. *tolup tashdi*). Although we cannot be in Beijing to participate in the 19th National Congress, many of us are able to watch it here, making it seem as if we are there in person (Uy. *naq meydenge barghandek hés qilduq*).... China is becoming a world superpower. The eyes of the world are directed at China right now (Uy. *pütün dunyaning diqqiti Junggogha*). The whole world holds high hopes (Uy. *chong ümid*) for the 19th Party Congress as well as for our country's future.[3]

I have not seen Mehrem since 2013, and increased surveillance of Uyghur social media accounts (Tong 2017) keeps our online conversations at a superficial level. Therefore, I can only surmise what circumstances changed the young woman's outlook. Now a wife and mother, Mehrem has understandably chosen to place the interests of her family ahead of her personal politics and religious beliefs. Joining the party, undoubtedly a prerequisite for her current position, may offer security to the young woman and her family's future. As one Uyghur friend explained to me, "Uyghurs often join the party, even if they disagree with its policies. When it rains, it's wise to have an umbrella."

Reestablishing Feelings of Belonging in Xinjiang

Once they return to the XUAR, Xinjiang Class graduates must reintegrate into communities wherein Uyghurs compose a significant proportion of the population. My research suggests that these individuals initially struggle to reestablish feelings of belonging, understood here as multilayered emotional attachments to a certain locale (Lovell 1998). Typically, the readjustment process is brief, especially for the young men I befriended. However, my female informants—who are expected to conform to rigid gender roles—tend to readapt to life in Xinjiang more slowly.

Sudden changes in social environment can be an immediate source of discomfort for Xinjiang Class graduates after their return. As noted above, Xinjiang

---

3. In order to protect the identity of this individual, I have decided against providing a URL link to the interview.

Class graduates typically live in neidi for a minimum of eight years—four years as Xinjiang Class students and four years as undergraduates. Those who pursue graduate degrees can extend their stays in neidi well into a decade. Removed from communities wherein Islamic and Central Asian social norms pervade when they are students, several individuals admitted to feeling alien in Xinjiang. Eziz, the individual who turned down a job offer with CSCEC, recalled:

> I remember feeling sad (Uy. *hesret chiqtim*) about returning. The people in Kashgar are still very poor; many are still uneducated (Uy. *bilim sapisining töwen*); and the farmers' lives are grueling (Uy. *bichare*). Even in my own home, I wasn't able to completely fit in (Uy. *a'ile muhitqa singip kirelmey*), and I felt as if I was a guest (Uy. *méhmande hés qildim*). In my mind, it felt as if other Uyghurs thought I was a Han. But I have been back for nearly a year now. Things have become much better (Uy. *yaxshi bop keldi*), and I have reconnected with many of my friends. (field notes, June 15, 2012)

Eziz's admission that he was misidentified as a Han person and regarded as a sinicized "guest"[4] by other Uyghurs appears to confirm the conclusions of studies examining the relationships between two types of educated Uyghurs. The research argues that minkaomin—those educated in Uyghur—rarely fully embrace their Chinese-educated peers, known as minkaohan (Taynen 2006; Smith 2000; Smith Finley 2007b). However, a closer examination of Eziz's statement casts further doubt on the depth of the minkaomin and minkaohan cleavage and underscores the social "flexibility" of young, well-educated Uyghurs in the twenty-first century (Smith Finley 2013, 389). Eziz's comment that his situation "has improved"— expressed by the phrase *yaxshi bop keldi*—insinuates that the hostility and mistrust he sensed from other Uyghurs dissipated. Indeed, during my visits with Eziz in 2012 and 2013, I witnessed ample evidence suggesting that he was popular among his (non–Xinjiang Class) peers. While strolling through Kashgar's old town (Uy. *kona sheher*), Eziz was regularly stopped by Uyghur friends and acquaintances, each greeting him warmly, shaking his hand and saying "essalamu eleykum."

Some Xinjiang Class graduates initially struggle over expectations to act as devout Muslims. In May 2015 I told Rashid about my upcoming trip to China. He excitedly requested some American cigarettes. I happily purchased packs of Marlboro and American Spirits, which I delivered to him in Beijing. He cradled the small bundle and pledged only to smoke them on special occasions. Rashid proceeded to describe his new career plan: he would no longer be a peripatetic trader in Beijing as he waited for a permanent position—his latest gig was dabbling in the saffron trade. With a master's degree in hand and his girlfriend, a Xinjiang

---

4. In the late 1990s the popular Uyghur musician Ömerjan Alim wrote a song entitled "Guest" (Uy. "Méhman"). The song compared Han migrants to guests who never left; it was eventually banned (Smith Finley 2013, 193–95).

Class classmate who worked in Ürümchi, he too agreed to return and take the civil service examination. We promised to meet again in the provincial capital.

During Ramadan in Ürümchi, as in other cities with large Muslim populations, excitement builds in the late afternoon in anticipation of iptar. Although Rashid was not fasting, the particular restaurant we would later dine at did not serve food until after sunset. Therefore, we met at Döngköwrük Mosque as the sun was setting. Before we departed together for the restaurant, Rashid's phone rang. "*Akam* [brother]!" he greeted. "Yes, I'm in Ürümchi now," he answered. Then panic seized his face. He quickly stubbed out his cigarette and stuffed the two packs I had given him into my hands. "Take these!" he commanded. Rashid waved his hand toward the mosque. His brother—who unbeknownst to Rashid had come to town on business from Kashgar—quickly made his way down the stairs, and the two embraced. Their reunion did not last long because his brother had other dinner plans. After his brother was at a safe distance, Rashid asked for his cigarettes. "My brother would beat me if he knew I smoked," he explained.

Rashid's decision to hide his smoking habit from his brother highlights the normative power of a common Islamic morality code respected by many Uyghurs (Byler 2017). It is unlikely that Rashid's brother would have become angry over the health risks of tobacco; rather, he would interpret his younger sibling's behavior as a deviation from Uyghur social and religious manners. Young Uyghurs abstain from smoking to demonstrate their respect to pious friends and relatives, as well as show renewed personal commitments to Islamic morals (Byler 2017; Smith Finley 2013, 110 and 282–83).[5] However, since 2017 CCP officials have politicized Uyghur abstention from smoking. Despite national antismoking campaigns (Rajagopalan and Campbell 2015), overzealous CCP officials in the XUAR now regard nonsmoking Uyghurs as potential "extremists." In April 2017 a Uyghur party chief was demoted because he refused to smoke. According to an anonymous party official familiar with the demotion, "smoking is a personal choice, and religious and ordinary people should respect each other, but his behavior of not daring to smoke conforms with extreme religious thought in Xinjiang" (Kentish 2017). Even choices about respect, healthy living, and religious ethics are associated with radical Islam (Byler 2017).

Rashid repeated his newfound piety when we met for iptar later that week. The gathering also reconnected me with his girlfriend, Jeher, whom I had not seen for almost two years. I arrived at the restaurant a few minutes before our scheduled meeting time and waited for the couple. Rashid and Jeher walked in shortly thereafter. The couple took their seats; Rashid appeared as if he was ill. "Don't worry about me," he reassured. "Jeher [who was fasting in secrecy while working at a state

---

5. Islamic jurists citing the Qur'an (2:195; 2:219; 4:27; 5:90–3, 17:26–7), hadith, and seeking *qiyas* (analogous situations) commonly rule smoking to be makruh (reprehensible) or *haram* (forbidden). For a detailed explanation on the permissibility of smoking in Islam, see Smith Finley 2013, 110.

publishing press] suggested I fast with her. This is day two. I'll be fine." Jeher giggled. "It's not hard. I've fasted every day," she boasted.

Diyanet, the individual who used marriage as an exit strategy to Turkey, similarly began to valorize his Muslim identity only after returning to Xinjiang. After proudly admitting to becoming a "good Muslim," Diyanet asked me about my own religious practices. Unprepared by the spontaneity of his question, I struggled to construct a coherent answer. As I desperately searched for words, he politely interjected:

> When I was a university student in Beijing, I drank, smoke, and went to Vic's and Mix [two popular dance clubs in Beijing] every weekend. Now, I realize the importance of being Muslim, and I pray five times a day. I even go to mosque for morning prayers. I know I am not permitted to go to mosque [because I work in a government office], but I am not afraid of getting fired. I hate my job anyway. But they [his superiors] also know they can't find a better replacement. Where are they going to find someone who speaks fluent Uyghur, Chinese, and English in Khotan? If you are a Muslim, you have to act like a Muslim. The same is true for Christians. It isn't enough just to say you are a Muslim or Christian. (field notes, June 13, 2012)

The two men's experiences illustrate the important role community pressure plays in shaping the religious practices of Xinjiang Class graduates. As students in Beijing, neither Rashid nor Diyanet maintained a prayer schedule, visited a mosque, or fasted during Ramadan. In fact, they engaged in behaviors frowned upon by observant Muslims (e.g., drinking and smoking). However, in Xinjiang and under the duress of communities wherein value is increasingly placed on religious piety (Bellér-Hann 2007; Smith Finley 2013, 235–93; Waite 2007), the two men were interpellated as Muslims.

Despite the risks, Xinjiang Class graduates often turn to Islam after their return. Public employees, such as the individuals profiled in this section, face dismissal if caught engaging in religious practice; "illegal religious activities" are punishable by imprisonment or "reeducation" (Ch. *jiaoyu zhuanhua*) (*Foreign Policy* 2018). Yet, embodiments of Islamic values (e.g., praying, fasting, and abstaining from smoking) provide Xinjiang Class graduates with important (and instant) access to communities from which they were separated for nearly a decade. In other words, piety is sometimes a prerequisite of (re)integration and suggests an embrace of a Uyghur identity emanating from Islamic Central Asia over the secular "Weiwu'er zu" identity promoted by the state.

Building a New Life in Xinjiang

Hectic works schedules distracted some Xinjiang Class graduates from pressures to conform to community expectations. In June 2012 I reconnected with Muhtar—the cocaptain of the "Uyghur" soccer team—in Ürümchi. Over the course of the evening, he described his new lifestyle. After returning to Xinjiang, Muhtar started working fifty hours per week at a local bank, a schedule that afforded him little time for leisure. His social life was limited to meals with his roommate—a colleague who also graduated from the Xinjiang Class—and weekend outings with a group of Muhtar's middle school classmates from Kashgar who were studying at Xinjiang University (field notes, June 7, 2012).

A year later, Muhtar was in the middle of several major life changes. He continued to log in over fifty hours a week at the bank but still managed to find time to gather with his friends on weekends. In the course of a year working as a bank teller—and with help from his parents—Muhtar purchased a flat in a high-rise apartment complex located just east of Döngköwrük. To help Muhtar maintain his new living space, his parents traveled from Kashgar to live with him. Muhtar insisted that I visit him at his new home. I gladly accepted the invitation. Seated on a large *gilem* rug and eating a hearty bowl of *lengmen* noodles prepared by his father, Muhtar shared more joyful news—he would marry in 2014. After making his announcement, Muhtar proceeded to share pictures of his fiancée, a young non–Xinjiang Class (minkaomin) Uyghur woman from Ürümchi whom he met through a work colleague. In preparation for his upcoming marriage, Muhtar was renovating the house's interior, installing internet service, and decorating the living room with large rugs and sitting mats (field notes, June 30, 2013).

Subtle but important details in Muhtar's routine—namely, his reconnection with primary and middle school classmates and his romantic relationship with a (minkaomin) Uyghur woman—allow us to assess the deportments of Xinjiang Class graduates. As noted above, some studies examining the social impact of Xinjiang's education system advance the argument that different modes of schooling stratify Uyghur communities. However, the lines dividing the so-called minkaomin and minkaohan Uyghurs may not be as clear as they were in the 1990s and early 2000s (cf. Grose 2014). Muhtar prefers the company of his minkaomin classmates over his Han colleagues and other "acculturated" Uyghurs despite his own status as a bilingual Uyghur who was educated in Han-dominated cities. His relationships with his childhood friends and his non–Xinjiang Class spouse highlight Muhtar's, along with other Xinjiang Class graduates', ability to navigate between and be accepted by various Uyghur social circles (Grose 2014; Smith Finley 2013, 360–66).

Balancing Acts: Women and the Struggles of Reintegration

Women, on the other hand, must carefully balance aspirations for successful careers with expectations tied to womanhood, marriage, and parenthood, or they risk becoming targets of stigmatization. Village matrons—who often expect young women to engage in trivial affairs—or *mish-mish*—were another source of tension for my female interlocutors. Gülnaz returned to rural Kashgar, where the provincial-level government had arranged a position (Ch. *fenpei*) for the young woman at a local school. Since the school was located near Gülnaz's natal home, she moved in with her parents. On weekends, she regularly accompanied her mother to informal social gatherings (Uy. *chay*). Although these get-togethers were meant to be a form of leisure, Gülnaz found the company of older women—who value commensality rituals, which appear to be in decline among young, educated Uyghurs (Smith Finley 2013, 391–92)—stressful. Here I paraphrase from my field notes:

> I felt uneasy after coming back to Xinjiang. As is pretty common if you live in a village [in Xinjiang], all of my mother's friends and neighbors come over to sit around the table to snack and talk. I attended these gatherings too, but I didn't speak or eat anything. My mother would get angry at me [for my impoliteness], but for some reason, I didn't know what to say. Looking back, I realize that life in the Xinjiang Class and college was too simple. I didn't do anything but study. I was never around adults, and as a young woman I didn't know how to talk with women older than me. Really, I didn't know how to act around adults. In the Xinjiang Class, I was only around my classmates. (July 7, 2013)

Kamirya, one of Gülnaz's Xinjiang Class schoolmates who also spent her childhood in Kashgar, felt equally despondent upon returning. After graduating from university in Hefei, Kamirya worked as an elementary school teacher for three years in rural Kashgar before moving to Ürümchi with her husband. While living in Kashgar, Kamirya felt alienated from the company of her mother's close female friends and ensconced herself in her bedroom. Again, I paraphrase my informant's response:

> I remember feeling mad when I was around my mother and her friends. I would go to the neighbor's or to my aunt's house, and they would force me to eat. [At times] I didn't want to eat anything [or] I was full. Actually, they were just being hospitable—making sure guests have enough to eat is part of Uyghur culture. But I was used to eating in cafeterias, and I only ate the food I wanted to eat [while studying in neidi]. I could eat as little or as much as I wanted. No one cared. I didn't have to be polite or think about how to act. I just did as I pleased. (July 7, 2013)

These two statements help to illustrate an apparent incompatibility between the (Han) cultural norms in which Xinjiang Class students are immersed while studying in neidi and those prevalent in Uyghur communities. After being removed from a Uyghur cultural milieu for nearly a decade, these two young women failed to comply with simple hospitality norms. Entertaining close friends and neighbors through conversation and offering tea, snacks, or cooked meals is a practice of Uyghur commensality culture that has persevered throughout the PRC's socialist era (Bellér-Hann 2008, 202–10; Dautcher 2009, 129–39). In order to play the role of a proper guest (Uy. *méhman bolush*) and correctly perform these commensality norms, Gülnaz and Kamirya should have accepted the offered food and drink and contributed to the conversation. Their nonparticipation was likely regarded by the other women present as impolite or even as a social offense (Bellér-Hann 2008, 208).

Female Xinjiang Class graduates also felt alienated when interacting with women of similar ages. Hajigül, the young woman who continued her studies in the Netherlands, remarked about feeling distant from her former (non–Xinjiang Class) schoolmates:

> While I was still in university [in China], I came home for each holiday, but every time [I came home], I began to feel more and more like a stranger (Uy. *barghansiri yat tuyulatti*). I still had girlfriends in my hometown [Aksu], but we are different (Uy. *perq bar*) [now], and we want to talk about different things. They wanted to discuss children and making money, but I wanted to discuss school and my dreams of going abroad. It was as if they thought I had become Westernized (Uy. *ghéripiliship ketkendek*). (field notes, September 1, 2011)

As a single woman in her late twenties pursuing a graduate degree, Hajigül was likely treated as an outcast by her peers (cf. Bellér-Hann 1998). Despite exposure to a secular education that values participation in the workforce, many Uyghur women still feel a strong sense of responsibility to fulfill maternal roles, especially in Xinjiang's rural southern communities (Huang 2009, 84; Smith Finley 2013, 143).

Some female graduates begrudgingly veiled post return. Gülnaz—the young teacher who felt uncomfortable at her mother's *chay* gatherings—was expected to wear a headscarf. Although her head was bare when we met, she covered it in the company of her husband. Gülnaz protested in a mix of Chinese and Uyghur:

> I never wore a headscarf as a child. My parents were part of the first cohort of Uyghurs who received a college education after the Cultural Revolution. My parents weren't conservative. My mother didn't wear a scarf while she was growing up either. So I don't think it feels natural to wear one now. I usually only wear it when I am with my husband or am at his family's home.

At the KFC in Ürümchi's International Grand Bazaar, Sumbul—the young woman who turned down the job at a cosmetics company in Shanghai—identified similar reasons for donning a headscarf. She said:

> My husband asked me . . . [*pause*] suggested that I cover my head, so now I wear a headscarf for most of the day [*pulls the scarf out of her purse*]. Umm, I take it off sometimes [*laughs*]. I am required [by my work] to remove my headscarf when I teach. If I go to a bank or have to do some "official" [relating to the government] business I don't wear it either. My husband has become very religious since graduating from the Xinjiang Class and returning to Xinjiang. He used to drink and smoke, but now he has given those up. He prays regularly and is fasting, so I prepare iptar for him. He also wants me to cover my head. I support his religious practice because now I don't worry about him finding another girl, smoking, or getting drunk. I think he is even kinder since becoming more religious.

For these two young women, veiling (in its various manifestations) is not principally an embodied Islamic practice or an assertion of Uyghur identity; nor does it reflect attempts to follow current fashions popular in Turkey, Central Asia, or the Middle East (Najafizadeh 2012, 87). These two interviewees suggest that veiling is indicative of the resilience of patriarchy in Uyghur society (Caprioni 2008; Zang 2011). Still, young women find creative ways in their daily routines to subvert their husbands' presumptions that, as married women, they must veil. Although they ultimately acquiesce to their husbands' demands in their presence, they also choose when and where to don headscarves once they are beyond their husbands' gaze.

Indeed, patriarchal attitudes remain widespread in contemporary Xinjiang (Bellér-Hann 1998; Caprioni 2008; Dautcher 2009). Before he returned to Xinjiang, I asked Muhtar who would be responsible for domestic tasks (Uy. *a'ile ishliri*), particularly the cooking, once he married. He answered emphatically, "Absolutely the woman" (Uy. *choqum ayal*) (field notes, June 19, 2011). One year later, after Muhtar shared the news about his upcoming marriage, I jokingly reminded him of the above exchange. Muhtar, blushing in embarrassment, confirmed that his fiancée "cooks very well." Muhtar's father, who, ironically enough, was preparing the meal in the kitchen, overheard our conversation, burst into the living room, and added, "It wouldn't be OK [i.e., he wouldn't marry her] if she couldn't cook" (Uy. *tamaq ételmisa bolmaydu*) (field notes, 30 June 2013).

Yet many female Xinjiang Class graduates challenged these gender norms. Educated in an environment wherein daily chores are not gendered, several of my informants admitted to not knowing how to perform domestic tasks—preparing meals being a notable example. Above all, most of my female informants criticized gender inequality in Uyghur society. Some young women even deferred marriage in favor of their own careers, despite the social risks this decision often invites. Hasiyet, the 2007 graduate of the Wuxi Xinjiang Class, complained:

> It's important for us [women] to know how to cook because 98 percent of Uyghur men think it is important. If we do not learn how to cook, we will lose face (Uy. *yüzi tökülgendek*) in front of our friends. Also, [after marriage] our husband's parents won't like us [if we can't cook] (Uy. *yaxshi körmeydu*). Actually, cooking and age are really important points. Most [Uyghur] girls marry before the age of twenty-five. The more successful we [Uyghur women] are, the harder it will be to find husbands. You see, it is hard to find someone as good as ourselves. There are very few Uyghur men who are hardworking (Uy. *tirishchan*), have dreams, and are responsible (Uy. *mesuliyetlik*). And then, we have to be able to cook for these guys (Uy. *tamaqni yaxshi étilishi kérek*) and wash their clothes. Of course, successful girls don't want to live like that. (field notes, July 27, 2013)

In her statement, Hasiyet tacitly expresses her unwillingness to submit to her future husband. That is, she accuses young Uyghur men of being unmotivated and intimidated by women who are career oriented, and she questions the existence of Uyghur men who are "good enough" for the growing number of highly educated Uyghur women.

Finding Place in Xinjiang

Grumblings about readapting to Uyghur social life are often drowned out by complaints over the lack of meaningful work in Xinjiang. Rather than spearheading government-planned development in the region, Xinjiang Class graduates are often stuck working menial jobs, if they are employed at all. To be sure, the CCP has taken measures to assist Xinjiang Class graduates in securing permanent employment. For example, in July 2011, the first job fair (Ch. *zhaopinhui*) specifically for Xinjiang Class graduates was held in Ürümchi. According to reports, over seventy employers—who hoped to fill 2,500 positions—attended the event. Before the job fair, the XUAR government distributed letters to employers that explained the boarding school program and guaranteed that its graduates possessed "high political quality" (Ch. *juyou zhengzhi suzhi gao*) (*China Education Newspaper* 2011). The event appears to have been very successful. Numbers provided by Xinjiang's Department of Education indicate nearly 520 Xinjiang Class graduates signed letters of intent, and over 800 Xinjiang Class graduates submitted their résumés to potential employers (Xinjiang Department of Education 2011).

According to my research, however, opportunities for Xinjiang Class graduates are limited to a few mostly undesirable professions. One Xinjiang Class graduate, a bank clerk in Ürümchi, reproached the CCP for this situation: "Xinjiang Class graduates can only be bank clerks, teachers, or police officers [in Xinjiang]. Really, the Xinjiang Class is about our assimilation (*Uy. assimiliyatsiye*)" (field notes, June 21, 2012). Many of my informants who have returned—themselves mostly engaged in these three professions—agreed with this assessment. They insisted that the best-paying, most prestigious jobs in Xinjiang are reserved for Han employees. Diyanet bluntly explained:

> It's simple. If a Uyghur with a master's degree who can speak perfect Chinese and a [Han] Chinese with a high school diploma apply for the same job, the Han will get the job every time. (field notes, June 13, 2012)

Sumbul, who spent six months looking for permanent work in Ürümchi added:

> It's so hard for me to get a job. You won't even believe how common it is for employers to be unwilling to hire Uyghurs. It is even harder for Uyghur women. You rarely find a company, a government office, or a school seeking Uyghur women. (field notes, July 17, 2013)

To be sure, Chinese laws seek to protect minority minzu from discriminatory hiring practices (see Law of the PRC on Regional Ethnic Autonomy 1984; Constitution of the PRC 1982), yet these laws appear to be sporadically enforced (see CECC 2010; Fay 2013). In fact, there are a number of documented cases in which employers specifically reserved vacancies for Han employees, especially in the private sector (CECC 2010).

Unemployed or unable to find meaningful work, Xinjiang Class graduates commonly direct their frustrations towards the CCP. Adalet protested:

> I don't think I belong here [in Xinjiang], not because I hate my hometown, but because I disagree with so many policies here. [The policies] are not based on principles at all, but always sway according to the government's own interests. You [as a Uyghur] are never treated like you are a person who has his or her own rights as a citizen. There is no fairness; power and money dominate all. (field notes, June 8, 2012)

Adalet's criticisms are vague. In public, they need to be. Nonetheless, having known Adalet for several years, I can speculate with some degree of certainty that, as a nonreligious young woman who planned to emigrate to Australia with her then fiancé (now husband)—who struggled to secure a Chinese passport—to further her education and eventually find employment, she is likely referring to discriminatory hiring practices and bureaucratic hurdles that ostensibly delay (or prevent) Uyghurs from going abroad.

Xinjiang Class graduates echo criticisms over the lack of meaningful work that have reverberated throughout China's Uyghur population for the last three decades (Bovingdon 2010; Dautcher 2000; Kaltman 2007; Mackerras 2001; Smith 2000, 2002; Smith Finley 2007a). But graduates of the Xinjiang Class are supposed to be different. The CCP pledged that these young Uyghurs would be a "new force" (Ch. *yi zhi xinsheng liliang*) behind Xinjiang's rapid economic and social development (*Xinjiang Daily* 2012). This promise is yet to be fulfilled.

Concluding Remarks

This chapter has shown that Xinjiang Class graduates have not returned to repay the CCP for its altruism. Nor have they returned as patriotic minority minzu who eagerly profess loyalty to the CCP. Rather, most graduates of the program return to Xinjiang only after exhausting other options or if they are under extreme pressure from their parents.

Reacclimating to life in Xinjiang can be vexing, especially for young women. Despite these difficulties, Xinjiang Class graduates can and do reestablish genuine feelings of belonging in Uyghur communities. However, finding suitable, well-paying work has been a more pressing concern for my informants. Xinjiang Class students have been promised the reins of Xinjiang's development programs, but they, like non–Xinjiang Class Uyghurs, often find themselves on the sidelines. My informants have complained bitterly about the dwindling, if not nonexistent, job opportunities available to them, and for those individuals fortunate enough to secure full-time employment, they are often forced to perform menial tasks for low wages.

Discontent simmers among my informants who have returned to Xinjiang. Some individuals attempt to pave new avenues leading to opportunities abroad. Others resort to expressing their disapproval of the CCP through vocal critiques (Bovingdon 2002; 2010, 88–94) and forms of media that the state cannot easily control (Dautcher 2000; Smith Finley 2007a, 2013). Regardless of the form of resistance, a sizeable group of the Uyghur intellectual elite is reluctantly reestablishing roots in Xinjiang's major oasis cities.

Conclusion

> I think that we will continue to thrive as a people. And I think that our future is going to be bright.
>
> Méningche bizning millet dawamliq güllep yashnaydu. Kelgülsimiz parlaq bolidu dep oylaymen
>
> —Ilham, Xinjiang Class Graduate, Hangzhou

In February 2015 the inconceivable happened. Tursun, a twenty-three-year-old Uyghur man, was placed into custody at an undisclosed detention center in China after allegedly traveling to Afghanistan to engage in global jihad. He had previously studied in the Xinjiang Class; in fact, he was only one of six students from his school in rural Khotan to be accepted into the program. In a nationally televised interview, the young Uyghur man—shackled in his chair and wearing a prison jumpsuit—spoke fondly of his days in the boarding school. The dorms were spacious, the food was delicious, and the teachers were caring, he recalled. Although he took the college entrance examination twice, his scores were not high enough to attend his university of choice. Disillusioned with China's education system and the likely impossibility of succeeding in Xinjiang without a university degree, Tursun sought another path. While working as a laborer in Xinjiang, he met a religious man who convinced Tursun to become his pupil, or *talip*. He even promised the young man a passport that would allow him to attend an Islamic university in Egypt. The document never materialized. According to Tursun, the man threatened him at knifepoint to either join jihadists in Central Asia or be killed. Fearing for his life, Tursun complied. He was loaded into a car with thirty other men and driven to a remote location in Afghanistan. Before long, he was detained during a raid and repatriated. Awaiting trial in Xinjiang, he hopes others can learn from his mistakes. He offered the following advice: "At all costs, do not be tricked by extremists and share my fate" (Sina 2015).

To be sure, cases similar to Tursun's are extremely rare, but the episodic antistate violence in Xinjiang that began thirty years ago has sent a clear warning to the CCP; it is losing precious ground in its struggle to integrate the Uyghurs into the Zhonghua minzu. In the short term, the party-state seeks to impose a semblance of stability with violence of its own. Paramilitary patrols regularly sweep through areas where Uyghurs predominate to snuff out "terrorism," "separatism," and "extremism" (Millward 2007, 341–43; Smith Finley 2013, 237–38). Armored vehicles parade through Xinjiang's major oasis cities in daily spectacles of strength. Government personnel stage public burnings of "illegal" religious paraphernalia to symbolically exorcise and purify the region (*People's Daily Online* 2014). Moreover, since Chen Quanguo's appointment as XUAR's Party Secretary in August 2016, authorities have detained thousands of Uyghurs in "concentration reeducation centers" (*Foreign Policy* 2018; Zenz 2018). The state's message is explicit: all forms of resistance—however peaceful—will be quashed.

Meanwhile, the CCP is waging an ideological war that reaches deep into Uyghur culture. Government censors have banned Uyghur-language books, songs, and poetry that may be interpreted as political critiques (Harris 2001; Smith Finley 2007c). State-employed historians and museum curators have rewritten the region's history to strengthen otherwise tenuous links between Xinjiang, its Turkic populations, and Chinese polities. For example, a statue of General Ban Chao (32–102 CE) towers over Kashgar to convince local Uyghurs that their home has been ruled by the Chinese since the Han dynasty (206 BCE–220 CE) (Bovingdon and Tursun 2004). Likewise, the Xinjiang Regional Museum in Ürümchi showcases Han-centric histories to undermine Uyghur claims to indigeneity (Hayes 2016). Officials even manufacture linguistic bonds between Uyghurs and Han by elevating Putonghua over minority minzu languages as the lingua franca for education, commerce, and law in Xinjiang (Dwyer 2005; Schluessel 2007). These measures share common goals—to pull the Uyghurs' allegiances eastward toward the Han "central plains" and push them away from their Turkic-Muslim neighbors in Central Asia.

State schooling is the frontline of this ideological fight. These tightly controlled spaces provide the CCP with bulwarks for the party's values and primed canvases on which the CCP's visions for the nation and national belonging are drawn and displayed (Joniak-Lüthi 2015, 58). However, many schools in Xinjiang lack basic classroom technology, their teachers are undertrained, and above all, after the final classes each day, students return to communities and homes where Uyghur culture pervades. Therefore, the state's idealized portraits of the "Weiwu'er" people and their place in the Zhonghua minzu are constantly being smudged.

Officials have responded to this interference with national boarding schools—the Xinjiang Class—to sculpt students into subjects of the state. Modeled after a similar program for Tibetans, the Xinjiang Class enrolls 80 percent of its student body from rural and nomadic areas, the vast majority of whom are Uyghur, and educates them for four years at schools scattered throughout central, eastern, and coastal China. The Xinjiang Class's goals are scholastic and political. Academically, the boarding schools prepare students for China's national college entrance examination. During their intensive coursework, students study the national curriculum

Conclusion

and Chinese language. In fact, Xinjiang Class students are expected to speak fluent Chinese after four years of immersive learning.

Politically, the Xinjiang Class is intended as a cultural and ideological boot camp to create a cohort of Uyghur elite who are grateful for the CCP and committed to protecting "minzu unity." To this end, Xinjiang Class students are thrust into a Han cultural milieu while they adhere to strict school policies, many of which are aimed at weakening religious consciousness. This sterilized environment—where information, daily routines, diets, and access to people and places beyond the gates of the boarding schools are scrupulously controlled by officials and teachers—is supposed to condition Uyghur students (or interpellate them) as always-already members of the Zhonghua minzu.

This examination of the memories and behaviors of Xinjiang Class graduates casts doubts on the party-state's interpellative potential. Despite lavishing energy and resources on the Xinjiang Class, the CCP is waging an endless war. Although the CCP controls the resources to define "Weiwu'er zu" and Zhonghua minzu categories and reify them in a boarding school education, it cannot contain countervailing, nonstate formulations of Uyghurness. Contrary to the CCP's plans, the Xinjiang Class has strengthened—and, in some cases, activated where it never existed—a specifically "Uyghur" consciousness.

At times, Xinjiang Class graduates identified, asserted, and even exaggerated key "ethnic markers" (Keyes 1976) of Uyghurness in contradistinction to Han ethnicity. In ways similar to Uyghurs in the XUAR (Béller-Hann 2002, 2007; Bovingdon 2010; Cesàro 2000; Smith Finley 2002, 2013), my informants segregated themselves from their Han peers. They organized "Uyghur"-only soccer teams, hosted exclusive cultural events, and avoided romantic relationships with Han people. Xinjiang Class graduates also maintained ethnic boundaries by demonstrating their preference to speak Uyghur, despite (or in spite of) their monolingual Chinese education. Concerned about the survival of their mother tongue, these individuals encouraged each other to speak and read Uyghur in otherwise Han environments. Finally, many of my informants embodied Islamic practices after they were no longer subject to the Xinjiang Class's harsh punishments for engaging in religious activity. Indeed, Islam remained an important reference point in Uyghur identity constellations among Xinjiang Class graduates (see Hale 2004).

Although they are perhaps the most salient, "Weiwu'er zu" and "Uyghur" collectivities are not the only social categorizations available to Xinjiang Class graduates. For instance, my informants often sought membership in transnational communities by stretching the boundaries of Uyghurness to overlap with global Muslim and Turkic identities, a strategy also employed by Uyghur elite in diaspora (Kuşçu Bonnenfant 2018, 92). To this end, Xinjiang Class graduates scoured websites hosted by Muslims in foreign countries for "authentic" instructions on pious behavior, participated in Qur'anic reading groups, adopted religious dress, and aspired to travel to countries with large Muslim and Turkic populations.

My informants' desire to establish feelings of belonging within the umma notwithstanding, I hesitate to describe their renewed interest in Islam with the term "re-Islamization"—a label applied to the increase of a highly visible form of religiosity practiced among some Uyghurs in Xinjiang that started in the early 2000s (Smith Finley 2013, 245). "Islamization"—or changed cultural frameworks spurred by an expansion or reinterpretation of Islam (Carvajal Lopez 2013)—does not capture my informants' motivations for openly expressing their religious identity. Turkic-language sources are making it increasingly clear that Islam has been a fundamental marker of Uyghur ethno-national (and protonational) identity for centuries (Béller-Hann 2008; Klimeš 2015; Thum 2014). To be sure, expressions of Muslim-ness within the paradigms of Uyghur ethno-religious and ethno-national identifies have changed over the centuries—as examples, according to intellectual trends within the umma, periods of violent religious persecution in China's recent history—such as the Cultural Revolution (1966–1976)—and more formulaic embodiments in the twenty-first century—but they have not radically altered Uyghur cultural reference points and will not in the future unless the CCP loosens its grip on religious activity.

Further complicating the assertion of "re-Islamization" is an apparent flaw in methodology. Researchers have pointed to government crackdowns on "illegally" produced religious materials (Dillon 2004, 88), pilgrimages to the tombs of important Islamic saints (Harris and Dawut 2002), and mosque attendance (Fuller and Lipman 2004) as evidence of surges in these practices. However, in his reevaluation of Islam in the former Soviet Union, the late Mark Saroyan (1997, 12) reminded us that "directly extrapolating social processes from ideological inspired declarations can be an extremely misleading interpretative practice, since there is no rigorous way to evaluate exactly what kinds of social processes are actually reflected in [state] polemics and political campaigns." In other words, a CCP-imposed crackdown does not necessarily mean that a given practice was undergoing revival. In fact, to date, a systematic study assessing the religious activities of Uyghurs from pre-1949 until the mid-1990s does not exist. Without this information, we cannot determine with confidence whether Xinjiang is currently witnessing a process of "re-Islamization."

It may be better to understand the embrace of Islam among Xinjiang Class graduates within the context of post-Soviet Central Asian Islam. That is, Central Asian Muslims often instrumentalize Islam to strengthen community and national bonds (Khalid 2007; Mishra 2017). Put another way, my informants' embrace of Islam occurred organically with their attempts at solidifying transregional bonds with other Uyghurs and creating entryways—sometimes "imagined" (Anderson 1991)—into the umma. In neidi, these connections were made by offering du'a, participating in informal Qur'anic reading groups, maintaining a prayer schedule, or simply by reading about other Muslims. After returning to Xinjiang, some of my informants—for the first time in their adult lives—abstained from smoking, fasted during Ramadan, and veiled to reestablish feelings of belonging in Uyghur communities. This type of situational religiosity—in which observances are flexible,

Conclusion

changing, but nonetheless form the foundations of ethno-national identity—often poses the most serious challenges to modern nation building (Rywkin 1990, 90–91).

To be sure, Xinjiang Class graduates did not simply reject the Zhonghua minzu identity. Similar to their instrumentalization of Islam, Xinjiang Class graduates activated their Chineseness when it was advantageous to do so. As members of the Zhonghua minzu, Uyghurs were offered a choice to participate in the Xinjiang Class. Many Uyghur families believed schooling in neidi provided their children with the best chances to succeed. These rationales are sensible. A Xinjiang Class education propels most Uyghurs into Chinese universities. Upon graduating from university, Xinjiang Class graduates are competent in an academic discipline as well as proficient in at least three languages—Uyghur, Chinese, and English. Theoretically, these skills offer Xinjiang Class graduates a competitive edge in both the Chinese and international job markets.

Despite their academic qualifications, many Xinjiang Class graduates struggled to secure meaningful employment in neidi and Xinjiang. Discriminatory hiring practices indisputably favor Han people in the private sector and forced many of my informants into working menial jobs. This reality evokes Amsler's (2009) exploration into the symbolic and political value of education: building on Bourdieu's (2001, 34) *idée-force*—or a socially powerful idea—she questions whether state-sponsored education provides students and their families with only the *hope* to better their lives. Under- and unemployed and living in a virtual police state, most of my informants in Xinjiang disparaged the CCP's boarding school experiment; it did not provide them the socioeconomic security authorities had promised.

To some extent, a Xinjiang Class diploma even contributed to the "Othering" and marginalization of my Uyghur informants. Throughout their adolescent and adult lives, Xinjiang Class Uyghurs were singled out as "Others." Before enrolling in the program, they underwent extensive academic testing and invasive political background checks. As Xinjiang Class students, they were segregated from their Han schoolmates in separate classroom buildings, cafeterias, and dormitories, effectively reproducing the asymmetrical relationship between Han people and minority minzu. Even after Xinjiang Class graduates left the boarding school behind, they were required to regularly report to state officials.

This conclusion began with the extraordinary case of Tursun—the young man who is accused of joining jihadist militants. Some readers may dismiss the report as fabricated or think it irrelevant because the young man has maintained his innocence and insisted he did not voluntarily join the Islamist group.[1] Nevertheless, Tursun's professional struggles and ensuing alienation are similar to those endured

---

1. Considering the harsh sentence Tursun will likely face if he is found guilty, I am not surprised by his plea of innocence. To be sure, Uyghurs have joined Islamist groups, albeit in small numbers. Ben Blanchard (2017) reported that nearly 5,000 Uyghurs have joined Islamic militant groups in Syria and Iraq. Meanwhile, the Trump administration has ramped up air attacks in Afghanistan to eliminate Uyghur combatants (Lamothe 2018).

by my informants. In other words, many Xinjiang Class graduates recognized that they were still marginalized and their religious practices were restricted despite excelling—as Chinese citizens—in China's education system. Rather than being content in the CCP defined and maintained "Weiwu'er zu" category—which requires secularization and subordination to Han people—Xinjiang Class graduates turned their backs on the Zhonghua minzu by asserting Uyghurness, Muslimness and (sometimes) Chineseness in ways that deviated from the state's vision.

This assessment rings especially true in the Chen Quanguo era. As I discussed previously, Chen has accelerated and expanded the use of "concentration reeducation" centers and installed state-of-the-art surveillance technology to monitor the activities of Uyghurs. Xinjiang Class graduates have not been spared. As I have during each visit to the region, I attempted to reconnect with my informants during my July 2017 trip to Xinjiang. By that time, most of my Uyghur friends had deleted me from their social networking apps for fear that their association with a foreigner would invite trouble. However, Rashid—the outspoken critic of the party and recently-turned-pious young man—risked his safety to meet with me. He confirmed the horror stories of mass disappearances. He shared more disturbing news; Murat—the religious man who studied in Turkey—"disappeared" when he returned to Xinjiang to attend a family wedding. He is likely being held in a "reeducation" camp. Married with one child, Muhtar—the young man who worked as a bank clerk—and his family were sent to Kashgar, his hometown, because he did not have proper documentation to work in Ürümchi. The whereabouts and safety of many others who returned to Xinjiang remain unknown.

Clearly, few would be satisfied with the pomegranate arrangement of ethnic unity, which requires totalitarianism to hold it together. My informants' resistance is symbolic of their relationship within the Zhonghua minzu turning sour and rotten. Perhaps this pomegranate system is squeezing too tightly, crushing the Uyghurs in the process.[2] It is in this politicized existence that Xinjiang Class graduates seek ways to negotiate inseparability.

---

2. I want to express my gratitude to Darren Byler (personal communication) for helping me tease out this powerful metaphor.

References

Ababekri Qari. 2006. "Du'a du'aning shertliri, du'a ijabet bolidighan waqitlar, we du'aning edpliri" [Du'a, the requirements of du'a, time du'a will be answered, and proper etiquette for du'a]. In *Hidayet Gülzari* [The Garden of Virtuous Guidance], edited by Shemshidin Haji, 293–300. Beijing: Minzu chubanshe.
AFP [Associated Foreign Press]. 2012. "China Region Bans Muslims from Fasting during Ramadan." *National.* August 1, 2012. http://www.thenational.ae/news/world/china-region-bans-muslims-from-fasting-during-ramadan.
Akiner, Shirin. 1997. "Melting Pot, Salad Bowl—Cauldron? Manipulation and Mobilization of Ethnic and Religious Identities in Central Asia." *Ethnic and Racial Studies* 20, no. 2: 362–98.
Al Jazeera. 2015. "China Bans Ramadan Fasting in Mainly Muslim Region." June 18, 2015. http://www.aljazeera.com/news/2015/06/china-bans-ramadan-fasting-muslim-region-150618070016245.html.
Al Jazeera. 2017. "China's Communist Party Hardens Rhetoric on Islam." March 12, 2017. http://www.aljazeera.com/news/2017/03/china-communist-party-hardens-rhetoric-islam-170312171857797.html.
Allen, Kerry. 2016. "China: Xinjiang Government to 'Clear Up' Ethnic Names." BBC, July 8, 2016. http://www.bbc.com/news/world-asia-china-36738682.
Allison, Anne. 2013. *Precarious Japan*. Durham, NC: Duke University Press.
Althusser, Louis. 1971. *Lenin and Philosophy and Other Essays*. New York: Monthly Review Press.
Amir, Ruth. 2015. "Killing them Softly: Forcible Transfers of Indigenous Children." *Genocide Studies and Prevention: An International Journal* 9, no. 2: 41–60.
Amsler, Sarah. 2009. "Promising Futures? Education as a Symbolic Resource of Hope in Kyrgyzstan." *Europe-Asia Studies* 61, no. 7: 1189–206.
Anderson, Benedict. 1991. *Imagined Communities: Reflections on the Origin and Spread of Nationalism*. Rev. ed. London: Verso.
Antoun, Richard. 1968. "On the Modesty of Women in Arab Muslim Villages: A Study in the Accommodation of Tradition." *American Anthropologist* 70, no. 4: 671–97.
Ardener, Edwin. 1972. "Language, Ethnicity and Population." *Journal of the Anthropological Society of Oxford* 3, no. 3: 125–32.
Atkin, Muriel. 1992. "Religious, National and Other Identities in Central Asia." In *Muslims of Central Asia: Expressions of identity and Change*, edited by Jo-Ann Gross, 46–72. Durham, NC: Duke University Press.

Baranovitch, Nimrod. 2003. "From the Margins to the Centre: The Uyghur Challenge in Beijing." *China Quarterly* 175, no. 44: 726–50.

Baranovitch, Nimrod. 2007. "Inverted Exile: Uyghur Writers and Artists in Beijing and the Political Implications of Their Work." *Modern China* 33, no. 4: 462–504.

Barth, Fredrik. 1969. "Introduction." In *Ethnic Groups and Boundaries: The Social Organization of Cultural Difference*, edited by Fredrik Barth, 9–38. Boston: Little, Brown and Company.

Bateson, Gregory. 1958. *Naven: A Survey of the Problems Suggested by a Composite Picture of the Culture of a New Guinea Tribe drawn from Three Points of View*. 2nd ed. Stanford, CA: Stanford University Press.

Baum, Richard. 1997. "The Road to Tiananmen: Chinese Politics in the 1980s." In *The Politics of China: The Eras of Mao and Deng*, edited by Roderick MacFarquhar, 340–471. Cambridge; Cambridge University Press.

BBC. 2009. "Scores Killed in China Protest." July 6, 2009. http://news.bbc.co.uk/1/hi/world/asia-pacific/8135203.stm.

BBC. 2014. "China Bans Xinjiang Officials from Observing Ramadan Fast." July 2, 2014. http://www.bbc.com/news/world-asia-china-28123267.

Bellér-Hann, Ildikó. 1998. "Work and Gender among Uighur Villagers in Southern Xinjiang." *Cahiers d'études sur la Méditerranée orientale et le monde turco-iranien* 25: 93–114.

Bellér-Hann, Ildikó. 2002. "Temperamental Neighbours: Uighur-Han Relations in Xinjiang, Northwest China." In *Imagined Differences: Hatred and the Construction of Identity*, edited by Günther Schlee, 57–81. Hamburg: LIT Verlag.

Bellér-Hann, Ildikó. 2007. "Situating Uyghur Life Cycle Rituals between China and Central Asia." In *Situating the Uyghurs between China and Central Asia*, edited by Ildikó Bellér-Hann, M. Cristina Cesàro, Rachel Harris, and Joanne Smith Finley, 131–48. Aldershot, UK: Ashgate.

Bellér-Hann, Ildikó. 2008. *Community Matters in Xinjiang: Towards a Historical Anthropology of the Uyghur*. Leiden: Brill.

Benson, Linda. 2004. "Education and Social Mobility among Minority Populations in Xinjiang." In Starr, *Xinjiang*, 190–215.

Bernard, H. Russell. 2006. *Research Methods in Anthropology: Qualitative and Quantitative Approaches*. Lanham and New York: Altamira Press.

Blanchard, Ben. 2017. "Syria Says up to 5,000 Chinese Uighurs Fighting in Militant Groups." Reuters, May 11, 2017. https://www.reuters.com/article/uk-mideast-crisis-syria-china/syria-says-up-to-5000-chinese-uighurs-fighting-in-militant-groups-idUSKBN1840UP.

Blum, Susan. 2001. *Portraits of "Primitives": Ordering Human Kinds in the Chinese Nation*. Oxford: Rowman & Littlefield.

Borchigud, Wurlig. 1995. "The Impact of Urban Ethnic Education on Modern Mongolian Ethnicity, 1949–1966." In *Cultural Encounters on China's Ethnic Frontiers*, edited by Stevan Harrell, 278–300. Seattle: University of Washington Press.

Bourdieu, Pierre. 1977. *Outline of a Theory of Practice*. Cambridge: Cambridge University Press.

Bourdieu, Pierre. 1989. "Social Space and Symbolic Power." *Sociological Theory* 7, no. 1: 14–25.

References

Bourdieu, Pierre. 1999. "Identity and Representation: Elements for a Critical Reflection on the Idea of Region." In *Language and Symbolic Power*, edited by John B. Thompson, 220–88. Cambridge, MA: Harvard University Press.

Bourdieu, Pierre. 2001. *Acts of Resistance*. Cambridge: Policy Press.

Bovingdon, Gardner. 1998. "From Qumulluq to Uyghur: The Role of Education in the Development of a Pan-Uyghur Identity." *Journal of Central Asian Studies* 3, no. 1: 19–29.

Bovingdon, Gardner. 2002. "The Not-So-Silent Majority: Uyghur Resistance to Han Rule in Xinjiang." *Modern China* 28, no. 1: 39–78.

Bovingdon, Gardner. 2004. *Autonomy in Xinjiang: Han Nationalist Imperatives and Uyghur Discontent*. Washington, DC: East-West Center.

Bovingdon, Gardner. 2010. *The Uyghurs: Strangers in their Own Land*. New York: Columbia University Press.

Bovingdon, Gardner, and Nabijan Tursun. 2004. "Contested Histories." In Starr, *Xinjiang*, 353–74.

Bromley, Julian, and Viktor Kozlov. 1989. "The Theory of Ethnos and Ethnic Processes in Soviet Social Science." *Comparative Studies in Society and History* 31, no. 3: 425–38.

Brophy, David. 2005. "Taranchis, Kashgaris, and the 'Uyghur Question' in Soviet Central Asia." *Inner Asia* 7(2): 163–84.

Brophy, David. 2015. "Little Apples in Xinjiang." *The China Story*. Accessed February 16, 2015. https://www.thechinastory.org/2015/02/little-apples-in-xinjiang.

Brophy, David. 2016. *Uyghur Nation: Reform and Revolution on the Russia-China Frontier*. Cambridge, MA: Harvard University Press.

Brubaker, Rogers. 1996. *Nationalism Reframed: Nationhood and the National Question in the New Europe*. Cambridge: Cambridge University Press.

Brubaker, Rogers. 2002. "Ethnicity without Groups." *Archives européennes de sociologie* 43, no. 2: 163–89.

Brubaker, Rogers, and Frederick Cooper. 2000. "Beyond 'Identity.'" *Theory and Society* 29, no. 1: 1–47.

Bucar, Elizabeth. 2012. *The Islamic Veil*. Oxford: One World.

Burawoy, Michael. 2003. "Revisits: An Outline of a Theory of Reflexive Ethnography." *American Sociological Review* 68 (October): 645–79.

Butler, Judith. 1990. *Gender Trouble: Feminism and the Subversion of Identity*. New York: Routledge.

Byler, Darren. 2017. "Imagining Re-engineered Muslims in Northwest China." *Milestone: Commentary on the Islamic World*. Accessed July 9, 2018. https://www.milestonesjournal.net/photo-essays/2017/4/20/imagining-re-engineered-muslims-in-northwest-china.

Caprioni, Elena. 2008. "A Look Inside the Heterogeneous World of Women in Northwestern China." *International Journal of Interdisciplinary Social Sciences* 3, no. 2: 149–60.

Caprioni, Elena. 2011. "Daily Encounters between Hans and Uyghurs in Xinjiang: Sinicization, Integration or Segregation?" *Pacific Affairs* 84, no. 2: 267–87.

Carvajal López, José. 2013. "Islamicisation or islamicisations? Islamic Expansion and Social Practice in the Vega of Granada (south east Spain)." *World Archaeology* 45, no. 1: 57–70.

Cassarino, Jean-Pierre. 2004. "Theorising Return Migration: The Conceptual Approach to Return Migrants Revisited." *International Journal on Multicultural Studies* 6, no. 2: 253–79.

CASTED [China Academy of Science and Technology for Development]. 2006. Xibu renmin de shenghuo [Life in Western China]. Beijing: China Statistical Press.
CECC [Congressional-Executive Commission on China]. 2009a. "Recruitment for State Jobs in Xinjiang Discriminates Against Ethnic Minorities." Last modified July 2, 2009. Accessed July 5, 2011. http://www.cecc.gov/publications/commission-analysis/recruitment-for-state-jobs-in-xinjiang-discriminates-against-ethnic.
CECC. 2009b. "Authorities Begin New Initiative to Continue Population Control in Xinjiang." Last modified December 11, 2009. Accessed June 1, 2013. https://www.cecc.gov/publications/commission-analysis/authorities-begin-new-incentive-initiative-to-continue-population.
CECC. 2010. "Discriminatory Job Hiring Practices Continue in Xinjiang." Last modified October 20, 2010. Accessed August 27, 2013. http://www.cecc.gov/publications/commission-analysis/discriminatory-job-hiring-practices-continue-in-xinjiang.
Central People's Government of the People's Republic of China. 1982. Zhonghua renmin gongheguo xianfa [Constitution of the People's Republic of China]. Accessed July 27, 2017. http://www.gov.cn/gongbao/content/2004/content_62714.htm.
Central People's Government of the People's Republic of China. 1984. *Zhongguo de minzu quyu zizhi zhidu* [China's system of regional ethnic autonomy]. Accessed July 27, 2017. http://www.gov.cn/test/2012-06/20/content_2165897_2.htm.
Cesàro, M. Christina. 2000. "Consuming Identities and Resistance among Uyghur in Contemporary Xinjiang." *Inner Asia* 2, no. 2: 225–38.
Cheboksarov, Nikolai. 1970. "Problems of the Typology of Ethnic Units in the Works of Soviet Scholars." *Soviet Anthropology and Archeology* 9, no. 2: 127–53.
Chen, Yangbin. 2008. *Muslim Uyghur Students in a Chinese Boarding School: Social Recapitalization as a Response to Ethnic Integration*. Lanham: Lexington Books.
Chen, Yangbin. 2014. "Towards Another Minority Educational Elite Group in Xinjiang?" In *Multicultural Education in China: Integration, Adaptation, and Resistance*, edited by James Leibold and Chen Yangbin, 198–215. Hong Kong: Hong Kong University Press, 2014.
Chen, Yangbin, and Gerard Postiglione. 2009. "Muslim Uyghur Students in a Dislocated Chinese Boarding School: Bonding Social Capital as a Response to Ethnic Integration." *Race/Ethnicity: Multidisciplinary Global Contexts* 2, no. 2: 287–309.
Cheng, Tiejun, and Mark Selden. 1994. "The Origins and Social Consequences of China's Hukou System." *China Quarterly* 139 (September): 644–68.
Child, Brenda. 2000. *Boarding School Seasons: American Indian Families, 1900–1940*. Lincoln: University of Nebraska Press.
China Daily. 2017. "Xinjiang to Send 5,000 Bilingual Teachers to Kindergartens Each Year." September 9, 2017. http://www.chinadaily.com.cn/china/2017-09/09/content_31769862.htm.
China Education Newspaper. 2011. "Xinjiang neigao ban gaoxiao biyesheng zhaopinhui juxing" [A job fair is organized for Xinjiang Class graduates]. July 18, 2011. http://www.jyb.cn/job/jysx/201107/t20110718_443200.html.
China Education Newspaper. 2014. "Xi Jinping qiangdiao: ge minzu yao xiang shiliu zi nayang jinjin bao zai yiqi" [Xi Jinping stresses that all ethnic groups must bind together as if they are pomegranate seeds]. May 30, 2014. http://www.jyb.cn/china/gnxw/201405/t20140530_583657.html.

China National Radio. 2015. "Xinchun 'zao' songfu quanguo gedi 3000 Xinjiang gezu xuesheng ganen" [3000 multi-minzu Xinjiang Class students give thanks by sending dates across China this new year]. February 3, 2015. http://xj.cnr.cn/2014xjfw/2014xjfw tpx/20150203/t20150203_517629661.shtml.
China Radio International Online. 2005. "Sixiang zhengzhi jiaoyu shi neidi Xinjiang ban de shouyao renwu" [Ideological and political education is the most important task of the Xinjiang Class]. June 24, 2005. http://gb.cri.cn/3821/2005/06/24/1385@596748.htm.
China State Council. 2009. "White Paper on Development and Progress in Xinjiang." Last modified September 21, 2009. Accessed October 31, 2017. https://www.chinadaily.com.cn/ethnic/2009-09/21/content_8717461_5.htm.
China State Council. 2015. "White Paper, Historical Witness to Ethnic Equality, Unity and Development in Xinjiang." Last modified September 24, 2015. Accessed September 19, 2017. http://www.chinadaily.com.cn/china/60thxjannivesary/2015-09/24/content_21970065.htm.
Çinar, Alev. 2008. "Subversion and Subjugation in the Public Sphere: Secularism and the Islamic Headscarf." *Signs: Journal of Women in Culture and Society* 33, no. 4: 891–913.
Clarke, Michael. 2007. "The Problematic Progress of "Integration' in the Chinese State's Approach to Xinjiang, 1759–2005." *Asian Ethnicity* 8, no. 3: 261–89.
Cliff, Thomas. 2016. "Lucrative Chaos: Inter-ethnic Conflict as a Function of the Economic 'Normalisation' of Southern Xinjiang." In *Ethnic Conflict and Protest in Tibet and Xinjiang*, edited by Ben Hillman and Gray Tuttle, 122–50. New York: Columbia University Press.
Clothey, Rebecca, and Emmanuel Koku. 2017. "Oppositional Consciousness, Cultural Preservation, and Everyday Resistance on the Uyghur Internet." *Asian Ethnicity* 18, no. 3: 351–70.
Cohen, Anthony. 1985. *The Symbolic Construction of Community*. London: Routledge.
Colmant, Stephen, Lahoma Schultz, Rockey Robbins, Peter Ciali, Julie Dorton, and Yvette Rivera-Colmant. 2004. "Constructing Meaning to the Indian Boarding School Experience." *Journal of American Indian Education* 43, no. 3: 22–40.
Communist Youth League Central Committee. 2009. *Minzu tuanjie jiaoyu: qingnian duben* [Minzu unity: A youth reader]. Beijing: Zhongguo qingnian chubanshe.
Connor, Walker. 1973. "The Politics of Ethnonationalism." *Journal of International Affairs* 27, 1, no. 1: 1–21.
Connor, Walker. 2004. "The Timelessness of Nations." *Nations and Nationalism* 10 (1/2): 35–47.
Constitution of the People's Republic of China. 1982. Adopted December 4, 1982. Accessed August 26, 2013. http://english.peopledaily.com.cn/constitution/constitution.html.
Côté, Isabelle. 2015. "The Enemies Within: Targeting Han Chinese and Hui Minorities in Xinjiang." *Asian Ethnicity* 16, no. 2: 136–51.
COX [Census Office of the Xinjiang Uyghur Autonomous Region]. 2002. *Xinjiang Weiwu'er zizhiqu 2000 nian renkou pucha ziliao* [The data of the 2000 Census of the Xinjiang Uyghur Autonomous Region]. Beijing: China Statistical Press.
Dautcher, Jay. 2000. "Reading Out-of-Print: Popular Culture and Protest on China's Western Frontier." In *China beyond the Headlines*, edited by Timothy Weston and Lionel Jensen, 273–94. Lanham, MD: Rowman and Littlefield.

Dautcher, Jay. 2004. "Public Health and Social Pathologies in Xinjiang." In Starr, *Xinjiang*, 276–98.
Dautcher, Jay. 2009. *Down a Narrow Road: Identity and Masculinity in a Uyghur Community in Xinjiang China*. Cambridge, MA: Harvard University Press.
de Bree, June, Tine Davids, and Hein de Haas. 2010. "Post-return Experiences and Transnational Belonging of Return Migrants: A Dutch-Moroccan Case Study." *Global Networks* 10, no. 4: 489–509.
Demick, Barbara. 2014. "China Releases Video of Tiananmen Square Attack." *Los Angeles Times*, June 24, 2014. http://beta.latimes.com/world/asia/la-fg-china-tiananmen-square-attack-video-20140624-story.html.
Deng Xiaoping. 1979. "Uphold the Four Cardinal Principles." Speech, March 30, 1979. Accessed July 28, 2017. *People's Daily*. http://en.people.cn/dengxp/vol2/text/b1290.html.
Denyer, Simon. 2015. "China Orders Muslim Shopkeepers to Sell Alcohol, Cigarettes, to 'Weaken' Islam." *Washington Post*, May 5, 2015. https://www.washingtonpost.com/news/worldviews/wp/2015/05/05/china-orders-muslim-shopkeepers-to-sell-alcohol-cigarettes-to-weaken-islam/.
Dillon, Michael. 2004. *Xinjiang: China's Muslim Far Northwest*. Durham East Asia Series. London: RoutledgeCurzon.
Dong Han. 2010. "Policing and Racialization of Rural Migrant Workers in Chinese Cities." *Ethnic and Racial Studies* 33, no. 4: 593–610.
DOS [Department of State]. 2004. *International Religious Freedom Report*. https://www.state.gov/j/drl/rls/irf/2004/35396.htm.
Dreyer, June. 1968. "China's Minority Nationalities in the Cultural Revolution." *China Quarterly* 35: 96–109.
Dreyer, June. 1976. *China's Forty Millions: Minority Nationalities and National Integration in the People's Republic of China*. Cambridge, MA: Harvard University Press.
Duara, Prasenjit. 1995. *Rescuing History from the Nation: Questions and Narratives of Modern China*. Chicago: The University of Chicago Press.
Dumont, Jean-Christophe, and Gilles Spielvogel. 2008. "Return Migration: A New Perspective." *Organization for Economic Co-operation and Development (OECD): International Migration Outlook—Annual Report 2008*. Paris: OECD. Accessed June 1, 2013. http://www.oecd.org/els/mig/43999382.pdf.
Dwyer, Arienne. 2005. *The Xinjiang Conflict: Uyghur Identity, Language Policy, and Political Discourse*. Washington, DC: East-West Center.
Economist. 2017a. "A Class Apart: China's Grim Rural Boarding Schools." April 12, 2017. https://www.economist.com/news/china/21720603-millions-children-countryside-attend-wretched-schools-far-home-chinas-grim-rural.
Economist. 2017b. "The Communist Party Is Redefining What It Means to Be Chinese." August 17, 2017. https://www.economist.com/news/china/21726748-and-glossing-over-its-own-history-mauling-chinese-culture-communist-party-redefining.
Edgar, Adrienne Lynn. 2004. *Tribal Nation: The Making of Soviet Turkmenistan*. Princeton and Oxford: Princeton University Press.
Elterish, Ablimit Baki. 2015. "The Construction of Uyghur Urban Youth Identity through Language." In *Language, Education, and Uyghur Identity in Urban Xinjiang*, edited by Joanne Smith Finley and Zang Xiaowei, 75–94. London and New York: Routledge.

Erie, Matthew. 2016. "In China, Fears of 'Creeping Sharia' Proliferate Online." *Tea Leaf Nation*. September 15, 2016. http://foreignpolicy.com/2016/09/15/in-china-fears-of-creeping-sharia-proliferate-online-muslims-islam-islamophobia.

Erkin, Adila. 2009. "Locally Modern, Globally Uyghur: Geography, Identity, and Consumer Culture in Contemporary Xinjiang." *Central Asian Survey* 28, no. 4: 417–28.

Fay, Gregory. 2013. "Uyghurs, Other Ethnic Groups Need Not Apply." Uyghur Human Rights Project Blog, August 7, 2013. http://weblog.uhrp.org/uyghurs-other-ethnic-groups-need-not-apply.

Fei Xiaotong. 1980. "Ethnic Classification in China." *Social Science in China* 1, no. 1: 94–107.

Fei Xiaotong. 2010. "Zhonghua minzu de duoyuan yiti geju" [The dualistic unified structure of the Zhonghua minzu]. In *Wenhua yu wenhua zijue* [Culture and cultural consciousness], edited by Fang Xing, 52–83. Beijing: Qunyan Press.

Fierman, William. 2009. "Identity, Symbolism, and the Politics of Language in Central Asia." *Europe-Asia Studies* 61, no. 7: 1207–28.

Fincher, Leta Hong. 2014. *Leftover Women: The Resurgence of Gender Inequality in China*. New York: Zed Books.

Forbes, Andrew. 1986. *Warlord and Muslims in Chinese Central Asia: A Political History of Republican Sinkiang 1911–1949*. Cambridge: Cambridge University Press.

Foreign Policy. 2018. "A Summer Vacation in China's Muslim Gulag." February 28, 2018. https://foreignpolicy.com/2018/02/28/a-summer-vacation-in-chinas-muslim-gulag.

Foster, George, Thayer Scudder, Elizabeth Colson, and Robert Kemper, eds. 1979. *Long-Term Field Research in Social Anthropology*. New York: Academic Press.

Foucault, Michel. 1984. *The Foucault Reader*. Edited by Paul Rainbow. New York: Pantheon Books.

Foucault, Michel. 1990. *The History of Sexuality: An Introduction*. Vol. 1. New York: Vintage.

Fuller, Graham, and Jonathan Lipman. 2004. "Islam in Xinjiang." In Starr, *Xinjiang*, 320–52.

Gaetano, Arianne. 2015. *Out to Work: Migration, Gender, and the Changing Lives of Rural Women in Contemporary China*. Honolulu: University of Hawai'i Press.

Geertz, Clifford. 1973. *The Interpretation of Cultures*. New York: Basic Books.

Gellner, Ernest. 1983. *Nations and Nationalism*. Ithaca, NY: Cornell University Press.

Gillette, Maris Boyd. 2000. *Between Mecca and Beijing: Modernization and Consumption Among Urban Chinese Muslims*. Stanford: Stanford University Press.

Gladney, Dru. 1990. "The Ethnogenesis of the Uighur." *Central Asian Survey* 9 1, no. 1: 1–28.

Gladney, Dru. 1991. *Muslim Chinese: Ethnic Nationalism in the People's Republic*. Cambridge, MA: Harvard University Press.

Gladney, Dru. 1994. "Representing Nationality in China: Refiguring Majority/Minority Identities." *The Journal of Asian Studies* 53, no. 1: 92–123.

Gladney, Dru. 1998. "Internal Colonialism and the Uyghur Nationality: Chinese Nationalism and Its Subaltern Subjects." *Cahiers d'études sur la Méditerranée orientale et le monde turco-iranien* 25: 47–63.

Gladney, Dru. 1999. "Making Muslims in China: Education, Islamicization and Representation." In *China's National Minority Education: Culture Schooling, and Development*, edited by Gerald A. Postiglione, 55–94. New York: Falmer Press.

Gladney, Dru. 2004. *Dislocating China: Muslims, Minorities, and Other Subaltern Subjects*. Chicago: University of Chicago Press.

Global Times. 2015a. "Xinjiang Official Calls for Fewer Births, Later Marriage in Rural South." January 23, 2015. Accessed October 23, 2017. http://www.globaltimes.cn/content/903539.shtml.

Global Times. 2015b. "Lanzhou lamian Chain Has Noodle Sector in a Tangle as Shops Expand." August 8, 2015. http://www.globaltimes.cn/content/938211.shtml.

Göle, Nilüfer. 1997. *The Forbidden Modern: Civilization and Veiling.* Ann Arbor: University of Michigan Press.

Goldstein, Melvyn, and Matthew Kapstein. 1998. *Buddhism in Contemporary Tibet: Religious Revival and Cultural Identity.* Berkeley: University of California Press.

Grose, Timothy. 2010. "The Xinjiang Class: Education, Integration, and the Uyghurs." *The Journal of Muslim Minority Affairs* 30, no. 1: 97–108.

Grose, Timothy. 2012. "Uyghur Language Textbooks: Competing Images of a Multi-ethnic China." *Asian Studies Review* 36, no. 3: 369–89.

Grose, Timothy. 2014. "Uyghurs and Ramadan: Challenging the *Minkaomin/Minkaohan* Labels." In *Multicultural Education in China: Integration, Adaptation, and Resistance,* edited by James Leibold and Chen Yangbin, 216–34. Hong Kong: Hong Kong University Press.

Grose, Timothy. 2015a. "Escaping 'Inseparability': How Uyghur Graduates of the 'Xinjiang Class' Contest Membership in the *Zhonghua Minzu*." In *Language, Education, and Uyghur Identity in Urban Xinjiang,* edited by Joanne Smith Finley and Zang Xiaowei, 157–75. New York: Routledge.

Grose, Timothy. 2015b. "(Re)Embracing Islam in *Neidi*: the 'Xinjiang Class' and the Dynamics of Uyghur Ethno-national Identity." *Journal of Contemporary China* 24, no. 91: 101–18.

Grose, Timothy. 2016a. "Protested Homecomings: Xinjiang Class Graduates and Reacclimating to Life in Xinjiang." In *Inside Xinjiang: Space, Place and Power in China's Muslim Far Northwest,* edited by Anna Hayes and Michael Clarke, 206–24. New York: Routledge.

Grose, Timothy. 2016b. "Reluctant to Serve Their Hometowns and Country: Xinjiang Class Graduates and Teaching in Xinjiang's 'Bilingual' Schools." In *Educational Development in Western China: Towards Quality and Equity,* edited by John Chi-Kin Lee, Zeyuan Yu, and Xianhan Huang, 163–76. Rotterdam, Boston, and Taipei: Sense.

Guanchazhe [Observer]. 2014. "Xinjiang jin dangyuan he gongzhi renyuan canjia zhaiyue deng zongjiao huodong [Xinjiang bans party members and civil servants from participating in Ramadan and other religious activities.] July 3, 2004. http://www.guancha.cn/politics/2014_07_03_243479.shtml.

Hale, Henry. 2004. "Explaining Ethnicity." *Comparative Political Studies* 37, no. 4: 458–85.

Hamut, Barargül, and Agnieszka Joniath-Lüthi. 2015. "The Language Choices and Script Debates among the Uyghur in Xinjiang Uyghur Autonomous Region, China." *Linguistik Online* 70, no. 1: 111–24. doi: 10.13092/lo.70.1745.

Han, Enze. 2010. "Boundaries, Discrimination, and Interethnic Conflict in Xinjiang, China." *International Journal of Conflict and Violence* 4, no. 2: 244–56.

Hansen, Mette Halskov. 1999. *Lessons in Being Chinese: Minority Education and Ethnic Identity in Southwest China.* Seattle: University of Washington Press.

Hansen, Mette Halskov. 2005. *Frontier People: Han Settlers in Minority Areas of China.* Vancouver and Toronto: The University of British Columbia Press.

Harrell, Stevan. 1995. "Introduction: Civilizing Projects and the Reactions to Them." In *Cultural Encounters on China's Ethnic Frontiers*, edited by Stevan Harrell, 3–36. Seattle: University of Washington Press.
Harrell, Stevan. 2001. *Ways of Being Ethnic in Southwest China*. Seattle: University of Washington Press.
Harris, Rachel. 2001. "Cassettes, Bazaars, and Saving the Nation: The Uyghur Music Industry in Xinjiang China." In *Global Goes Local: Popular Culture in Asia*, edited by Timothy Craig and Richard King, 265–83. Vancouver: University of British Columbia Press.
Harris, Rachel. 2005. "Wang Luobin: Folk Song King of the Northwest or Song Thief. Copyright, Representation, and Chinese Folk Songs." *Modern China* 31, no. 3: 381–408.
Harris, Rachel. 2008. *The Making of a Musical Canon in Chinese Central Asia: The Uyghur Twelve Muqam*. Farnham, UK: Ashgate Press.
Harris, Rachel. 2012. "Tracks: Temporal Shifts and Transnational Networks of Sentiment in Uyghur Song." *Ethnomusicology* 56, no. 3: 450–75.
Harris, Rachel, and Rahile Dawut. 2002. "Mazar Festivals of the Uyghurs: Music, Islam and the Chinese State." *British Journal of Ethnomusicology* 11, no. 1: 101–18.
Hasmath, Reza. 2011. "The Education of Ethnic Minorities in Beijing." *Ethnic and Racial Studies* 34, no. 11: 1835–54.
Hayes, Anna. 2016. "Space, Place, and Ethnic Identity in the Xinjiang Regional Museum." In *Inside Xinjiang: Space, Place, and Power in China's Muslim Far Northwest*, edited by Anna Hayes and Michael Clarke, 52–72. New York: Routledge.
Hillman, Ben. 2004. "The Rise of the Community in Rural China: Village Politics, Cultural Identity and Religious Revival in a Hui Hamlet." *China Journal* 51 (January): 53–73.
Hillman, Ben, and Lee-Anne Henfry. 2006. "Macho Minority: Masculinity and Ethnicity on the Edge of Tibet." *Modern China* 32, no. 2: 251–72.
Hillman, Ben, and Gray Tuttle, eds. 2016. *Ethnic Conflict and Protest in Tibet and Xinjiang: Unrest in China's West*. New York: Columbia University Press.
Hirsch, Francine. 2005. *Empire of Nations: Ethnographic Knowledge and the Making of the Soviet Union*. Ithaca and London: Cornell University Press.
Hobsbawm, Eric. 1983. "Mass-Producing Traditions: Europe, 1870–1914." In *The Invention of Tradition*, edited by Eric Hobsbawm and Terence Ranger, 263–308. Cambridge: Cambridge University Press.
Hobsbawm, Eric. 1990. *Nations and Nationalism since 1780: Programme, Myth, Reality*. Cambridge: Cambridge University Press.
Horowitz, Donald. 1981. "Patterns of Ethnic Separatism." *Comparative Studies in Society and History* 23, no. 2: 165–95.
Howell, Anthony, and C. Cindy Fan. 2011. "Migration and Inequality in Xinjiang: A Survey of Han and Uyghur Migrants in Urumqi." *Eurasian Geography and Economics* 52, no. 1: 119–39.
Hoy, Caroline, and Ren Qiang. 2003. "Socioeconomic Impacts of Uyghur movement to Beijing." In *China's Minorities on the Move: Selected Case Studies*, edited by Robyn Iredale, Naran Bilik, and Fei Guo, 155–74. Armonk and London: M. E. Sharpe.
Huang, Cindy. 2009. "Faith and Ethics in the Time of Postcommunism." *Soundings: An Interdisciplinary Journal* 92, no. 1/2: 77–98.
Hughes, Aaron. 2013. *Muslim Identities: An Introduction to Islam*. New York: Columbia University Press.

Human Rights Watch. 2005. "Devastating Blows: Religious Repression of Uighurs in Xinjiang." *Human Rights in China Special Report*, 17, no. 2: 1–115.
Huq, Maimuna. 2008. "Reading the Qur'an in Bangladesh: The Politics of 'Belief' Among Islamist Women." *Modern Asian Studies* 42, no. 2/3: 457–88.
Hyer, Eric. 2016. "China's Policy towards Uighur Nationalism." *Journal of Muslim Minority Affairs* 26, no. 1: 75–86.
Iredale, Robyn, Naran Bilik, and Fei Guo, eds. 2003. *China's Minorities on the Move: Selected Case Studies*. New York: M. E. Sharpe.
Iredale, Robyn, Naran Bilik, and Wang Su. 2001. *Contemporary Minority Migration, Education and Ethnicity in China*. Cheltenham, UK: Elgar.
Isma'il, Ekber. 2013. "Ichkiri Shinjang toluq ottura siniplirigha oqughuchi qobul qilish ongushluq boluwatidu" [The enrollment procedures for the Xinjiang Class are moving along smoothly]. Tianshan Net, August 8, 2013. http://uy.ts.cn/news/content/2013-08/05/content_296025.htm.
Jacka, Tamara. 2009. "Cultivating Citizens: *Suzhi* (Quality) Discourse in the PRC." *Positions: East Asia Cultures Critique* 17, no. 3: 523–35.
Jacobs, Andrew. 2014. "A Devotion to Language Proves Risky." *New York Times*, May 11, 2014. https://www.nytimes.com/2014/05/12/world/asia/a-devotion-to-language-proves-risky.html.
Jacobs, Justin. 2016. *Xinjiang and the Modern Chinese State*. Seattle: University of Washington Press.
Jacobs, Margaret. 2006. "Indian Boarding Schools in Comparative Perspective: The Removal of Indigenous Children in the United States and Australia, 1880–1940." In *Boarding School Blues: Revisiting American Indian Educational Experiences*, edited by Clifford Trafzer and Jean Keller, 202–31. Lincoln and London: University of Nebraska Press.
Jaschok, Maria, and Jingjun Shui. 2000. *The History of Women's Mosques in Chinese Islam*. Richmond, UK: Curzon Press.
Jiangsu Ethnic Religions. 2011. "Tachengshi tianjiabing zhongxue zuzhi Xinjiang ban shisheng qingming jie jisao geming lieshi mu" [Tacheng's Tianjiabing Middle School organizes Qing Ming activity for teachers and students of the Xinjiang Class to sweep the tombs of revolutionary martyrs]. Accessed November 19, 2012. http://www.jsmzzj.gov.cn/art/2011/4/6/art_14_13273.html.
Joniak-Lüthi, Agnieszka. 2015. *The Han: China's Diverse Majority*. Seattle and London: Washington University Press.
Johansson, Perry. 1998. "White Skin, Large Breasts: Chinese Beauty Product Advertising as Cultural Discourse." *China Information* 13, no. 59: 59–84.
Kaltman, Blaine. 2007. *Under the Heel of the Dragon: Islam, Racism, Crime, and the Uighur in China*. Athens: Ohio University Press.
Kaup, Katharine. 2000. *Creating the Zhuang: Ethnic Politics in China*. Boulder, CO: Lynne Rienner.
Kentish, Ben. 2017. "Chinese Official Demoted 'for Refusing to Smoke in front of Religious Figures in Muslim Province." *Independent*. April 11, 2017. http://www.independent.co.uk/news/world/asia/chinese-communist-party-official-demoted-smoking-xinjiang-province-uyghur-minority-group-a7678896.html.
Keyes, Charles. 1976. "Towards a New Formulation of the Concept of Ethnic Groups." *Ethnicity* 3: 202–13.

References

Khalid, Adeeb. 2007. *Islam after Communism: Religion and Politics in Central Asia*. Berkeley: University of California Press.

Kim, Hodong. 2004. *Holy War in China: The Muslim Rebellion and State in Chinese Central Asia, 1864–1867*. Stanford: Stanford University Press.

Klimeš, Ondřej. 2015. *Struggle by the Pen: The Uyghur Discourse of Nation and National Interest, c. 1900–1940*. Leiden and Boston: Brill.

Klimeš, Ondřej. 2018. "Advancing 'Ethnic Unity' and 'De-extremization': Ideational Governance in Xinjiang under 'New Circumstances' (2012–2017). *Journal of Chinese Political Science* 23, no. 3: 413–36. doi:10.1007/s11366-018-9537-8.

Kirkwood, Michael. 1991. "'Glasnost', 'the National Question' and Soviet Language Policy." *Soviet Studies* 43, no. 1: 61–81.

Kormondy, Edward. 2002. "Minority Education in Inner Mongolia and Tibet." *Internationale Zeitschrift für Erziehungswissenschaft* 48, no. 5: 377–401.

Kuşçu Bonnenfant, Işık. 2018. "Constructing the Uyghur Diaspora: Identity Politics and the Transnational Uyghur Community." In *The Uyghur Community: Diaspora, Identity, and Geopolitics*, edited by Güljanat Kurmangaliyeva Ercilasun and Konuralp Ercilasun, 85–103. New York: Palgrave Macmillan.

Laitin, David. 1996. "Language Planning in the Former Soviet Union: The Case of Estonia." *International Journal of the Sociology of Language* 118: 43–62.

Lamothe, Dan. 2018. "Bombing of Chinese Separatists in Afghanistan Is a Sign of How Trump's War There Has Changed." *Washington Post*, February 10, 2018. https://www.washingtonpost.com/news/checkpoint/wp/2018/02/10/bombing-of-chinese-separatists-in-afghanistan-is-a-sign-of-how-trumps-war-there-has-changed.

Law of the People's Republic of China on Regional National Autonomy. 1984. Adopted May 31, 1984. Accessed August 26, 2013. http://www.china.org.cn/english/government/207138.htm.

Lee, Raymond. 2014. "Unrest in Xinjiang, Uyghur Province [sic] in China." Al Jazeera, February 20, 2014. http://studies.aljazeera.net/en/reports/2014/02/201421281846110687.html.

Leibold, James. 2006. "Comparative Narratives of Racial Unity in Republican China: From Yellow Emperor to Peking Man." *Modern China* 32, no. 2: 181–220.

Leibold, James. 2007. *Reconfiguring the Chinese Nation: How the Qing Frontier and Its Indigenes Became Chinese*. New York: Palgrave Macmillan.

Leibold, James. 2010. "More Than a Category: Han Racial Nationalism on the Chinese Internet." *China Quarterly* 203: 539–59.

Leibold, James. 2013. *Ethnic Policy in China: Is Reform Inevitable?* Policy Studies 68. Washington: East-West Center.

Leibold, James. 2014a. "Han Chinese Reactions to Preferential Minority Education in the PRC." In *Multicultural Education in China: Integration, Adaptation, and Resistance*, edited by James Leibold and Chen Yangbin, 299–319. Hong Kong: Hong Kong University Press.

Leibold, James. 2014b. "Xinjiang Work Forum Marks New Policy of 'Ethnic Mingling.'" *China Brief* 14, no. 12. http://www.jamestown.org/programs/chinabrief/single/?tx_ttnews%5btt_news%5d=42518&#.V4ShbKL4ZBK.

Leibold, James. 2015. "Carrot and Stick Tactics Fail to Calm China's Ethnic Antagonism." *East Asia Forum*. Accessed April 28, 2015. http://www.eastasiaforum.org/2015/04/28/carrot-and-stick-tactics-fail-to-calm-chinas-ethnic-antagonism.

Leibold, James. 2016a. "China's Minority Report: When Racial Harmony Means Homogenization." *Foreign Policy*, March 23, 2016. Accessed March 24, 2016. https://www.foreignaffairs.com/articles/china/2016-03-23/chinas-minority-report.

Leibold, James. 2016b. "Interethnic Conflict in the PRC: Xinjiang and Tibet as Exceptions?" In *Ethnic Conflict and Protest in Tibet and Xinjiang: Unrest in China's West*, edited by Ben Hillman and Gray Tuttle, 223–50. New York: Columbia University Press.

Leibold, James, and Chen Yangbin. 2014. "Introduction." In *Minority Education in China: Balancing Unity and Diversity in an Era of Critical Pluralism*, edited by James Leibold and Chen Yangbin, 1–24. Hong Kong: Hong Kong University Press.

Leibold, James, and Timothy Grose. 2016. "Islamic Veiling in Xinjiang: The Political and Societal Struggle to Define Uyghur Female Adornment." *China Journal* 76 (July): 78–102.

Leibold, James, and Timothy Grose. 2019. "Inculcating Chineseness: Cultural and Political Disciplining inside China's Dislocated Minority Schooling System." *Asian Studies Review*, DOI: 10.1080/10357823.2018.1548571.

Li, Xiaoxia. 2005. "Regional Ethnic Autonomy." In *Xinjiang of China: Its Past and Present*, edited by Li Sheng, 175–204. Ürümchi: Xinjiang People's Publishing House.

Lim, Louisa. 2013. "For Chinese Women, Marriage Depends on Right 'Bride Price.'" NPR, April 23, 2013. http://www.npr.org/2013/04/23/176326713/for-chinese-women-marriage-depends-on-right-bride-price.

Lings, Martin. 1983. *Muhammad: His Life Based on the Earliest Sources*. London: Islamic Texts Society.

Litzinger, Ralph A. 2000. *Other Chinas: The Yao and the Politics of National Belonging*. Durham and London: Duke University Press.

Liu Caiyu. 2017. "Revised Regulation Emphasizes Religious Freedom, Interests of Groups." *Global Times*, September 7, 2017. http://www.globaltimes.cn/content/1065390.shtml.

Liu Xiaochun. 2014. "Jiyu renkou pucha de zhongguo musilin renkou tezheng fenxi" [Traits of the Muslims of China based on census data analysis]. *Journal of Hui Muslim Studies* 93, no. 1: 70–76.

Liu Yong. 2010. "An Economic Band-Aid: Beijing's New Approach to Xinjiang." *China Security* 6, no. 2: 27–40.

Lomawaima, K. Tsianina. 1994. *They Called It Prairie Light: The Story of Chilocco Indian School*. Lincoln: University of Nebraska Press.

Lovell, Nadia. 1998. "Introduction." In *Locality and Belonging*, edited by Nadia Lovell, 1–24. New York: Routledge.

Luo Jihua. 2010. "Multicultural Education and the Acculturation of Students in the Interior-Region Xinjiang Senior Middle School Classes." *Chinese Education and Society* 43, no. 3: 22–34.

Luo, Wei, and Zhen Sun. 2015. "Are You the One? China's TV Dating Shows and the Sheng Nü Predicament." *Feminist Media Studies* 15, no. 2: 239–56.

Ma Rong. 2008. *Ethnic Relations in China*. Beijing: China Tibetology Press.

Ma Rong. 2009. "The Development of Minority Education and the Practice of Bilingual Education in [sic] Xinjiang Uyghur Autonomous Region." *Frontiers of Education in China* 4, no. 2: 188–251.

Ma Rong. 2010. "The 'Politicization' and 'Culturalization' of Ethnic Groups." *Chinese Sociology & Anthropology* 42, no. 4: 31–45.

Ma Rong. 2011. "Income Gaps in Economic Development: Differences among Regions, Occupational Groups, and Ethnic Groups." *ProtoSociology* 28: 101–29.

Ma Rong. 2012. *Zuqun, Minzu yu Guojia Goujian* [Ethnic groups, minzu, and nation building]. Beijing: Shehui kexue wenxian chubanshe.

Ma Yunfu. 2008. "Xin Zhongguo chengli hou Zhongguo Musilin chaojin shiji [A record of the Chinese hajj after the founding of New China]. *Zhongguo Huizu Xue* [Hui Nationality Studies] 3: 3–18.

Macaulay, Thomas B. 1835. "Minute on Education." Accessed October 11, 2017. http://www.columbia.edu/itc/mealac/pritchett/00generallinks/macaulay/txt_minute_education_1835.html.

Mackerras, Colin. 1994. *China's Minorities: Integration and Modernization in the Twentieth Century*. Oxford: Oxford University Press.

Mackerras, Colin. 2001. "Xinjiang at the Turn of the Century: The Causes of Separatism." *Central Asian Survey* 20, no. 3: 289–303.

Martines, Jamie. 2016. "Despite Policy Reform, Barriers to Obtaining Hukou Persist." *Diplomat*, February 27, 2016. http://thediplomat.com/2016/02/despite-policy-reforms-barriers-to-obtaining-hukou-persist.

Maurer-Fazio, Margaret, James Hughes, and Dandan Zhang. 2007. "An Ocean Formed from One Hundred Rivers: The Effects of Ethnicity, Gender, Marriage, and Location, on Labor Force Participation in China." *Feminist Economics* 13 (3–4): 159–87.

McBeth, Sally. 1983. "Indian Boarding Schools and Ethnic Identity: An Example from the Southern Plains Tribes of Oklahoma." *Plains Anthropologist* 28, no. 100: 119–28.

McCarthy, Susan. 2009. *Communist Multiculturalism: Ethnic Revival in Southwest China*. Seattle: University of Washington Press.

McKenzie, David. 2014. "Is China's Grand Ethnic Experiment Working?" CNN, November 2, 2014. http://www.cnn.com/2014/11/02/world/asia/china-ethnic-experiment.

McMillen, Donald. 1979. *Chinese Communist Power and Policy in Xinjiang, 1949–1977*. Boulder, CO: Westview Press.

Melucci, Alberto. 1995. "The Process of Collective Identity." In *Social Movements and Culture*, edited by Hank Johnston and Bert Klandermans, 41–63. Minneapolis: University of Minnesota Press.

Millward, James. 2004. *Violent Separatism in Xinjiang: A Critical Assessment*. Washington, DC: East West Center.

Millward, James. 2007. *Eurasian Crossroads: A History of Xinjiang*. New York: Columbia University Press.

Millward, James. 2009. "Introduction: Does the 2009 Urumchi Violence Mark a Turning Point?" *Central Asian Survey* 28, no. 4: 347–60.

Millward, James. 2014. "China's Fruitless Repression of the Uighurs." *New York Times*, September 28, 2014. Accessed October 1, 2014. https://www.nytimes.com/2014/09/29/opinion/chinas-fruitless-repression-of-the-uighurs.html

Millward James, and Nabijan Tursun. 2004. "Political History and Strategies of Control, 1884–1978." In Starr, *Xinjiang*, 63–98.

Mishra, Manoj. 2017. "Rise of Ethnicity, Islam, and Nationalism in Central Asia." *Peaceworks* 7, no. 1: 38–62.

Montag, Warren. 1995. "'The Soul Is the Prison of the Body': Althusser and Foucault, 1970–1975." *Yale French Studies* 88: 53–77.

Mullaney, Thomas. 2011. *Coming to Terms with the Nation: Ethnic Classification in Modern China*. Berkeley, CA: University of California Press.

Murata, Sachiko, and William Chittick. 1994. *The Vision of Islam*. New York: Paragon House.

Nagel, Joane. 1994. "Constructing Ethnicity: Creating and Recreating Ethnic Identity and Culture." *Social Problems* 41, no. 1: 152–76.

Najafizadeh, Mehrangiz. 2012. "Gender and Ideology." *Journal of Third World Studies* 29, no. 1: 81–101.

Newby, Laura. 2007. "'Us and Them' in Eighteenth and Nineteenth Century Xinjiang." In *Situating the Uyghurs between China and Central Asia*, edited by Ildikó Bellér-Hann, Joanne Smith Finley, M. Cristina Cesàro, and Rachel Harris, 15–29. Farnham, UK: Ashgate.

New Oriental [*Xin Dongfang*]. 2015. "2015 nian neidi Xinjiang gaozhong ban luqu reshu [Enrollment figures for the 2015 Xinjiang Class]. August 10, 2015. http://bj.xdf.cn/publish/portal24/tab16573/info854022.htm.

NurMuhammad, Rizwangul, Heather Horst, Evangelia Papoutsaki, and Giles Dodson. 2016. "Uyghur Transnational Identity on Facebook: On the Development of a Young Diaspora." *Global Studies in Culture and Power* 23, no. 4: 485–99.

Oakes, Timothy. 1993. "The Cultural Space of Modernity: Ethnic Tourism and Place Identity in China." *Environment and Planning D: Society and Space* 11, no. 1: 47–66.

Oudengcaowa. 2014. "Tamen ruhe zai shehui shang zhaodao ziji de weizhi: neidi Xinjiang gaozhong ban biyesheng jiuye zhuangkuang diaochao" [How do they find their places in society? Investigation on high school graduates' employment situation of Inland Xinjiang Class]. *Qinghai Journal of Ethnology* 25, no. 2: 64–70.

Party Committee Organization Department of the Xinjiang Uyghur Autonomous Region. 2011. "Zizhiqu juban neigao ban gaoxiao biyesheng shoujie zhuanchang zhaopinhui" [The Autonomous Region holds first job fair for Xinjiang Class graduates]. July 27, 2011. Accessed October 25, 2012. http://www.xjkunlun.cn/zzgz/rcgz/2011/2155468.htm.

Pêcheux, Michel. 1982. *Language, Semantics and Ideology: Stating the Obvious*. London: Macmillan.

People's Daily Online. 2011. "Sun Qi: zai neidi 'baba,' 'mama' de guanai xia neidi Xinjiang gaozhong ban de xuesheng zhuozhuang chengzhang" [Sun Qi: Under the love and care of their neidi fathers and mothers, Xinjiang Class students thrive]. August 1, 2011. http://news.xinmin.cn/rollnews/2011/08/01/11587174.html.

People's Daily Online. 2014. "Xinjiang yuepuhu baohu zhishi chanquan jizhong xiaohui 'san fei' wupin" [Xinjiang's Yuepuhu protects intellectual property with its destruction of the "three-illegals"]. November 11, 2014. http://news.163.com/14/0111/23/9IBI3F1T00014JB6.html.

People's Daily Online. 2015. "Neidi Xinjiang gaozhong ban buzai kuozhao" [The Xinjiang Class will not expand enrollment]. June 20, 2015. http://edu.people.com.cn/n/2015/0620/c1053-27185485.html.

Pessar, Patricia. 1997. "Introduction: New Approaches to Caribbean Emigration and Return." In *Caribbean Circuits, New Directions in the Study of Caribbean Migration*, edited by Patrica Pessar, 1–12. New York: Center for Migration Studies.

Phoenix Weekly. 2014. "Xinjiang bu jinzhi jinze de jiaoshi" [The dutiful teachers of the Xinjiang Class]. November 11, 2014. http://news.ifeng.com/a/20141128/42589491_0.shtml.

Piao Shengyi. 1990. *Zhongguo shaoshu minzu jiaoyu fazhan yu zhanwang* [The development and prospectus of Chinese minority education]. Hohhot, Inner Mongolia: Neimenggu jiaoyu chubanshe.

Pierson, David. 2010. "China's Housing Boom Spells Trouble for Boyfriends." *Los Angeles Times*, June 21, 2010. http://articles.latimes.com/2010/jun/21/business/la-fi-china-bachelor-20100621.

Postiglione, Gerard. 2008. "Making Tibetans in China: The Educational Challenges of Harmonious Multiculturalism." *Education Review* 60, no. 1: 1–20.

Postiglione, Gerard. 2009. "Dislocated Education: The Case of Tibet." *Comparative Education Review* 53, no. 4: 483–512.

Postiglione, Gerard, and Ben Jiao. 2009. "Tibet's Relocated Schooling: Popularization Reconsidered." *Asian Survey* 49, no. 5: 895–914.

Powers, Liam. 2013. "Xinjiang: Reassessing the Recent Violence." *The Diplomat*, August 4, 2013. https://thediplomat.com/2013/08/xinjiang-reassessing-the-recent-violence/.

Powers, Liam. 2014a. "Beyond the Kunming attack." openDemocracy, March 18, 2014. https://www.opendemocracy.net/opensecurity/liam-powers/beyond-kunming-attack.

Powers, Liam. 2014b. "Kashgar's Redevelopment Is about More than Anti-Uyghur Sentiment." *Open Democracy*, March 28, 2014. https://www.opendemocracy.net/opensecurity/liam-powers/kashgars-redevelopment-is-about-more-than-antiuyghur-sentiment-0.

Radio Free Asia. n.d. "Xinjiang Unrest Timeline." http://www.rfa.org/english/multimedia/timeline/UyghurUnrest.html.

Radio Free Asia. 2007. "China Confiscates Muslims' Passports." June 27, 2007. http://www.rfa.org/english/uyghur/uyghur_passports-20070627.html.

Radio Free Asia. 2011. "Xitaydiki 'hinjang sinipliri' da oquwatqan ikki neper Uyghur oqughuchi namaz oqughanliqi üchün mektepin heydeleän" [Two Uyghurs students studying in China's "Xinjiang Class" have been expelled for praying]. July 11, 2011. http://www.rfa.org/uyghur/xewerler/qisqa_xewerler/shinjiang-sinipi-07112011160911.html.

Radio Free Asia. 2012. "Student Battles Travel Ban." December 20, 2012. http://www.rfa.org/english/news/uyghur/travel-12202012143138.html.

Radio Free Asia. 2017a. "China Extends Ban on 'Extreme' Uyghur Baby Names to Children under 16." June 1, 2017. http://www.rfa.org/english/news/uyghur/ban-06012017165249.html.

Radio Free Asia. 2017b. "Restaurants Ordered to Remain Open in Xinjiang amid Ramadan Fast." May 26, 2017. http://www.rfa.org/english/news/uyghur/ramadan-05262017080553.html.

Rajagopalan, Megha. 2017. "This Is What a 21st Century Police State Really Looks Like." BuzzFeed, October 17, 2017. https://www.buzzfeed.com/megharaj/the-police-state-of-the-future-is-already-here.

Rajagopalan, Megha. 2018. "Spy for US—or Never Speak to your Family Again." BuzzFeed, July 9, 2018. https://www.buzzfeednews.com/article/meghara/china-uighur-spies-surveillance.

Rajagopalan, Megha, and Joseph Campbell. 2015. "China Launches Campaign to Snuff Out Smoking in Beijing." Reuters, June 1, 2015. http://www.reuters.com/article/us-china-smoking/china-launches-campaign-to-snuff-out-smoking-in-beijing-idUSKBN0OH26M20150601.

Ramzy, Austin. 2009. "Why the Uighurs Feel Left Out of China's Boom." *Time*, July 14, 2009. http://www.time.com/time/world/article/0,8599,1910302,00.html.

Ramzy, Austin. 2010. "A Year after Xinjiang Riots, Ethnic Tensions Remain." *Time*, July 5, 2010. http://www.time.com/time/world/article/0,8599,2001311,00.html.

Raudvere, Catharina. 2002. *The Book and the Roses: Sufi Women, Visibility and Zikr in Contemporary Istanbul*. Sweden: I.B. Tauris.

Rehangu, Maimaiti. 2006. "Wushiyi tuan shixue ertong xiankuang diaochao baogao" [An investigative report on student drop-outs in Kashgar's 51st District]. Unpublished senior thesis, Minzu University of China.

Reuters. 2009. "Wushi 'qiwu' shijian chuli jinzhan: xingju 718 ren pibu 83 ren" [The handling of Ürümqi's 7-5 Incident is making progress: 718 people have been arrested; 83 have been detained]. August 5, 2009. http://cn.reuters.com/article/CNTopGenNews/idCNCHINA-249320090805.

Reuters. 2016. "China to Expand Bilingual Schooling in Xinjiang: Xinhua." May 6, 2016. http://www.reuters.com/article/us-china-xinjiang/china-to-expand-bilingual-schooling-in-xinjiang-xinhua-idUSKCN0XX1NT.

Richburg, Keith. 2010. "China 'Hukou' System Deemed Outdated as Way of Controlling Access to Services." *Washington Post*, August 15, 2010. http://www.washingtonpost.com/wp-dyn/content/article/2010/08/14/AR2010081402009.html.

Roberts, Sean. 2009. "Imagining Uyghurstan: Re-evaluating the Birth of the Modern Uyghur Nation." *Central Asian Survey* 28, no. 4: 361–81.

Ross, Heidi. 2000. "In the Moment – Discourse of Power, Narratives of Relationship: Framing Ethnography of Chinese Schooling, 1981–1997." In *The Ethnographic Eye: An Interpretative Study of Education in China*, edited by Judith Liu, Heidi A. Ross, and Donald P. Kelly, 123–52. New York and London: Falmer Press.

Royce, Anya. 1982. *Ethnic Identity: Strategies and Diversity*. Bloomington: Indiana University Press.

Rudelson, Justin Jon. 1997. *Oasis Identities: Uyghur Nationalism along China's Silk Road*. New York: Columbia University Press.

Rudelson, Justin, and William Jankowiak. 2004. "Acculturation and Resistance: Xinjiang Identities in Flux." In Starr, *Xinjiang*, 299–319.

Rywkin, Michael. 1990. *Moscow's Muslim Challenge: Soviet Central Asia*. Armonk, NY: M.E. Sharpe.

Saroyan, Mark. 1997. "Rethinking Islam in the Soviet Union." In *Minorities, Mullahs, and Modernity: Reshaping Community in the Former Soviet Union*, edited by Edward W. Walker, 8–42. Berkeley: University of California Press.

Sautman, Barry. 1998. "Preferential Policies for Ethnic Minorities in China: The Case of Xinjiang." *Nationalism and Ethnic Politics* 4 (1–2): 86–118.

References

Sautman, Barry. 1999. "Expanding Access to Higher Education for China's National Minorities: Policies of Preferential Admissions." In *China's National Minority Education: Culture Schooling, and Development*, edited by Gerald A. Postiglione, 173–210. New York: Falmer Press.

Sautman, Barry. 2005. "China's Strategic Vulnerability to Minority Separatism in Tibet." *Asian Affairs* 32, no. 2: 87–118.

Sawut, Pawan, Rahile Dawut, and Saadet Kurban. 2017. "Uyghur Meshrep Culture and Its Social Functions." *Fourth World Journal* 15, no. 2: 81–90.

SBX [State Statistical Bureau]. 2010. *Xinjiang tongji nianjian* [Xinjiang statistical yearbook]. Beijing: China Statistical Press.

Sewell, William. 1992. "A Theory of Structure: Duality, Agency, and Transformation." *American Journal of Sociology* 98, no. 1: 1–29.

Schein, Louisa. 1997. "Gender and Internal Orientalism in China." *Modern China*. 23, no. 1: 69–98.

Schein, Louisa. 2000. *Minority Rules: The Miao and the Feminine in China's Cultural Politics*. Durham, NC: Duke University Press.

Schluessel, Eric. 2007. "'Bilingual' Education and Discontent in Xinjiang." *Central Asian Survey* 26, no. 2: 251–77.

Schluessel, Eric. 2009. "History, Identity, and Mother-Tongue Education in Xinjiang." *Central Asian Survey* 28, no. 4: 383–402.

Schmitz, Rob. 2017. "Wary of Unrest Among Uighur Minority, China Locks Down Xinjiang Region." *NPR*, September 26, 2017. https://www.npr.org/sections/parallels/2017/09/26/553463964/wary-of-unrest-among-uighur-minority-china-locks-down-xinjiang-province.

Schwab, Wendell. 2012. "Traditions and Texts: How Two Young Women Learned to Interpret the Qur'an and Hadiths in Kazakhstan." *Contemporary Islam* 6, no. 2: 173–97.

Scott, James C. 1989. "Everyday Forms of Resistance." *Copenhagen Papers* 4: 33–62.

Scott, James C. 1990. *Domination and the Arts of Resistance: Hidden Transcripts*. New Haven, CT: Yale University Press.

Şenyürekli, Aysem, and Cecilia Menjívar. 2012. "Turkish Immigrants' Hopes and Fears around Return Migration." *International Migration* 50, no. 1: 3–19.

Shahrani, Nazif. 1984. "From Tribe to Umma': Comments on the Dynamics of Identity in Muslim Central Asia." *Central Asian Survey* 3, no. 3: 27–38.

Shanin, Theodor. 1989. "Ethnicity in the Soviet Union: Analytical Perceptions and Political Strategies." *Comparative Studies in Society and History* 31, no. 3: 409–24.

Shichor, Yitzhak. 2005. "Blow Up: Internal and External Challenge of Uyghur Separatism and Islamic Radicalism to Chinese Rule in Xinjiang." *Asian Affairs: An American Review* 32, no. 2: 119–35.

Sidiq, Mutellip. 2013. *Isim Quyush Qollanmisi* [A handbook for naming]. Kashgar: Kashgar Uyghur neshriyati.

Simayi, Zuliyati. 2014. "The Practice of Ethnic Policy in Education: Xinjiang's Bilingual Education System." In *Multicultural Education in China: Integration, Adaptation, and Resistance*, edited by James Leibold and Chen Yangbin, 131–60. Hong Kong: Hong Kong University Press.

Sina. 2015. "Migration to Jihad Exposed: University Student Forced to Take Part in Jihad in Afghanistan" [Jiemi qianxi shengzhan: gaokaosheng bei qiangpo dao Afugan shengzhan]. June 8, 2015. http://news.sina.com.cn/c/2015-06-08/081631925189.shtml [URL no longer active].

Slezkine, Yuri. 1994. "The USSR as a Communal Apartment, or How a Socialist State Promoted Ethnic Particularism." *Slavic Review* 53, no. 2: 414–52.

Slobodník, Martin. 2004. "Destruction and Revival: The Fate of the Tibetan Buddhist Monastery Labrang in the People's Republic of China." *Religion, State, & Society* 32, no. 1: 7–19.

Smith, Anthony. 1979. "Towards a Theory of Ethnic Separatism." *Ethnic and Racial Studies* 2, no. 1: 21–37.

Smith, Anthony. 1998. *Nationalism and Modernism*. New York: Routledge.

Smith, Jeremy. 1997. "The Education of National Minorities: The Early Soviet Experience." *The Slavonic and East European Review* 75, no. 2: 281–307.

Smith, Joanne. 2000. "Four Generations of Uyghurs: The Shift towards Ethno-political Ideologies among Xinjiang's Youth." *Inner Asia* 2, no. 2: 195–224.

Smith, Joanne. 2002. "'Making Culture Matter': Symbolic, Spatial and Social Boundaries between Uyghurs and Han Chinese." *Asian Ethnicity* 3, no. 2: 153–74.

Smith Finley, Joanne. 2006. "Maintaining Margins: The Politics of Ethnographic Fieldwork in Chinese Central Asia." *China Journal* 56: 131–47.

Smith Finley, Joanne. 2007a. "Chinese Oppression in Xinjiang, Middle Eastern Conflicts and Global Islamic Solidarities among the Uyghurs." *Journal of Contemporary China* 16, no. 53: 627–54.

Smith Finley, Joanne. 2007b. "'Ethnic Anomaly' or Modern Uyghur Survivor? A Case Study of the *Minkaohan* Hybrid Identity in Xinjiang." In *Situating the Uyghurs between China and Central Asia*, edited by Ildikó Beller-Hann, Joanne Smith Finley, M. Cristina Cesàro, and Rachel Harris, 219–38. Farnham, UK: Ashgate.

Smith Finley, Joanne. 2007c. "The Quest for National Unity in Uyghur Popular Song: Barren Chickens, Stray Dogs, Fake Immortals and Thieves." In *Music, National Identity and the Politics of Location: Between the Global and the Local*, edited by Ian Biddle and Vanessa Knights, 115–41. Aldershot, UK: Ashgate.

Smith Finley, Joanne. 2011. "No Rights without Duties. Minzu Pingdeng [Nationality Equality] in Xinjiang since the 1997 Ghulja Disturbances." *Inner Asia* 13, no. 1: 73–96.

Smith Finley, Joanne. 2013. *The Art of Symbolic Resistance: Uyghur Identities and Uyghur-Han Relations in Contemporary Xinjiang*. Leiden: Brill.

Smith Finley, Joanne. 2016. "Whose Xinjiang? Space, Place, and Power in the Rock Fusion of *Xin Xinjiang Ren*, Dao Lang." In *Inside Xinjiang: Space, Place, and Power in China's Muslim Far West*, edited by Anna Hayes and Michael Clarke, 75–99. London: Routledge.

Smith Finley, Joanne, and Zang Xiaowei, eds. 2015. *Language, Education, and Uyghur Identity in Urban Xinjiang*. London and New York: Routledge.

Song, Jesook. 2014. *Living on Your Own: Single Women, Rental Housing, and Post-revolutionary Affect in Contemporary South Korea*. Albany, NY: SUNY Press.

Starn, Orin. 2011. "Here Come the Anthros (Again): The Strange Marriage of Anthropology and Native Americans." *Cultural Anthropology* 26, no. 2: 179–204.

Starr, Frederick, ed. 2004. *Xinjiang: China's Muslim Borderland*. Studies of Central Asia and the Caucasus. New York: M. E. Sharpe.

SCCO [State Council Census Office]. 2002. *China 2000 Census Data*. Beijing: Statistical Press of China.

Sulayman, Äsäd. 2007. "Hybrid Name Culture in Xinjiang: Problems Surrounding Uyghur Name/Surname Practices and Their Reform." In *Situating the Uyghurs between China and Central Asia*, edited by Ildikó Beller-Hann, Joanne Smith Finley, M. Cristina Cesàro, and Rachel Harris, 109–30. Farnham, UK: Ashgate.

Szasz, Margaret. 2005. "'I Knew How to Be Moderate. And I Knew How to Obey': The Commonality of American Indian Boarding School Experiences, 1750s–1920s." *American Indian Culture and Research Journal* 29, no. 4: 75–94.

Tang, Wenfang, and Gaochao He. 2010. *Separate but Loyal: Ethnicity and Nationalism in China*. Honolulu: East-West Center.

Tang Yong, ed. 2011. *Milletler ittipaqliqi terbiyesi oqushluqi / minzu tuanjie jiaoyu duben* [Ethnic unity education: A reader]. Ürümchi: Xinjiang meishu sheying chubanshe.

Tao Jiaqing, and Yang Xiaohua. 2010. "Our Good Han Mothers." *Chinese Education and Society* 43, no. 3: 64–72.

Tapper, Nancy, and Richard Tapper. 1987. "The Birth of the Prophet: Ritual and Gender in Turkish Islam." *Man: Journal of the Royal Anthropological Institute* 22, no. 1: 69–92.

Taynen, Jennifer. 2006. "Interpreters, Arbiters, or Outsides: The Role of the Min Kao Han in Xinjiang Society." *Journal of Muslim Minority Affairs* 26, no. 1: 45–62.

Teo, Sin Yih. 2011. "'The Moon Back Home Is Brighter'? Return Migration and the Cultural Politics of Belonging." *Journal of Ethnic and Migration Studies* 37, no. 5: 805–20.

Thornham, Sue, and Pengpeng Feng. 2010. "'Just a Slogan': Individualism, Post-feminism, and Female Subjectivity in Consumerist China." *Feminist Media Studies* 10, no. 2: 195–211.

Thum, Rian. 2012. "Modular History: Identity Maintenance before Uyghur Nationalism." *The Journal of Asian Studies* 71, no. 3: 627–53.

Thum, Rian. 2014. *The Sacred Routes of Uyghur History*. Cambridge, MA and London: Harvard University Press.

Tianshan Net. 2005. "Xinjiang fangkuan neigaoban zhaosheng tijian biaozhun" [Xinjiang broadens the standards for the Xinjiang Class' mandatory physical examinations]. November 5, 2005. http://www.tianshannet.com.cn/GB/channel3/18/200505/25/158969.html.

Tianshan Net. 2007. "Neigaoban zhaosheng shoushe jiafen zhengce" [The Xinjiang Class institutes bonus point policy]. June 24, 2007. http://www.tianshannet.com.cn/news/content/2007-06/24/content_2013760.htm.

Tianshan Net. 2009. "Xinjiang: 98% de neidi ban biyesheng kaoshang daxue" [Xinjiang: 98% of all Xinjiang Class Graduates test into university]. August 11, 2009. http://www.ts.cn/news/content/2009-08/11/content_4387854.htm.

Tianshan Net. 2011. "Neidi Xinjiang gaozhong ban jiazhang daibiao dao ban xuexiao kanwang haizi" [Xinjiang Class parent representatives arrive at Xinjiang Class schools to visit the children]. October 21, 2011. http://www.ts.cn/news/content/2011-10/21/content_6264251.htm.

Tianshan Net. 2015a. "Ichki ölke-sheherlerdiki Shinjang toluq ottura sinipi oqughuchiliri chaghnni shadaliq we minnetdarliq ichide ötküzdi" [Xinjiang Class students in neidi celebrate new year's with joy and gratitude]. February 25, 2015. http://uy.ts.cn/news/content/2015-02/25/content_402725.htm.

Tianshan Net. 2015b. "Xinjiang neidi gaozhong ban kaoshi 2015 nian 6 yue 20 ri—22 ri jinxing" [The 2015 Xinjiang Class exam will be held from June 20 to June 22.] June 15, 2015. http://news.ts.cn/content/2015-06/15/content_11370124.htm.

Tianshan Net. 2015c. "Dianying 'Meng kaishi de difang' juxing meiti guanpian hui chuandi Xinjiang neigao ban zhengneng liang" [The Film *A Place Where the Dream Begins* holds film screening to transmit the positive energy of the Xinjiang Class]. August 10, 2015. http://news.hexun.com/2015-08-10/178218301.html.

Tibet News Web. 2015. "Jujiao: neidi Xizang ban 30 nian" [Focus: 30 years of the Tibet Class]. October 16, 2015. http://www.chinatibetnews.com/yz/yzzx/201510/t20151016_864289.html.

Tobin, David. 2011. "Competing Communities: Ethnic Unity and Ethnic Violence on China's North-West Frontier." *Inner Asia* 13, no. 1: 7–25.

Tong, Elson. 2017. "Xinjiang woman detained for sharing praise for Allah on social media-reports." *Hong Kong Free Press*, May 10, 2017. https://www.hongkongfp.com/2017/05/10/xinjiang-woman-detained-sharing-praise-allah-social-media-reports/.

Toops, Stanley. 2004. "The Demography of Xinjiang." In Starr, *Xinjiang*, 241–63.

Toops, Stanley. 2016. "Spatial Results of the 2010 Census in Xinjiang." *China Policy Institute Analysis*, March 7, 2016. Accessed July 31, 2017. https://cpianalysis.org/2016/03/07/spatial-results-of-the-2010-census-in-xinjiang.

Turnbull, Lesley. 2014. "In Pursuit of Islamic 'Authenticity': Locating Muslim Identity on China's Peripheries." *Cross-Currents: East Asian History and Culture Review* 12: 35–67.

Usborne, David. 2013. "New York Police's Use of Stop and Search Powers Is Racist, Says Judge." *Independent*, August 12, 2013. https://www.independent.co.uk/news/world/americas/new-york-police-s-use-of-stop-and-search-powers-is-racist-says-judge-8758200.html.

US Congress-Senate Indian Affairs Committee 2010. "S. J. Res. 14-A Joint Resolution to Acknowledge a Long History and Ill-Conceived Policies by the Federal Government Regarding Indian Tribes and Offer an Apology to All Native Peoples on Behalf of the United States." https://www.congress.gov/bill/111th-congress/senate-joint-resolution/14.

Utley, Robert, ed. 1964. *Battlefield and Classroom: Four Decades with the American Indian, the Memoirs of Richard H. Pratt*. New Haven: Yale University Press.

VanderKlippe, Nathan. 2017. "How China Is Targeting Its Uyghur Ethnic Minority Abroad." *The Globe and Mail*, October 29, 2017. https://beta.theglobeandmail.com/news/world/uyghurs-around-the-world-feel-new-pressure-as-china-increases-its-focus-on-those-abroad/article36759591.

van Doorn-Harder, Pieternella. 2006. *Women Shaping Islam: Reading the Qur'an in Indonesia*. Champaign, IL: University of Illinois Press.

Waite, Edmund. 2007. "The Emergence of Muslim Reformism in Contemporary Xinjiang: Implications for the Uyghurs' Positioning Between a Central Asian and Chinese Context." In *Situating the Uyghurs between China and Central Asia*, edited by Ildikó Bellér-Hann, Joanne Smith Finley, M. Cristina Cesàro, and Rachel Harris, 165–81. Aldershot, UK: Ashgate.

Wang, Fei-Ling. 2004. "Reformed Migration Control and New Targeted People: China's Hukou System in the 2000s." *China Quarterly* 177: 115–32.

Wang Hongman. 2000. *Xin Zhongguo minzu zhengce gailun* [An introduction to New China's policy towards minority nationalities] [*sic*]. Beijing: Minzu daxue chubanshe.

Wang Lijuan. 2016. "Hetian diqu zongjiao shiwu guanli ji qu jiduanzhuyi wenti yanjiu" [Research on the issues with Khotan's religious affairs and de-extremification]. MA Thesis, Shihezi University.

Wang, Wenfei Winnie, and C. Cindy Fan. 2006. "Success or Failure: Selectivity and Reasons of Return Migration in Sichuan and Anhui, China." *Environment and Planning A* 38, no. 5: 939–58.

Wang, Chengzhi, and Zhou Quanhou. 2003. "Minority Education in China: From State's Preferential Policies to Dislocated Tibetan School." *Educational Studies* 29, no. 1: 85–106.

Wang, Edward. 2014. "To Quell Unrest, Beijing Movies to Scatter Uighurs across China." *New York Times*, November 6, 2014. https://www.nytimes.com/2014/11/07/world/asia/labor-program-in-china-moves-to-scatter-uighurs-across-han-territory.html.

Weber, Eugen. 1976. *From Peasants into Frenchmen: The Modernization of Rural France, 1870–1914*. Stanford: Stanford University Press.

Wright, Robin. 2005. "Chinese Detainees Are Men without a Country." *Washington Post*, August 24, 2005. http://www.washingtonpost.com/wp-dyn/content/article/2005/08/23/AR2005082301362.html.

Wu, David. 1990. "Chinese Minority Policy and the Meaning of Minority Culture: The Example of the Bai in Yunnan, China." *Human Organization* 49, no. 1: 1–13.

Wu Haiying. 2013. "Neidi Xinjiang gaozhongban zhaosheng zhengce yanjiu" [Study on enrollment policy for students from Xinjiang to high school classes in inland China]. PhD dissertation, Northeast Normal University.

Xiao Ying and Baihetiye'er Tu'ersun. 2004. *Weiwu'erzu: Xinjiang Mulaoma cun diaochao* [The Uyghurs: An investigation of Mulaomacun Village]. Yunnan: Yunnan daxue chubanshe.

Xinhua. 2008. "Xinjiang Sends More Students to High Schools in China's Inland." August 5, 2008. http://news.xinhuanet.com/english2010/culture/2011-08/05/c_131032080.htm.

Xinhua. 2009. "Evidence Shows Rabiya Kadeer behind Urumqi Riot: Chinese Gov't." July 9, 2009. http://news.xinhuanet.com/english/2009-07/09/content_11676293.htm.

Xinhua. 2011. "Xinjiang Sends More Students to High Schools in China's Inland." August 5, 2011. http://news.xinhuanet.com/english2010/culture/2011-08/05/c_131032080.htm.

Xinhua. 2012. "Xinjiang Sets World Record for Cotton Production. October 15, 2012. http://english.people.com.cn/90778/7976252.html.

Xinhua. 2013. "Xinjiang neigao ban jinnian zhaosheng 9122 ren xin zeng 6 suo xuexiao [The Xinjiang Class plans to enroll 9,122 students and increase schools by 6 this year]. May 11, 2013. http://news.xinhuanet.com/edu/2013-05/11/c_115727788.htm.

Xinhua. 2014. "China stresses Ethnic Integration in Cities." September 29, 2014. http://en.ce.cn/main/latest/201409/30/t20140930_3631877.shtml.

Xinhua. 2015. "Xinjiang Short of Bilingual Teachers." February 24, 2015. http://www.xinhuanet.com/english/china/2015-02/24/c_134014656.htm.

Xinjiang Daily. 2005. "Neidi Xinjiang gaozhong ban zouguo wu nian" [The Xinjiang Class goes into its fifth year]. November 25, 2005. No active link.

Xinjiang Daily. 2008. "Xinjiang ban xuesheng: lizhi chengcai, baoxiao zuguo" [Xinjiang Class students: Determined to become successful and repay their country]. January 1, 2008. http://www.xjdaily.com.cn/news/xinjiang/218352.shtml.

Xinjiang Daily. 2010. "Laizi Xinjiang neigao ban xuesheng de shuxin" [A letter from a Xinjiang Class student]. December 23, 2010. http://www.ts.cn/news/content/2010-12/23/content_5466047.htm.

Xinjiang Daily. 2012. "Zizhiqu neixue ban fuzeren zuoke benbao minsheng lianxian shi jieshao neigao ban jinnian qi shixing tanxing xuezhi" [An administrator representing the Xinjiang Class is guest interviewed to introduce the connections with the livelihood

of people and this year's flexible education program]. March 3, 2012. http://xjrb.xjdaily.com/msms/671947.shtml.
Xinjiang Daily. 2017. "Shinjang toluq ottura siniplirigha oqughuchi qobul qilish hizmiti axirlashti" [Acceptance decision work for the Xinjiang Class is complete]. August 8, 2017. http://uyghur.xjdaily.com/47/40779.html.
Xinjiang Health Inspection [Xinjiang weisheng jiandu]. 2017. "Xinjiang Weiwu'er zizhiqu renkou yu jihua shengyu tiaoli" [Xinjiang Uyghur Autonomous Region's Population and Family Planning Regulation." Last modified August 4, 2017. Accessed July 11, 2018. http://www.xjwsjd.gov.cn/flfg/jgsyfg/xjwwezcgbb/14509.htm.
Xinjiang Net. 2016. "Neidi Xinjiang ban zhuanti peixun juban" [The Xinjiang Class holds special topics training]. May 23, 2016. http://www.xinjiangnet.com.cn/2016/0523/1568883.shtml.
Xinjiang Normal Middle School [Xinjiang shida fuzhong]. 2015. "Xinjiang shida fuzhong 2015 nian gaozhong zhaosheng wenda" [FAQs concerning enrollment at Xinjiang Normal Middle School in 2015]. Accessed September 15, 2015. http://fz.xjnu.edu.cn/s/85/t/201/3e/25/info81445.htm.
Yang, Mayfair Mei-hui. 1994. *Gifts, Favors, and Banquets: The Art of Social Relationships in China.* Ithaca and London: Cornell University Press.
Yang, Miaoyan. 2017. *Learning to Be Tibetan: The Construction of Ethnic Identity at Minzu University of China.* Lanham, MD: Lexington Books.
Yang Shengmin. 2006. "Xinjiang wei han minzu guanxi de chubu diaocha yu fenxi" [A preliminary investigation and analysis of Uyghur-Han relations in Xinjiang]. In *Zuqun yu Shehui* [Ethnic groups and society], edited by Wu Tiantai, 261–78. Taipei: Wunan Book Inc.
Yao Wenxia. 2013. "Dui neidi Xinjiang ban sixiang zhengzhi yu jiaoyu guanli de sikao" [On the politics and education management of Inland Xinjiang Class]. *Journal of Bingtuan Education Institute* 23, no. 3: 19–23.
Yee, Herbert. 2003. "Ethnic Relations in Xinjiang: A Survey of Uygur-Han Relation in Ürümqi." *Journal of Contemporary China* 6, no. 1: 431–52.
Yeh, Emily. 2013. *Taming Tibet: Landscape Transformation and the Gift of Chinese Development.* Ithaca, NY and London: Cornell University Press.
Yorkshire Evening Post. 2015. "Exclusive: Report Reveals Young Leeds Muslims Blame Government for 'Serious Failures' on Counter-extremism." July 7, 2015. https://www.yorkshireeveningpost.co.uk/news/crime/exclusive-report-reveals-young-leeds-muslims-blame-government-for-serious-failures-on-counter-extremism-1-7345281.
Yu, Haibo. 2010. *Identity and Schooling among the Naxi.* Lanham, MD: Lexington Books.
Yuen, Lotus. 2013. "Why Chinese College Graduates Aren't Getting Jobs." *The Atlantic,* May 23, 2013. https://www.theatlantic.com/china/archive/2013/05/why-chinese-college-graduates-arent-getting-jobs/276187.
Zang, Xiaowei. 2011. *Islam, Family Life, and Gender Inequality in Urban China.* London: Routledge.
Zang, Xiaowei. 2015. *Ethnicity in China.* Cambridge, UK: Polity Press.
Zenz, Adrian. 2018. "New Evidence for China's Political Re-Education Campaign in Xinjiang." *China Brief* 18, no. 10: https://jamestown.org/program/evidence-for-chinas-political-re-education-campaign-in-xinjiang.

Zenz, Adrian, and James Leibold. 2017. "Xinjiang's Rapidly Evolving Security State." *China Brief.* Accessed September 8, 2017. https://jamestown.org/program/xinjiangs-rapidly-evolving-security-state.

Zhang, Shaoying, and Derek McGhee. 2014. *Social Policies and Ethnic Conflict in China: Lessons from Xinjiang.* New York: Palgrave.

Zhang Shiyi. 2010. "Ban hao neidi Xinjiang gaozhong ban, ba minzu tuanjie jiaoyu luodao shichu" [Effectively managing the Xinjiang Class, implementing ethnic unity education]. In *Minzu tuanjie jiaoyu gongzuo jingyan xuanbian* [Selected work experiences on ethnic unity education], edited by Li Yi, 125–36. Beijing: Minzu chubanshe.

Zhang, Xinmin. 2014. "Soccer on the Silk Road: How the 'Beautiful Game' Came to Xinjiang." *China File*, July 12, 2014. http://www.chinafile.com/multimedia/photo-gallery/soccer-silk-road.

Zhao, Jie. 2007. *Minzu hexie yu minzu fazhan* [Ethnic harmony and ethnic development]. Beijing: Minzu chubanshe.

Zhao, Zhenzhou. 2010. *China's Mongols at University: Contesting Cultural Recognition.* Lanham, MD: Lexington Books.

Zhu, Zhiyong. 2007a. *State Schooling and Ethnic Identity: The Politics of a Tibetan Neidi School in China.* New York: Lexington Books.

Zhu, Zhiyong. 2007b. "Ethnic Identity Construction in the Schooling Context: A Case Study of a Tibetan Neidi Boarding School in China." *Chinese Education and Society* 40, no. 2: 38–59.

Xinjiang Class Documents

Beijing No. 10 Middle School. 2013. "Xuesheng guanli zhidu" [System of student management]. *Xinjiang Xiaoqu*. Last modified March 23, 2013. http://www.bj10z.com.cn/include/TEXTShow.asp?cataid=A00710001&id=129.

Bureau of Education of Turpan. 2011a. "Xinjiang Weiwu'er zizhiqu 2011 nian neidi Xinjiang gaozhong ban zhaosheng gongzuo guiding" [Enrollment requirements for the Xinjiang Uyghur Autonomous Region's Xinjiang Class for 2011]. Last modified February 14, 2011. Accessed March 7, 2011. http://jyj.tlf.gov.cn/ny.jsp?urltype=news.NewsContentUrl&wbnewsid=67188&w btreeid=1582.

Bureau of Education of Turpan. 2011b. "Xinjiang Weiwu'er zizhiqu 2011 nian neidi Xinjiang gaozhong ban zhaosheng kaoshi guanli shishi xize" [Implementation of rules for the Xinjiang Uyghur Autonomous Region's Xinjiang Class's 2011 entrance examination]. Accessed November 12, 2012. http://tlf.gov.cn/ssjg.jsp?wbtreeid=1.

Bureau of Education of Ürümchi. 2006. "Guanyu zuohao 2006 nian neidi Xinjiang gaozhong ban zhaosheng gongzuo de tongzhi" [Notice about the 2006 Xinjiang Class student recruitment work]. Accessed November 1, 2012. http://www.wlmqedu.gov.cn/www/wsbs/bszn/rxzsks/1638.htm

China Education and Research Network. 2000. "Neidi Xinjiang gaozhong ban guanli banfa (shixing)" [Administrative procedures for the Xinjiang Class (trial)]. June 5, 2000. Accessed October 15, 2008. http://www.edu.cn/xie_zuo_826/20060323/t20060323_110910.shtml.

China Testing Online. 2012. "Xinjiang Weiwu'er zizhiqu 2012 nian neidi Xinjiang gaozhong ban zhaosheng jihua fenpeibiao" [The Xinjiang Uyghur Autonomous Region's enrollment plan and distribution list for the Xinjiang Class's 2012 recruitment cycle]. July 7, 2012. Accessed September 1, 2012. http://www.3773.com.cn/zhongkao/NEIGAOBAN/632600.shtml.

Dongguan Education Online. 2012. "Xinjiang ban minzu tuanjie banji jiaoyu moshi yanjiu" [Research on the educational model of the Xinjiang Class's minzu unity classes]. Last modified June 11, 2012. Accessed July 12, 2018. http://www.dgjy.net/info/71739.

General Office of the Ministry of Education. 2000. "Guanyu neidi Xinjiang gaozhong ban xuesheng guo Gu'erbang jie he Rouzi jie youguan wenti de tongzhi" [A notice about questions related to how Xinjiang Class students will celebrate the Qurban and Roza holidays]. December 15, 2000. Accessed November 19, 2012. http://school.sjyz.sjedu.cn/yz/Article/Article_Print.asp?ArticleID=12509.

General Office of the MOE [Ministry of Education] and General Office of the SEAC [State Ethnic Affairs Commission]. 2008. "Guanyu zuo hao putong gaoxiao zhaoshou de neidi Xinjiang gaozhong ban xuesheng daxue biye jiuye gongzuo de yijian" [Opinions concerning employment efforts for colleges and universities who have Xinjiang Class university graduates]. Accessed April 19, 2011. http://zbb.shu.edu.cn/graduateweb/news/viewnews.asp?id=2528&type=8.

General Office of the MOE and General Office of the SEAC. 2011. "Guanyu jinyibu jiaqiang neidi Xinjiang gaozhong ban qingzhen shitang guanli gongzuo de tongzhi" [A notice on further strengthening the Xinjiang Class's administration of halal cafeterias]. Last modified August 2, 2011. Accessed July 12, 2018. http://www.seac.gov.cn/art/2011/8/2/art_142_131796.html

General Office of the State Council of the PRC. 1999. "Guowuyuan bangongting zhuanfa jiaoyubu deng bumen guanyu jinyibu jiaqiang shaoshu minzu diqu rencai peiyang gongzuo yijian de tongzhi" [Information about suggestions of the State Council's General Office's to the Ministry of Education and other relevant departments concerning the work for strengthening education in minority areas]. September 30, 1999. Accessed April 9, 2012. http://www.xjdrc.gov.cn/copy_3_copy_1_second.jsp?urltype=news.NewsContent Url&wbtreeid=11118&wbnewsid=122283.

Laoshan No. 2 Middle School. 2006. "Yi renwu qudong guanchuan jiaoxue shizhong—yuke xinxi jishu ke jiaoxue qingkuang yu yidian tihui" [Carrying out the task of driven-led education—Conditions and experiences from teaching preparatory studies information technology classes]. September 12, 2006. Accessed July 12, 2018. http://www.lsez.qdedu.net/newsInfo.aspx?pkId=49535.

MOE [Ministry of Education of the People's Republic of China]. 1995. "Education Law of the People's Republic of China." Last updated March 18, 1995. Accessed October 1, 2008. http://www.china.org.cn/english/education/184669.htm.

MOE. 2000. "Neidi Xinjiang gaozhong ban gongzuo huiyi jiyao" [Summary of the Xinjiang Class Work Meeting]. May 30, 2000. Accessed September 1, 2008. http://old.moe.gov.cn/publicfiles/business/htmlfiles/moe/moe_752/200407/1010.html.

Shanghai Fengxian Middle School. 2006a. "Xinjiang ban xuesheng qianghua putonghua kouyu xunlian de guiding" [Provisions for strengthening Xinjiang Class students' training in spoken Chinese]. June 2006. Accessed September 10, 2012. http://www.fxzx.fx.edu.sh.cn/xjbfm/open.asp?articleID=88&classid=163.

Shanghai Fengxian Middle School. 2006b. "Fengxian zhongxue Xinjiang ban qingkuang" [The Conditions of Fengxian Middle School's Xinjiang Class]. 2006. Accessed September 10, 2012. http://www.fxzx.fx.edu.sh.cn/xjbfm/open.asp?articleID=2732&classid=162.

Shanghai JinShan High School. 2011. "Baozi he mijiu, weixiangqing geng nong" [Steamed dumpling and rice wine richens the flavors of the spirit]. December 12, 2011. Accessed July 12, 2018. http://jszx.jsedu.sh.cn/p/3351.html.

Shanghai Songjiang No. 1 High School. 2010a. "Neidi Xinjiang gaozhong ban pinkun xuesheng rending biaozhun ji pingshen shishi xize" [Details on the implementation of the Xinjiang Class's standards and evaluations for students in poverty]. September 25, 2010. Accessed December 4, 2012. http://school.sjyz.sjedu.cn/yz/Article/Article_Show.asp?ArticleID=12510.

Shanghai Songjiang No. 1 High School. 2010. "Neidi Xinjiang gaozhong ban kaosheng jiazhang chengnuo shu" [Contract for guardians of Xinjiang Class students]. September 25, 2010. Accessed June 20, 2016. http://school.sjyz.sjedu.cn/yz/Article/Article_Show.asp?ArticleID=12513.

Shanghai Yucai Middle School. 2016. "Yucai zhongxue Xinjiang ban xueshang jiangli tiaoli" [Regulation to encourage rewards in Yucai Junior Middle School's Xinjiang Class]. April 28, 2016. Accessed December 15, 2016. http://www.yucai.sh.cn/uploadfile/20164221420168636.pdf.

Shenzhen No. 2 Vocational School of Technology. 2015. "Xinjiang Bu: Yingzao Nianwei Huandu Chunjie" [Xinjiang Department of Education: Creating a festive and joyful Spring Festival]. February 24, 2015. Accessed July 7, 2016. http://www.szped.com/client/20150224000000/20150224000000_1425093736554.html.

State Ethnic Affairs Commission of the People's Republic of China (SEAC). 2004. "Neidi Xinjiang gaozhong ban banxue gongzuo qude chubu chengxiao" [The work of the Xinjiang Class gains first stages of success]. July 16, 2004. Accessed July 12, 2018. http://www.seac.gov.cn/jks/xgyw/2004-07-16/1169515214826957.htm.

State Ethnic Affairs Commission of the People's Republic of China. 2008. "Xuexiao minzu tuanjie zhidao gangyao, shixing" [Outline for schools' ethnic unity education (trial)]. November 26, 2008. Accessed July 12, 2018. http://old.moe.gov.cn/publicfiles/business/htmlfiles/moe/s3081/201001/77787.html.

UIBE [University of International Business and Economics]. 2008. "Changjian wenti ji jieda" [Frequently asked questions and their answers]. Accessed September 24, 2012. http://sit.uibe.edu.cn/bencandy.php?id=243.

Xinjiang Class Online. 2008. "Guanyu xiada Xinjiang 2008 nian neidi gaozhong ban zhaosheng jihua" [About the Xinjiang Uyghur Autonomous Region's 2008 Xinjiang Class recruitment plan]. Accessed October 1, 2008. http://www.xjban.com/ReadNews.asp?NewsID=682.

Xinjiang Class Online. 2011. "Neigao ban daxue biyesheng jiuye zhengce wenda" [Questions and answers about the employment policies for Xinjiang Class graduates]. June 2011. Accessed July 12, 2018. http://www.docin.com/p-720474377.html.

Xinjiang Class Online. 2012. "Qiantan neidi Xinjiang gaozhong ban minzu tuanjie jiaoyu de youxiao tujing" [A brief discussion on the Xinjiang Class's effective channels for "ethnic unity" education]. 2012. Accessed November 19, 2012. http://www.xjban.com/kanwu/dysxyj/2012/50523.htm.

Xinjiang Class Online. 2013a. "Guo xinchun dajia xue chuantong wenhua" [Celebrating the New Year's Festival and learning traditional culture]. Accessed July 7, 2016. http://www.xjban.com/xjb/ngbxw/2013/57446.htm.

Xinjiang Class Online. 2013b. "Neigao ban daxue biyesheng jiyue zhengce wenda" [Questions and answers concerning employment policies for Xinjiang Class graduates]. Accessed January 11, 2016. http://www.xjban.com/xjb/bysjyzd/tzgg/2013/65613.htm.

Xinjiang Class Online. 2015a. "Neidi Xinjiang gaozhong ban gaoxiao biyesheng liu neidi jiuye (shengxue) shengqing biao" [Neidi employment (and continuing education) form for Xinjiang Class graduates]. Accessed January 11, 2016. http://www.xjban.com/xjb/bysjyzd/tzgg/2015/85892.htm.

Xinjiang Class Online. 2015b. "Peiyang yin sixiang zhuanbian, xuexi cu jihua luoshi—yukeban zhuren gongzuo tansuo" [Training as a way to transform thinking and studying as a way to realize our goals—Exploring the work of a preparatory studies' director]. Accessed September 19, 2017. http://www.xjban.com/xjb/kw/bzrgz/2015/85578.htm.

Xinjiang Class Online. 2015c. "Shaoxingshi zhijao zhongxin Xinjiang ban xiying chunjie quwei duo" [The Shaoxing's Vocational Education Center's Xinjiang Class welcomes an interesting new year]. Accessed July 7, 2016. http://www.xjban.com/xjb/nzbxw/2015/85399.htm.

Xinjiang Class Online. 2015d. "2015 nian neigao ban zhaosheng gongzuo richeng anpai biao" [The Xinjiang Class's 2015 recruitment work schedule]. Accessed July 13, 2018. https://zixun.7139.com/11/20/225075.html.

Xinjiang Department of Education. 2007. "2007 nian putong gaodeng xuexiao zhaoshou neidi Xinjiang gaozhong ban biyesheng zhaosheng jihua renwu he luoshi zhuanye jianyi biao" [Suggestions for the 2007 recruitment plan for colleges and university to enroll Xinjiang Class graduates]. Accessed July 13, 2018. http://www.docin.com/p-20323643.html.

Xinjiang Department of Education. 2011. "Neidi Xinjiang gaozhong ban xuesheng shouze" [Xinjiang Class student regulations]. April 26, 2011. Accessed November 12, 2012. http://www.dhzx.net/xjb/gzzd/201104/20110426141617.html.

Xinjiang Uyghur Autonomous Region (XUAR). 2014. "2013 nian Xinjiang Weiwu'er zizhiqu neidi Xinjiang gaozhong ban kaosheng huji shenhe ji zhengshen biao" [The 2013 Xinjiang Uyghur Autonomous Region's household registration and political status form for Xinjiang Class students]. June 25, 2014. Accessed September 4, 2015. http://www.iliyu.com/zhongkao/zixun/zhaosheng/694885.

Index

Arabic, 9, 59, 63n10, 64–65, 67n13
Arman supermarket, 95
Australia, 7, 20, 87, 94, 109

Bekri, Nur, 1, 45
Beijing, 2–4, 2n2, 10, 12, 14, 26, 31–33, 35, 39, 41–43, 46, 50, 52, 58, 61, 63–65, 67–70, 69n16, 72, 74, 76–85, 81n9, 92–97, 99–101, 103
boundary/boundaries: construction and maintenance, 6, 9–10, 42–29, 58–59, 113; ethnic segregation 30–32, 42–49, 51–53, 76–77, 104, 113; food 45–47, 54–55, 68–70, 97–98; linguistic, 11, 55–59, 113; political, 86–88; psychological 43–44; religious 11, 54–55, 69, 101–3, 113–15; symbolic, 68–69
Buddhism, 9, 13

Canada, 7, 20, 66
Central Asia, 1, 12, 32, 34, 62, 64, 101, 103, 107, 111–12, 114. *See also* Kazakhstan; Kyrgyzstan; Tajikistan
Chen Quanguo, 112, 116
China Islamic Association, 63
China State Construction Engineering Corporation (CSCEC), 98, 101
Chinese civilizing project, 4, 75
Chinese Communist Party (CCP), 38, 73–74, 77, 82–83; Document No. 7, 14; "double exposure" to party values, 32, 32n13; and ethnic practices, 1n2, 8–12, 19, 29; naming policies for government documents, 33–34; and

preferential policies (*youhui zhengce*), 9, 9n13, 22n7, 27, 27n10; restrictions on religious expressions in Xinjiang, 34, 36, 62–64, 63n8, 66–67, 66n12, 69, 73, 79–81, 99–100, 112; Uyghur attitudes toward, 4, 16, 26–27, 78, 100, 108–10, 115
Chinese Muslims. *See Hui*
Chinese Nation. *See* Zhonghua minzu
Christianity, 8, 34, 103
civil unrest: Baren riots, 80; Beijing/Tiananmen, 3; Ghulja disturbances, 14, 14n21; Kunming railway station attacks, 3–4; Lukchun violence, 3; Ürümchi riots of 2009, 3, 3n6, 24, 80
concentration reeducation centers, 103, 112, 116
Confucianism, 75

Daolang, 33, 33n14
Dawes General Allotment Act, 7–8
Demonstrations. *See* civil unrest
Deng Xiaoping, 19n2, 21, 21n4, 80; and theory, 19
Döngköwrük, 2, 94, 102, 104

East Turkestan, 11n15, 66, 84, 88
East Turkestan Islamic Movement (ETIM), 80
East Turkestan Republic (ETR), 10
Eid al-Adha (*Qurban héyt*). *See* Islamic feasts
Eid al-Fitr (*Roza héyt*). *See* Islamic feasts

employment: and discrimination, 77, 81, 83–85, 92–93, 108; in neidi, 74–77, 81–82, 85, 92–97, 115; in Xinjiang, 74–76, 76n5, 77, 81, 83–85, 93–95, 97–100, 103–6, 108–9, 115
Erdaoqiao. See Döngköwrük
ethnic: amalgamation, 8, 19; assimilation, 7, 38, 60, 108; conflict, 3, 3n6, 7, 24, 80; consciousness, 5–7, 9, 11, 43–44, 113; markers, 5–6, 43, 51, 55, 86, 113; minority (minority *minzu*), x, 6, 8–10, 12–16, 18–20, 21n6, 22n7–8, 25–26, 27n10, 28–30, 33, 40, 43, 47–49, 58–59, 62, 72–74, 78, 86, 88, 91–92, 96, 108–9, 115

family planning (birth control) policies, 9, 22, 22nn7–8, 36, 74
fasting (*roza tutmaq*). *See* Islam: Ramadan
Four Cardinal Principles, 21, 21n4
Four Identities, 29

General Office of the State Council, 18
Guantanamo Bay, 39
guanxi (interpersonal relationships), 73, 84
Guomindang (GMD), 10

Han: Central Plains Culture, 50, 74–75, 112; discrimination against Uyghurs, 78, 83–84, 91; festivals, 31, 37–38, 37n20, 59, 78n8; interactions with Uyghurs in the Xinjiang Class, 42–44; as "killjoys," 53; migrants, 43, 81, 83, 91, 101n4. *See also* marriage, Uyghur-Han intermarriage
Hui (Chinese Muslims), 9–10, 22–23, 46, 54–55, 58, 69–70, 78n7, 82
hukou (residency permit), 91

Indian Emancipation Act. *See* Dawes General Allotment Act
Interpellation, 4, 7, 10, 51, 72, 74, 87, 103, 113
Islam: Islamic feasts, 47–48, 53, 53 fig. 2.1, 54 fig 2.2, 60, 96; hadith, 50n2, 51n4, 64, 65n11, 66, 67n13, 102n5; *hajj*, 9, 67; halal, 42, 46–47, 69–70, 70n18, 97–98; obligatory prayer (*namaz*), 35, 35n17, 51n3, 66–68, 100; overtly Islamic names, 12, 12n17, 34; prayers of supplication (*du'a*), 35n17, 50–51, 50n2, 51n4, 68–69, 114; *qadar* (predestination), 92; *qiyas*, 102n5; Qur'an, 47, 51n3, 54, 62–65, 65n11, 67n13, 68–69, 81, 102n5, 113–14; Ramadan, 60, 69, 69n17, 80, 99–100, 102–3, 114; *umma* (global community of Muslims), 5, 38, 51–52, 61–66, 69–71, 81, 113–14; Uyghurs conversion to, 11; veiling, 12, 34–35, 34n15, 65–66, 80, 106–7
Islamic Institute of Xinjiang, 63

Jadidism, 52, 52n5
Jiti hukou (group residency permit), 86–87, 91

Kashgar, 1n3, 10, 11n15, 12, 15, 21n5, 23–25, 23 table 1.1, 27, 32, 38–39, 41–42, 52–53, 59, 61, 64, 66–67, 76n5, 79, 81–82, 84–85, 98, 101–2, 104–5, 112, 116
Kazakhs, 22–23, 23 table 1.1, 65n11
Kazakhstan, 1n1, 52–53, 65n11
Khotan, 1n2, 2, 11n15, 13, 15, 21n5, 23, 23 table1.1, 25, 27–28, 30, 38, 42–44, 64–65, 76n5, 81–82, 97, 103, 111
Korla, 32, 42
Kyrgyzstan, 1n1

Law of Regional Ethnic Autonomy, 40
"Leftover women," 93–96, 106–7
Lenin, Vladimir, 7, 9, 21n4
Lukchun, xi. *See also* civil unrest, Lukchun

Macaulay, Thomas, 7
Manchu Qing empire, 4n8, 10–11
Mao Zedong, 2, 2n4, 33; and Mao Zedong Thought, 19, 21n4
marriage: endogamy, 59–60, 94, 104, 113; exogamy, 60–61; pressure to marry, 93–97; Uyghur-Han intermarriage, 60–61

mehelle (neighborhood), 12
meshrep, 14n21, 47
migration, 90–91; emigration, 5, 76–77, 78–80, 82, 84, 86–87, 92, 109; to neidi, 74, 85–86, 96–97
Ministry of Education, 17–19, 74
minkaohan, 21n6, 52, 55–57, 57 table2.1, 101, 104
minkaomin, 21n6, 26, 55, 57, 57 table2.1, 101, 104
minzu unity, 19–21, 25, 30, 37–38, 42, 49, 52, 75
Minzu University of China, xi, 12, 14
Mongols, 11, 22–23, 78n7
Musabayov, Hussein and Bawudun, 52, 52n5

Native American Boarding Schools, 7–8, 20, 23, 30, 34, 49
neidi: and employment, 74–77, 81–82, 85, 92–97, 115; discrimination in, 58, 91; loosened political climate in, 62, 80, 90, 93, 97

passport application process, 86–87, 86n12, 109, 111
pomegranate: as symbol of minzu unity, 2–3, 2 fig. 0.1, 116
Pratt, Richard, 8, 30

qingzhen ("pure and true"), 42, 46, 70, 70n18. *See also* halal

sama (dance), 53, 54 fig. 2.2
Shaoguan Incident, 3
shenfen zheng (identification cards), 77–80
Shihezi, 41
Sinopec, 61
soccer, 16, 52, 60–61, 103, 113
Soviet Union, 7, 114
Stalin, Joseph, 1n2, 7
Star Wars, 25
State Ethnic Affairs Commission (SEAC), 20, 46, 74

stereotypes: "backwardness," 32, 38; 42–43; of Han, 44–45, 53, 55, 98; Uyghurs as singing and dancing minorities, 26, 48
Strike Hard campaigns, 80
Sun Qi, 18, 46, 75
suzhi (personal quality), 74, 74n3, 108

Tajik, 23
Tajikistan, 1n1
Taranchis, 11
targeted population, 91
Three Evil Forces, 1, 28, 80, 112
Tibetans, 13, 46n25, 112
Tibet Boarding School (*Xizang neidi gaozhong ban*), 13, 15, 20, 45, 46n25, 112
Tohti, Ilham, 88
Tukey, 50, 52, 66–67, 80, 94, 97, 103, 107, 116
Tulum, Qurban, 2, 2n4
Turkish-Islamic Republic of Eastern Turkestan, 10

United States of America, 7–8, 20, 33, 80, 82, 84, 87; 9/11 attacks, 14, 80
Ürümchi, 1, 2 fig. 0.1, 3, 14, 27, 30–31, 40–43, 45, 56–57, 61, 68, 75, 77, 79–80, 94–95, 98, 102–6, 108, 112. *See also* civil unrest, Ürümchi riots, and Döngköwrük

Wang Lequan, 28
WeChat, 57–58, 57 table2.1, 57n7, 58 fig. 2.3
Weiwu'er zu (CCP defined category for Uyghurs), 5, 5n11, 10, 12, 32, 48, 67, 71–72, 87, 103, 112–13, 118
World Uyghur Congress, 3

Xi Jinping, 2, 9, 38, 51, 91
Xinjiang Education, 12–13, 12n18, 22, 25–28, 40–41, 55–56, 58, 72, 104, 112. *See also minkaohan* and *minkaomin*
Xinjiang Class policy: appearance/dress code, 32, 34–35; dorm inspections, 35, 37; enrollment, 15, 20–27, 23 table 1.1, 24 fig.1.1; Han holidays, 37–38, 47;

language, 18, 20, 23, 36, 38–41, 113; naming, 33–34; *qingzhen* cafeterias, 42, 46–47; religion, 34–36, 34–35n16, 113; resistance to, 35–36, 41–42, 45, 49, 86

Yaqub Beg, 10

Zhonghua minzu (Chinese Nation), 4–5, 4n8, 12, 19, 21–22, 29, 37, 49, 70, 72–74, 86, 111–13, 115–16